D0207524

SOUTHERN LITERARY STUDIES

Fred Hobson, Editor

WALKER PERCY, THE LAST CATHOLIC NOVELIST

WALKER PERCY
THE LAST CATHOLIC NOVELIST

Kieran Quinlan

LOUISIANA STATE UNIVERSITY PRESS   Baton Rouge and London

For Mary and Kate—
in different ways

Copyright © 1996 by Louisiana State University Press
All rights reserved
Manufactured in the United States of America
First printing

05 04 03 02 01 00 99 98 97 96   5 4 3 2 1

Designer: Glynnis Weston
Typeface: Times Roman
Typesetter: Impressions Book & Journal Services, Inc.
Printer and binder: Thomson-Shore, Inc.

Library of Congress Cataloging-in-Publication Data

Quinlan, Kieran, 1945–
    Walker Percy : the last Catholic novelist / Kieran Quinlan.
        p.   cm. — (Southern literary studies)
    Includes bibliographical references (p.   ) and index.
    ISBN 0-8071-2044-8 (cloth : alk. paper)
    1. Percy, Walker, 1916– —Religion.   2. Christian fiction,
American—History and criticism.   3. Christianity and literature
—Southern States.   4. Fiction—Religious aspects—Christianity.
5. Southern States—In literature.   6. Catholic Church—In
literature.   I. Title.   II. Series
PS3566.E6912Z832   1996
813'.54—dc20   95-44232
                                                                                       CIP

The excerpt from Walker Percy's 1951 letter to Caroline Gordon, shelfmark bMS Am 1905 (513-522), is published by permission of the Houghton Library, Harvard University.
    Portions of Chapter 5 appeared originally in somewhat different form in the author's essay *"The Moviegoer:* The Dilemma of Walker Percy's Scholastic Existentialism," in *Modern American Fiction: Form and Function,* ed. Thomas Daniel Young (Baton Rouge, 1989), 213–24.

The paper in this book meets the guidelines for permanence and durability of the Committee on Production Guidelines for Book Longevity of the Council on Library Resources. ♾

Remember that I die in the Communion of the Catholic Church, and that I am a Percy in life and death.

—Blessed Thomas Percy, Martyr, 1572

My memory fills with the ghosts of dead phrases—salvation, washed in the blood of the Lamb, He descended into hell, the resurrection of the body, born of the Virgin Mary. They are not the sort of ghosts I care to meet. Where lies the virtue in attempting to persuade honest young minds to entertain such outworn rubbish?

—William Alexander Percy
Lanterns on the Levee

The reason I am a Catholic is that I believe that what the Catholic Church proposes is true.

—Walker Percy, 1989

CONTENTS

Acknowledgments

I want to express my gratitude to the following, who, in various ways and at various times, have helped me complete this study, though they are of course in no way responsible for its conclusions (with which I know that some of them will strongly disagree), much less its deficiencies: Dan Young, Terrye Newkirk, Lewis Lawson, Susan Donaldson, Jay Lamar, Lewis P. Simpson, Dan Schwarz, Bertram Wyatt-Brown, Jay Tolson, Patrick Samway, William Rodney Allen, Fred Hobson, and above all my wife, Mary Kaiser, to whom the work is dedicated.

Walker Percy, the Last Catholic Novelist

INTRODUCTION

A few months before his death in May, 1990, Walker Percy was invited by Clifton Fadiman to contribute a "kind of informal intellectual and spiritual testament" to a forthcoming volume entitled *Living Philosophies: The Reflections of Some Eminent Men and Women of Our Time*.[1] Percy's piece would be called "Why Are You a Catholic?"—a heading the novelist admittedly found somewhat embarrassing. Nevertheless, the topic suggested hardly came as a surprise to anyone who had been following Percy's career over the previous three decades, nor was he himself altogether displeased with it. In fact, though the essay never answers the question with either the precision of argument or the unbuttoned intimacy that one might wish for, it is the most explicitly denominational credo in a collection that includes two priests (Hans Küng and Theodore Hesburgh), an Anglican bishop (Desmond Tutu), a prominent conservative Catholic journalist (William F. Buckley, Jr.), and others of equally strong, if somewhat more circumspect, religious persuasion (biographer Lady Elizabeth Longford and poet Czeslaw Milosz). In spite of the essay's moments of evasion and ironic humor—both very characteristic of its author—there is never any doubt as to Percy's stance on the fundamental issue: "The reason I am a Catholic is that I believe that what the Catholic Church proposes is true" (166).

The centrality of religious belief, and of a very Roman Catholic form of that belief, to Walker Percy's life and *oeuvre* is indisputable. Statement after statement in his essays and interviews attest to this fact, his declarations of faith seeming to grow only stronger and more fervent with each passing year. In regard to his novels, Percy himself has said that "there is hardly a moment in my writing when I am not aware of where, say, my main character—who is usually some kind of Catholic, bad, half-baked, lapsed, whatever . . . stands vis-à-vis the Catholic

1.   Clifton Fadiman, ed., *Living Philosophies: The Reflections of Some Eminent Men and Women of Our Time* (New York, 1990). Subsequent in-text references are to this collection.

faith." Critic Alfred Kazin, who visited Percy at his home in Louisiana for several days in the 1970s, concluded that his novels are "essentially the self-determination of a religious personality." Jay Tolson's biography, composed after extensive interviews with its subject, confirms this perception for every stage in the author's career. It is a stance, moreover, that is of great significance for an understanding of the author's work: Percy once explained the situation succinctly by observing, "It would not have mattered a great deal if Margaret Mitchell were a Methodist or an atheist. But it does matter what Sartre's allegiance is, or Camus's, or Flannery O'Connor's. For what his allegiance is is what he is writing about." [2]

But not only was Percy's commitment deeply religious, it was also polemically such, forever taking on those he liked to refer to as the "denizens of the age": scientists (physical and social), anthropologists, liberal theologians, philosophers, linguists, sometimes even other novelists. In a 1971 essay entitled "Notes for a Novel About the End of the World," Percy claims that "not being called by God to be a prophet, he [the novelist] nevertheless pretends to a certain prescience. If he did not think he saw something other people didn't see or at least didn't pay much attention to, he would be wasting his time writing and they reading." [3] Later in the same essay, he offers a list of adjectives that one can apply to the kind of novelist he is commending: "philosophical," "metaphysical," "prophetic," "eschatological," "religious" (102). Percy was equally convinced that his own position within such a prophetic context was specifically Catholic—and Catholic in a highly orthodox way.

Thus, Walker Percy was conscious of being at odds with many of the "accepted" intellectual and social positions of the day, including those of some of his fellow Catholics. He had arguments to propose against them and alternatives to offer. In fact, the Fadiman collection provides a convenient illustration of the overall situation, for there Percy's testament appears among a number of positions toward which he himself was quite explicitly opposed: those of psychologist B. F. Skinner, philosopher Sidney Hook, and evolutionary biologist Stephen Jay

2. Walker Percy, "The Holiness of the Ordinary," in *Signposts in a Strange Land*, ed. Patrick Samway (New York, 1991), 368; Alfred Kazin, *Bright Book of Life: American Novelists and Story-tellers from Hemingway to Mailer* (Notre Dame, 1980), 66; Jay Tolson, *Pilgrim in the Ruins: A Life of Walker Percy* (New York, 1992); Percy, *Signposts,* 110–11.

3. Walker Percy, *The Message in the Bottle: How Queer Man Is, How Queer Language Is, and What One Has to Do with the Other* (New York, 1975), 101.

Gould in particular, those of several others in more general ways. Of course, it is not hard to find blatant contradictions between the points of view of the various contributors to Fadiman's book, though it is also significant that all were thought in some way "worthy" of inclusion, all of them being men and women "of good will and high intelligence," as the editor put it.[4] If anything, the selection might be criticized for not being inclusive enough, since all those chosen are, in spite of their divergent views, fairly "establishment" figures, their various iconoclasms very much within the boundaries of generally accepted discourse: not a single one of those more recent thinkers who would question the very bases of Western epistemological constructions is present. But, in any case, while professing there his own Christian beliefs, Percy attacks a theoretical, scientific view of the world—one proximately derived from Newton, Darwin, and Freud, he claims—which, though possibly valid in its limited sphere, is ultimately totalitarian and opposed to the spiritual dimension of human existence. It is a view that, from Percy's perspective, has led indirectly to the extermination of millions of Jews, since human beings are no longer seen as having a metaphysical value. More explicitly, it is a post-Christian worldview "in the sense that people no longer understand themselves, as they understood themselves for some fifteen hundred years, as ensouled creatures under God, born to trouble and whose salvation depends upon the entrance of God into history as Jesus Christ" (171).

Many of the other essayists in Fadiman's volume represent, as already noted, precisely the outlook that Percy is here criticizing. Physicist and science-fiction writer Arthur C. Clarke, for example, suggests that the "Problem of Evil" does not exist, but is rather "an inevitable consequence of the bell-shaped curve of normal distribution" of natural occurrences (51). Stephen Jay Gould reminds us (in phrases reminiscent of some of the stoic characters that regularly appear in Percy's novels and of which Percy is sympathetically critical) that "we can anticipate no geologically long duration of our species, as no entity survives for very long on our changing planet. . . . We must eventually go under. We can only strive to hang on as long as possible, have some fun while we're at the table, and, since we happen to be moral agents as well, to stay the course with honor" (141–42). Sociobiologist Edward O. Wilson (brought up a Baptist in Percy's Alabama)

---

4. Fadiman, *Living Philosophies,* xii.

posits that "the mystery of life . . . has been largely solved," that "human tragedy is . . . to some degree Darwinian noise, the expected result of ordinary genetic innovation," and that "naturalism (or secular humanism if you prefer) will gain credence as time passes and knowledge accumulates. If not, then I am prepared to join the philosopher Sidney Hook in saying, Lord, you didn't give me enough evidence" (280–81). Anthropologist Jane Goodall contends that "we humans are not, after all, set apart, separated from the rest of the animal kingdom by an unbridgeable chasm. The hyena, like the chimpanzee, can think and reason. . . . It is in the *sophistication* of the intellect and the uses to which it is put, that Man differs from Beast" (82). In short, although Lady Longford, representing a position similar to Walker Percy's, states that she cannot imagine what life would be like without belief in God, an afterlife, and so on, others in the volume obviously can.

But it is also easy to find a measure of overlap between Percy's ideas and those of even some of his opponents. Several believe, for instance, that since science does not answer all the questions posed by man's existence, there is room and even need for human creativity. Skeptics of traditional religion such as Gould and physicist Steven Weinberg concede that there is a distinct, if not perhaps unbridgeable, gap between evolutionary processes and moral behavior. Thus Gould: "Many people view the existential solution—that we are alone as moral agents, by virtue of consciousness, and must seek the guidelines of action by ourselves— as either terrifying or depressing. I regard it as exhilarating, the greatest testimony of, and challenge to, our human evolutionary uniqueness" (142). And Weinberg, admitting the apparent fact that human beings have no special place in the universe to be a "rather melancholy view," concludes his essay with the flourish that "melancholy is one of the distinctive creations of our species, and not without its own consolations" (269). More important, nearly all the contributors to Fadiman's volume are appalled by the degree of human cruelty that has characterized the twentieth century. Literary critic and novelist George Steiner, for example, shares Percy's acute awareness that "a man can play Bach and Schubert in the morning and torture or incinerate other human beings after lunch" and that "liberal eclecticism [does not] seem to give insight much purchase on the actual fabric of history." In the light of such disturbing reflections on the human enterprise, Steiner finds himself forced to resort to a rather unfashionable explanation: the possibility of an Original Sin (220).

Taking into account Walker Percy's embattled stance, then, his being at odds with the "wisdom" of the age, the present study is concerned with the validity or otherwise of the religious, social, and scientific views he himself held and so consistently argued for in essay after essay and novel after novel. These views were grounded not merely in Roman Catholicism as such, but specifically in the *kind* of Catholicism that Percy embraced in the late 1940s. The matter of Percy's Catholicism has, of course, been dealt with by almost all the author's critics to date.[5] But it has not, it seems to me, been dealt with in either the way or with the degree of importance it deserves. Just as much criticism of Percy has overassociated him with his early and continuing interest in existentialist philosophy—understandable in that this mode of thinking has been particularly accessible to those engaged in the literary disciplines in a way that has not been the case with analytic philosophy—or with his acknowledged need to use the medium of fiction to come to terms with the suicides in his family, or, more recently, with his Southern heritage (all of these quite valid, but limited, approaches), it has correspondingly suffered from an inadequate perception of the circumstances and influence of his religious conversion.

So, for example, the fact that Percy's foster parent, William Alexander Percy, had given much attention to his own Catholic background in his autobiographical *Lanterns on the Levee,* published in 1941, had more to do with his young cousin's conversion than is generally acknowledged. Much more important, however, the ambiance of Roman Catholic intellectual life in the 1940s, which was to have such a lasting effect on Walker Percy's views, has been almost totally ignored. Although Percy would make the partly surprising claim in later years that it was mainly the Danish philosopher Søren Kierkegaard who had brought about his conversion to the Church of Rome, the reading that influenced his decision also included such thinkers as Etienne Gilson and Jacques Maritain, both neo-Thomist philosophers who enjoyed enormous prestige among certain American intellectuals in the 1930s and 1940s and were responsible for a great number of conversions—those of Thomas Merton, who went on to become a Trappist monk and write his best-selling autobiography, *The Seven Storey Mountain,* and Robert Low-

---

5. See especially Jac Tharpe, *Walker Percy* (Boston, 1983), and Robert H. Brinkmeyer, Jr., *Three Catholic Writers of the Modern South* (Jackson, Miss., 1985).

ell, who chronicled some of his journey in the poems of *Land of Unlikeness,* being among the most notable.[6] Percy's academic background may have been more in the sciences than in the arts, but the factors that led him to embrace Catholicism were not so very different from those that were influencing a variety of fellow seekers at the time.[7] In other words, Percy's conversion took place as part of what he himself once described as the postwar generation's "tremendous spiritual awakening." [8]

The event involved more than simple conversion, however, for the provenance of Percy's change of belief also gave it its peculiar character. Entering the Church in the 1940s, Percy began—and remained—a sympathizer with thinkers who were considered "progressive" at the time, but who would later become quite conservative (or simply stay consistent with their original principles) as the changes brought about by the Second Vatican Council in the early 1960s seemed to them to be effecting excessive compromises with a secular world. Maritain, once viewed as a dangerous radical by the orthodox establishment in Rome, would finally reject what he saw as unwise change and publish his frustrations in *The Peasant of the Garonne* in 1967.[9] In the main, they were thinkers who stressed the intelligence of faith, the ultimate harmony between scientific investigation and religious belief, but who also saw the Church as a bulwark against the chaos of the twentieth century. In fact, Gilson, Maritain, and another thinker in whom Percy

6. William Alexander Percy, *Lanterns on the Levee: Recollections of a Planter's Son* (Baton Rouge, 1973); Thomas Merton, *The Seven Storey Mountain* (New York, 1948); Robert Lowell, *Land of Unlikeness* (Cummington, Mass., 1943).

7. Jay Tolson suggests that Percy's conversion was different from those of most others at the time in that they had backgrounds mainly in literature whereas his had been in science (*Pilgrim in the Ruins,* 198). However, insofar as many of these converts (including Jacques Maritain himself and Allen Tate) were engaged in a cautionary attack on an all-encompassing science and scientism, it seems to me that there was not quite as much difference as Tolson supposes. Maritain had, in fact, studied in Heidelberg with the distinguished biologist and neovitalist Hans Dreisch. Moreover, one can easily exaggerate Percy's "scientific" background: the medical sciences, however vigorously pursued, hardly rate the same intellectual status as physics and mathematics; certainly Percy's attacks on "scientists" tend to include a far broader range of thinkers than that with which a purist would be comfortable.

8. Lewis A. Lawson and Victor A. Kramer, eds., *Conversations with Walker Percy* (Jackson, Miss., 1985), 316.

9. Jacques Maritain, *The Peasant of the Garonne: An Old Layman Questions Himself About the Present Time,* trans. Michael Cuddihy and Elizabeth Hughes (New York, 1968). The French original, *Le Paysan de la Garonne,* was published in 1967.

was specifically interested, the German theologian Romano Guardini, are usually associated with an interim phase in Catholic intellectual life between the old debased Scholasticism of the early-twentieth-century Church and the newer, secular-influenced theologies that flourished in the sixties and seventies. That is to say that Percy's theological understanding tended to be that of a well-informed lay Catholic of the postwar years, at once sensitive to certain modern scientific developments and yet determined to resist any secularizing interpretation of the religious phenomenon. Percy remained skeptical of the ideas not only of the new thinkers, but even more so of those Catholics involved in Liberation Theology and other attempts at bringing the Church into the twentieth century (or at least into a particular conception of it). Indeed, in its absolute dedication to the view of the Church enunciated by Pope John Paul II, Walker Percy's final position was not too unlike that of William F. Buckley at the *National Review,* theologian and social critic Michael Novak, or the well-known English political journalist and conservative Catholic convert Malcolm Muggeridge. Novak, for example, originally a champion of *aggiornamento,* has expressed the dismay he felt in the post–Vatican II era thus:

I did not expect a mandatory Latin Mass to be replaced by a mandatory English Mass; nor the virtual disappearance of Gregorian chant and the classical musical patrimony; nor the collapse of the vital Thomistic revival led by Jacques Maritain and Etienne Gilson, Bernard Lonergan and Karl Rahner, M. D. Chenu and so many others; nor the swift withering away of the great intellectual tradition nourished at so much cost by Jean Danielou and Henri de Lubac, Hans Urs von Balthasar and Louis Bouyer. I did not expect scriptural studies so to eclipse systematic theological reflection; nor Catholic preaching and practice to become evermore untheological and uncritical, in favor of the experiential and fervent ways of Baptists and Methodists; nor the charismatic style so to replace the style of realism; nor easy prophecy so thoroughly to dominate the tradition of prudence.[10]

10. Michael Novak, *Confession of a Catholic* (San Francisco, 1983), 170. William F. Buckley, Jr., regards Percy as one of his heroes (see Mark Royden Winchell, *William F. Buckley, Jr.,* Boston, 1984, p. 12).

Walker Percy might not have agreed with every single one of the criticisms listed above—he was irritated with those "who think you have to cling to every accidental of the faith as it was 50 years ago"—but there is no doubt that his general response to the situation was along similar lines.[11]

One might even go so far as to say that Percy's Catholicism had a strong ideological flavor. Although the word *ideology* is one that occurs frequently in his writing, Percy himself has usually associated it with an extremity of outlook, a slavery to some theoretical viewpoint or other, toward which he was thoroughly opposed. But he has also accused himself of at least temporarily adopting such a position. In the Summer, 1987, issue of the *Paris Review,* in answer to a question about his fundamental beliefs, Percy replied: "If you mean, am I still a Catholic, the answer is yes. The main difference after thirty-five years is that my belief is less self-conscious, less ideological, less polemical."[12] In light of his frequent engagement with theological issues in the last decade of his life, one might want to dispute this claim. In any case, the clear implication is that he was once ideological, even if he now perceives himself as being less so. In fact, Percy referred to both Christianity and Catholicism on a number of occasions as ideological.[13] Again, when the manuscript of *The Moviegoer,* his first novel, arrived at the offices of Alfred A. Knopf in 1960, its editor found it to consist of "only forty good pages and a rather evangelical Catholic ending."[14] And as novel follows novel, there is what Harold Bloom has referred to as "a metamorphosis from the language of story to the urgencies that transcend art."[15] Adherence to a faith such as Catholicism tends to prescribe a certain outcome, however achieved, and perhaps renders Walker Percy's fictions less interesting, if more comforting, than those of writers more openly responsive to the unpredictabilities of the human adventure.[16] At all events, Catholicism is an ideology that for good and for bad

---

11. Lewis A. Lawson and Victor A. Kramer, eds., *More Conversations with Walker Percy* (Jackson, Miss., 1993), 117.

12. Percy, *Signposts,* 375.

13. See, for example, Percy, *Signposts,* 332, and Lawson and Kramer, eds., *Conversations,* 157.

14. Quoted in Alfred Kazin, "The Pilgrimage of Walker Percy," *Harper's,* CCXLII (June, 1971), 81.

15. Harold Bloom, ed., *Walker Percy* (New York, 1986), 1.

16. Writers as diverse as Cardinal Newman, André Gide, and George Orwell have been skeptical about the possibility of a good Catholic novel.

has determined Percy's attitudes on far more issues—about human life, culture, race, gender—than is initially apparent and, as such, its influence needs to be fully explored.[17]

Walker Percy is the "last" Catholic novelist, then, in the sense that his vision of the world has been profoundly shaped by a particular period in recent Catholic history, and such a vision (as will be argued) is no longer viable.[18] There are, of course, other Catholic novelists in the English-speaking world—Muriel Spark, Auberon Waugh, David Lodge, Wilfrid Sheed, Mary Gordon, David Plante, Louise Erdrich, to name just a few—some of whom are "cultural Catholics," others true believers. But in no case is their vision immersed in the technicalities of a philosophical and theological Catholicism in the way that Percy's was. The Irish novelist Brian Moore is well known for his treatment of Catholic issues, but he himself does not profess such a faith, and his explorations are far less affirmative, or philosophically informed, than anything in Percy. Will Barrett, Percy's "last" gentleman in the novel of that title, did not bring southern chivalry to a complete end, but he did signal the demise of a notable form of that institution.[19] Likewise, although much of what Walker Percy did was unique to him, he too heralded the death of a certain type, or tradition, of Catholic novel writing.

In any attempt at giving a full presentation of Percy's thought, it is necessary to deal with both his philosophical essays and his novels. This is not quite a matter of following Jean-Paul Sartre's advice in regard to William Faulkner that "a fictional technique always relates back to the novelist's metaphysics," for Percy intended the two to be taken together.[20] Indeed, his case is more like that

17. For further discussion of Catholicism as an ideology, see Paul Giles, *American Catholic Arts and Fictions: Culture, Ideology, Aesthetics* (New York, 1992), 1–31.

18. In *Testing the Faith: The New Catholic Fiction in America* (New York, 1992), Anita Gandolfo holds out more hope for a new Catholic novel and a new Catholic paradigm than I do, though she acknowledges that it does not yet exist. Not being concerned with the kinds of philosophical issues that seem to me to invalidate any form of Catholic belief, she also sees Percy as more religiously innovative than I argue in the present study.

19. Walker Percy, *The Last Gentleman* (New York, 1966).

20. Jean-Paul Sartre, "On *The Sound and the Fury:* Time in the Work of Faulkner," in *Literary and Philosophical Essays,* trans. Annette Michelson (London, 1955), 79. When, in *Walker Percy and the Old Modern Age: Reflections on Language, Argument, and the Telling of Stories* (Baton Rouge, 1985), Patricia Lewis Poteat criticized Percy's philosophical as opposed to novelistic excursions as "the peculiar perils of seeking to construct a radical philosophical anthropology by using the conceptual tools of one's antagonists . . . [which] turn in his hands against him" (3), Percy's response,

of Sartre himself, who claimed that though he would have preferred to express all his ideas through fiction, there were matters that were too technically philosophical for such treatment, and so he felt obliged "to duplicate each novel with an essay." [21] Percy has explained his alternations between writing philosophical essays and novels as "the fruit of twenty years' off-and-on thinking about the subject [of man], of coming at it from one direction, followed by failure and depression and giving up, followed by making up novels to raise my spirits, followed by a new try from a different direction or from an old direction but at a different level, followed by failure, followed by making up another novel, and so on." [22] The novels and the nonfiction together are meant to present a theory of man, an anthropology, to use an expression that occurs frequently in Percy.[23]

In regard to Walker Percy's fiction, the connection between an idea and its imaginative representation is never, of course, direct or necessarily lacking in subtlety—Percy alludes often to the novelist as being indirect and even "devious." But while one must in this sense tease out each novel's meaning from the narrative, allusions, and tropes employed by the author, since one is trying to understand Percy in his totality, those additional comments he has offered on his intentions are just as relevant as the text itself. The most detailed, and, in my estimation, stimulating readings (occasionally overreadings) of all Percy's novels are to be found in John Edward Hardy's *Fiction of Walker Percy*. I agree with his judgment (specifically alluding to *The Moviegoer*, but with a wider reference implied) about Percy's "marvelously evocative urban and rural landscapes . . . acute and meticulously discriminate renderings of idiom and accent," and his impressive "rendering of marginal states of consciousness." My interest here, however, is to confine each story to its thematic essentials without losing sight of whatever narrative detail is relevant to this purpose. I am aware that this search

---

according to Tolson, was that she was "partly a victim of the old humanities-science split" (*Pilgrim in the Ruins,* 459–60).

21. Quoted in Ronald Hayman, *Sartre: A Biography* (New York, 1987), 136–37.

22. Percy, *The Message in the Bottle,* 10.

23. In his Jefferson Lecture in Washington in 1989, Percy said, "What I've been doing, both in the novels and in the nonfiction, is to make the beginnings of an anthropology, a coherent theory of man" (quoted in Ellen K. Coughlin, "Walker Percy, a Physician Turned Novelist, Chastises the Sciences for Failing to Explicate the Human Mind," *Chronicle of Higher Education,* May 10, 1989, p. A5; this quotation is not found exactly as such in the version of the lecture in *Signposts,* 271–91).

for theological structure rather than theological texture implicitly denies one of the strongest elements in Percy's religious outlook, his celebration of a sacramental universe—the "ordinary things of this world, bread, wine, water, touch, breath, words, talking, listening" have the "highest significance"—but feel equally that the religious argument is present *explicitly* in Percy's work in a way that is not the case with, for example, Flannery O'Connor. Hardy is especially unwilling to let Percy himself dictate (in interviews and essays) what his fictions are about. I, on the contrary, wish to present the "mind" of the author irrespective of the medium of its expression.[24] Moreover, in recent years, we have become less willing to admit an absolute distinction between those texts that are designated "discursive" and those usually referred to as "literary"; rather are the two perceived as mutually interactive, commenting on and informing each other, even pressuring the strategies of their respective narrations and arguments. So, again, the larger question is, Is Percy's anthropology, as expressed in his novels and essays, convincing? Is Percy's anthropology coherent? And if he is right, then is everyone else—the scientists whose credos appear in *Living Philosophies,* for example—wrong?

In his time, Walker Percy felt himself not quite at one *with* his time. He believed in the existence of evil, in an evolutionary process that had been interrupted by a supernatural force to make man qualitatively different from other species, in a subsequent divine intervention in human history, in the absolute authority of the Roman Church. How this set him in opposition to other contemporary thinkers has already been suggested in the selections given above from the contributors to Fadiman's *Living Philosophies* and in the references to recent Catholic thought. In the chapters that follow, I attempt to bring Percy into clearer confrontation with some of the ideas and people he is attacking—or with alternative positions on the thinkers he is sympathetically expounding. Thus, in Percy's first novel, *The Moviegoer,* the hero at one stage comes to realize how inadequate his reading of scientific books has been in helping him cope with the realities of daily existence. Among the volumes Binx lists—popular works of the first half of the

24. Percy, *Signposts,* 369; John Edward Hardy, *The Fiction of Walker Percy* (Urbana, 1987), 56, 57.

century—are Erwin Shrödinger's *What Is Life?*, Albert Einstein's *The Universe as I See It*, Sir Arthur Eddington's *The Expanding Universe*, and *The Chemistry of Life*. The popular scientific works that one must now confront (and that Percy has often confronted in his various essays and, by implication, in his novels) include Carl Sagan's *Cosmos*, Stephen Hawking's *A Brief History of Time*, Gould's *Wonderful Life*, Daniel C. Dennett's *Consciousness Explained*, and so forth, and the question still remains as to how "adequate" they are as guides to life. After all, Fadiman chose to begin his 1990 collection with a piece from Einstein that he had included in the original 1931 edition of *Living Philosophies*, an essay in which the famous physicist denies the existence of a God of reward and punishment made in man's image, or the survival of the individual after death, showing that, whatever Percy's opinion, many still find Einstein's thoughts satisfying and perfectly adequate. In *The Last Gentleman*, reflecting on his father's suicide, Will Barrett realizes that "it was not in the Brahms that one looked" for the meaning of things. In William Styron's 1990 account of how he resisted the temptation to do the deed, however, it is precisely the Brahms *Alto Rhapsody* that saves him.[25]

This study begins by examining the development of Walker Percy's literary career, particularly three major influences: his father's suicide, his adolescence in the home of his cousin and foster parent William Alexander Percy, and his bout with tuberculosis in the early 1940s, which led him to abandon medicine as a profession and to pursue instead his latent philosophical interests and eventually convert to the Roman Catholic faith. I sketch the milieu of American Catholicism in that period and the arguments of its opponents at the *Partisan Review* and elsewhere, and then I look at the various essays in the field of religious philosophy that Percy published during the 1950s as he attempted to become a specifically Catholic philosopher. The later circumstances in which Percy decided to turn (return, in fact, as we know from Tolson's biography) to novel writing and his first novel,

25. Walker Percy, *The Moviegoer* (New York, 1961), 59–60; Carl Sagan, *Cosmos* (New York, 1980); Stephen Hawking, *A Brief History of Time: From the Big Bang to Black Holes* (New York, 1988); Stephen Jay Gould, *Wonderful Life: The Burgess Shale and the Nature of History* (New York, 1989); Daniel C. Dennett, *Consciousness Explained* (Boston, 1991); Albert Einstein, "From *Living Philosophies*" (1931), in Fadiman, *Living Philosophies*, 3–6; Percy, *The Last Gentleman*, 260; William Styron, *Darkness Visible* (New York, 1990), 66–67.

are dealt with in Chapter 5. Since Percy alternated novel and essay after that, the remaining chapters pursue his publishing career in both endeavors right up to his death in 1990. My principle throughout what follows is that if Percy deals with an issue—in whatever field—I examine other important perspectives on that subject, especially those he criticizes by name, but also those he commends. I explore his positions on such topics as evolution, consciousness, abortion, and euthanasia, and finally attempt to place him in the context of the current intellectual thought that seems most relevant to his case, particularly as expressed by the former Catholic theologian, and now religiously agnostic analytic philosopher, Anthony Kenny.

Walker Percy is one of the few contemporary novelists who has made a difference in the lives of many of his readers. So it is no accident that one of his best critics, Lewis Lawson, uses the title *Following Percy* for his most recent collection of essays on the author, and then goes on to preface his volume with a personal note on what Percy has meant to him as a human being. Child psychologist Robert Coles constantly acknowledges Percy's influence on his life and work and has dedicated *The Spiritual Life of Children* to his memory. Within the present century, one has to look back to T. S. Eliot, or to the more personal writings of C. S. Lewis or Thomas Merton, to find a similar response. Such appeal is, of course, a reason for caution in judging Percy's work—James Atlas has referred to some of Percy's followers as "fanatical."[26] It is noticeable, too, I think, that almost all those who have written book-length studies of Percy have been quite sympathetic with his ideas, while his harshest critics are to be found among reviewers (some of them philosophers or linguists irritated by Percy's presumptions) less familiar with the totality of Percy's writings. In this sense, Percy has tended to become an author with a well-defined, if eclectic, audience, whose work stands somewhat apart from the main currents of contemporary critical interest, a writer engaged in an illusory spiritual pursuit that was merely the belated product of a discredited bourgeois individualism. In the light of such cautionary ob-

---

26. Lewis Lawson, *Following Percy: Essays on Walker Percy's Work* (Troy, N.Y., 1988); Robert Coles, *The Spiritual Life of Children* (Boston, 1990); Lawson and Kramer, eds., *Conversations,* 186.

servations, the reader of the present volume may legitimately wonder what this critic's stance is in regard to the subject of his inquiry.

My background has been in philosophy and theology in a Roman Catholic setting, subsequently in the British and American analytic tradition, and later still in literature. My convictions now, however, are perhaps best reflected in David Lodge's comment on his own present religious perspective as "demythologized, provisional, and in many ways [theologically] agnostic."[27] Nevertheless, while fundamentally critical of Percy, I am not unsympathetic with his purposes, and I consider that his was a successful life in a deeply meaningful way. After all, Percy's best friend, Shelby Foote, constantly—and often irritatingly—expressed dissent from Percy's religious opinions. It is possible to give a thoughtful response to an author who has raised thought-provoking questions without necessarily agreeing with him. So, if I can no longer consider myself a pilgrim in the strictly Christian sense, I am, I trust, a wayfarer who retains a knack for listening. Both what Walker Percy himself has had to say and the fact that numerous others have found his message appealing are phenomena that provoke serious interest whatever one's final judgment on them. To put the matter another way: in reading the personal accounts of the Catholic revival period of the 1930s to the 1950s in Wilfrid Sheed's memoir of his parents, *Frank and Maisie* (of the publishing house Sheed and Ward), and in Richard Gilman's *Faith, Sex, Mystery: A Memoir,* I have felt a sense of liberation from a burdensome and not fully understood past, a nostalgia for former certainties, and an admiration for the fortitude (and compassion) of many of those who survived faithfully into the more complex and (for them) depressing 1970s and 1980s; it is with such contesting emotions that I write.[28]

27. See David Lodge's introduction to a reissue of his 1960 novel *The Picturegoers* (London, 1993), ix. Lodge refers in passing to Percy's *Moviegoer,* which appeared a year later with a similar theme, as "a much better novel than mine . . . written by a much more mature author" (x).

28. Wilfrid Sheed, *Frank and Maisie: A Memoir with Parents* (New York, 1985); Richard Gilman, *Faith, Sex, Mystery: A Memoir* (New York, 1986).

1
FATES OF OUR FATHERS

At one point in "Why Are You a Catholic?" Walker Percy imagines a Presbyterian lady, a distant kin, asking him incredulously how a person of his social class could have become one of *them*.[1] But, in fact, when in the late 1940s Percy arrived at the conviction that he should join the Roman Catholic church, the prospect was not altogether without precedent in his family's history. Indeed, if it is true—as tradition has it—that the American Percys were in some way descended from the English earls of Northumberland (the most famous of whom was the fourteenth-century Sir Henry Percy, better known as Hotspur), then one of the novelist's ancestors was Blessed Thomas Percy, the Catholic martyr executed in 1572 (beatified in 1896) for his rebellion against Queen Elizabeth I, who died declaring that he remained "in the Communion of the Catholic church" and "a Percy in life and death." In the case of Charles Percy, the founder of the American line, it is uncertain whether this Irish-born adventurer was of Anglican or Catholic persuasion. It is known that his children by his second wife were all baptized in Natchez, Mississippi, by a Spanish priest.[2] Indeed, though many of the details were unavailable to Walker Percy himself, there had always been Catholic members of the Percy family, through either marriage or religious conversion.[3]

1. Clifton Fadiman, ed., *Living Philosophies: The Reflections of Some Eminent Men and Women of Our Time* (New York, 1990), 169.

2. See Bertram Wyatt-Brown, *The House of Percy: Honor, Melancholy, and Imagination in a Southern Family* (New York, 1994), 33. One of the most interesting and even amusing parts of Wyatt-Brown's study is devoted to showing how the Percy family, caught up in the Anglo-Saxon ancestor-hunting rage at the end of the nineteenth century, suppressed for several decades the definitive information it had received from the Public Record Office in London on its immediate *Irish* origins (339–49).

3. See Bertram Wyatt-Brown, *The House of Percy, passim.* A ninteenth-century relative, Eleanor Percy Lee, also a novelist, had converted to Catholicism. Wyatt-Brown even interprets a cautionary remark by the mother of one of Walker Percy's early girlfriends that her potential husband had

Most important of all, of course, the person mainly responsible for bringing Walker Percy up after the age of fourteen—his cousin, William Alexander Percy—had begun life as a member of that faith and was, in spite of his current agnosticism, to retain his affiliation throughout his life. If "Uncle" Will's understanding of Catholicism was not quite that which his young cousin was to adopt—it seems to have been strongly colored by Arnoldian and Hardyesque doubt of the late nineteeth century—it nevertheless provided Walker Percy with a model that would be relevant to his own later choice and perhaps render the decision less exotic than it might otherwise have been. "My Uncle Will was a Catholic, a lapsed Catholic; he didn't go to church but he was always talking about the great Catholic tradition," the younger Percy commented in 1988. Besides, in 1941, several years prior to Walker Percy's conversion, William Alexander Percy had published a best-selling account of his life as the son of a Mississippi Delta plantation owner, an account dedicated in part to Walker Percy and one providing a good deal of information about Will Percy's views and history on the subject of religious belief. Much has been written about the commitment to the Stoic philosophy of Marcus Aurelius that is so evident in the pages of *Lanterns on the Levee: Recollections of a Planter's Son,* but the book is pervaded also by the remembrance of a lost Roman Catholicism that seemed to its author to be no longer available to a thinking man. Moreover, in spite of his often-proclaimed unbelief, when William Alexander Percy died in the year following the book's publication, the funeral services were conducted by a Catholic priest (in the kind of hurried and distracted manner, in fact, that Walker Percy would use for the final scene of *The Last Gentleman*).[4] The twenty-five-year-old unconverted Walker Percy, by then a medical student at Columbia, can hardly have failed to take note of the circumstance.

His father's suicide in 1929 was the traumatic event that had brought Walker Percy, his mother (who was shortly to die in a mysterious car accident), and two

---

tuberculosis and was, besides, "poles apart" from her as referring to the Percys' reputed Catholicism—and this occurred several years before the future novelist converted (305).

4. Phil McCombs, "Century of Thanatos: Walker Percy and His Subversive Message," in Lewis A. Lawson and Victor A. Kramer, eds., *More Conversations with Walker Percy* (Jackson, Miss., 1994), 203; William Alexander Percy, *Lanterns on the Levee: Recollections of a Planter's Son* (Baton Rouge, 1973); Jay Tolson, *Pilgrim in the Ruins: A Life of Walker Percy* (New York, 1992), 161.

younger brothers from their country club home in the New South city of Birmingham, Alabama, to the very Old South residence of their distinguished—"legendary" is the word most frequently used of him—cousin in Greenville, Mississippi, about a year later. The suicide itself, while distressing, was not exceptional in the Percy clan, however. In 1794, following the exposure of certain matrimonial irregularities, his own ill health, and the deaths of two sons—and while under attack from French forces trying to retake the Spanish part of Mississippi (then West Florida) that his plantation occupied—the founder of the American Percy line had, as his great-great-grandson rather nonchalantly put it, "walked down to the creek with a sugar kettle, tied it round his neck, and hopped in." In the intervening years, there were to be many Percys who suffered various forms of mental illness—the family's most recent biographer, Bertram Wyatt-Brown, attributes this ongoing melancholia to genetic factors—right up to Walker Percy's grandfather, a prominent corporate lawyer, who had also committed suicide in Birmingham.[5]

Whatever the causes both biological and psychological for LeRoy Percy's fate in 1929, his oldest son's reaction, as he himself explained years later, was that he "didn't feel guilty or responsible the way some children of suicides do. . . . I was angry. And I was determined not only to find out why he did it but also to make damn sure that it didn't happen to me." So, the "central mystery" of Walker Percy's life would "always be why my father killed himself."[6] He would ponder thereafter the kind of man his father was, the apparent inadequacy of his father's inheritance of ethical Stoicism and religious agnosticism (in the Liberal Protestant tradition of the late nineteenth century), in an effort not only to protect himself, a depressive, from coming to a similar fate, but also in the hope of finding a more positive alternative. Walker Percy would often refer to the novelist as a "post-suicide" and examine in several of his works the mind-set of those about to perpetrate the act. He would maintain a lifelong interest in the career and death of Albert Camus, an author well known for his proposition—much quoted by Percy—that suicide poses the only real philosophical question. Dostoevsky, a

5. Lewis Baker, *The Percys of Mississippi: Politics and Literature in the New South* (Baton Rouge, 1983), 3–4; William Alexander Percy, *Lanterns on the Levee*, 39–40; Wyatt-Brown, *The House of Percy*, 55–73; Tolson, *Pilgrim in the Ruins*, 32.

6. Tolson, *Pilgrim in the Ruins*, 73, 396.

novelist in whose works suicides are by no means uncommon, would become his favorite writer. But he would also never cease looking for a better way, a cure rather than a mere antidote.[7]

At fourteen, then, Walker Percy had already experienced the defining moment of his life, the one that would pose the most basic questions about the meaning of things for him. Shortly thereafter, he left his "rotten childhood" (which, however, seems to have had many happy moments) behind him, the country club culture that, quite apart from his father's suicide, made him feel rootless and alienated ever afterwards, and he began the formation of what he later called his "second self" under the tutelage of his bachelor cousin, a lawyer, a plantation owner, and, most important of all for Walker Percy, a poet of some standing.[8] In the introduction that Walker Percy wrote for a new edition of *Lanterns on the Levee* in 1973, he recounts his first meeting with his cousin, when he was struck by the latter's "beautiful and terrible eyes" which were "shadowed by sadness" (viii). The description nicely points out both the stubborn independence and the absolute integrity of the older man and his sense of being disappointed in himself and in the times. But perhaps from the very beginning Walker Percy's questioning of his father's suicide had caused him to be a little suspicious of the kind of depressive Stoicism that his father had shared with their Greenville cousin and to look elsewhere, even in Uncle Will's own history, for the kind of truth that might make life physically and psychologically bearable.

Quite apart from its presumed origins in the English aristocracy, William Alexander Percy's ancestry was a distinguished one. In fact, in the late eighteenth century, precisely when the fame of the Northumberland Percys had died out, the family's reputation in America (or at least in Mississippi's Delta) was just beginning. By the time that William Alexander Percy was born there in 1885, the family had long been a dominant force in the political and social life of the region. Will Percy was an exceptional child, however, unlike any of his ancestors on either side of the family, less robust and much more artistic than an older brother who had died as a youth. Nevertheless, he had distinguished himself as an officer in

7. See N. N. Shneidman's *Dostoevsky and Suicide* (New York, 1977). The author arrives at a total of 31 suicides made up of actual (22), attempted (6), and contemplated (3).

8. William Alexander Percy, *Lanterns on the Levee*, ix.

World War I (he would seem to Walker to be a kind of American Rupert Brooke), campaigned hard for his father's reelection as a United States senator, and courageously opposed the Ku Klux Klan in the 1920s even while he himself held firm to the old paternalism in regard to his black sharecroppers. But whereas his father had entertained American presidents at his home, William Alexander Percy was more inclined to open his doors to scholars and artists, William Faulkner, Harry Stack Sullivan, and Langston Hughes being among the more notable of his many guests.

As a poet, Will Percy—whose work was published by Knopf in New York and by Yale University Press (for which he also acted as editor)—was of the age of Thomas Hardy, A. E. Housman, Robert Frost, and the Nashville Fugitives in that his poetry, though strongly resistant to the modernist aesthetic and less accomplished and more sentimental than theirs, expresses some of the same poignancy about the human condition when traditional religious belief is no longer possible. Thus, in a 1923 poem titled "A Canticle," the speaker asks a series of questions about the origins of the world's beauty in the vein: "Was there no love conceived the one-starred, rivered evening, / And dipped in crocus fire the gray horns of the moon?" He answers (somewhat in the manner, if not the idiom, of Wallace Stevens):

> They say there never was a god men loved but died—
> Dead is Astarte, Astoreth is dead, and Baal;
> Zeus and Jehovah share a single grave and deep;
> Olympus brings no laughter, Sinai no voice.

If there is a "loveliness" that outlasts such "temporal" beings (Percy never indicates very clearly what this loveliness is), the one thing certain is that the gods of the old time are now, for whatever reason, silent.[9]

Walker Percy has indicated what the effect of living with such a person was on a "raw" youth of an unusually receptive disposition: it was "nothing less than to be informed in the deepest sense of the word. What was to be listened to, dwelled on, pondered over for the next thirty years was of course the man himself,

9. William Alexander Percy, *Collected Poems* (New York, 1943), 208–209.

the unique human being, and when I say unique I mean it in its most literal sense: he was one of a kind: I never met anyone remotely like him. It was to encounter a complete, articulated view of the world as tragic as it was noble." [10] Uncle Will was for Percy "a fixed point in a confusing world," so that "even when I did not follow him [in intellectual commitments], it was usually in *relation* to him, whether with him or against him, that I defined myself and my own direction" (xi). So, while Walker Percy's relationship with his cousin may have been complicated by the latter's discreet and sexually repressed homoerotic orientation (the future novelist seems never to have been quite comfortable with such a world and has made no allusion to this aspect of his foster parent's life), and though he has claimed on occasion that back then he was more interested in the pure certainties of science than in either the teachings of Sunday school or the philosophical outlook of his uncle, that life obviously did preoccupy him. [11] Most of all, and in retrospect, it did so not in its witness to the viability of the Stoic ethic but rather in its nostalgia for a lost religious faith.

William Alexander Percy's memoir, *Lanterns on the Levee,* in which he recounts this loss, is an extraordinary work that represents the totality of the man who wrote it, giving voice to thoughts and attitudes that have rarely been articulated so clearly, engaging because of the self-deprecatory tone of its author even while certain of its observations on race and class especially now must sound highly offensive, and while the entire enterprise seems astonishingly unaware of its own political and social self-interest. Perceptive, romantic, realistic, sentimental, condescending, and diffident by turns, it is a work that—as Walker Percy was only too well aware—has its misguided enthusiasts among certain conservative southerners just as it has its vehement detractors among those of more liberal persuasion. Percy's overall tone is one of Spenglerian pessimism about a world

10. William Alexander Percy, *Lanterns on the Levee,* x.

11. Bertram Wyatt-Brown notes the intensity of William Alexander Percy's male friendships and his association with English writer Norman Douglas at Taormina, a resort well known for its "Uranian" clientele (*The House of Percy,* 217–22). Taking account of Walker's later acts of rebellion—such as his spending a year in Germany (a country that his cousin loathed) rather than France in the 1930s—William Rodney Allen surmises that he was seeking a stronger, less homosexual "father" and that his subsequent adoption of an autocratic Catholicism was an example of this (*Walker Percy: A Southern Wayfarer* [Jackson, Miss., 1986], 12). But whatever questions his uncle's proclivities may have aroused in him, the evidence suggests that Walker Percy's conversion was a response to his uncle's past interests rather than a reaction against him.

undergoing what he sees as a process of deterioration; the decline of his own class, the changing situation of blacks (regarded as children and unequals, who are now foolishly breaking away from the old white paternalism as they follow illusory promises of a better life elsewhere), and the rise of poor whites to political office (and, in Europe, of nazism) are but symptoms of this phenomenon. Convinced that "we are now watching the followers of Jesus and Buddha and Socrates being driven from the face of the earth," Percy finds his only consolation in his own inner resources and in a loneliness that he so touchingly describes as to appear actually to revel in its bleakness (313).

Part of Will Percy's loneliness undoubtedly sprang from the sense of religious abandonment that had come to him in his teens, an event which he recounts with telling detail in his autobiography. Thus, because his mother was a French Catholic, he had begun life as a member of that faith and was for a time fervent in his beliefs and critical of the "unchurchliness" of his father (nominally an Episcopalian). Indeed, he recalls that reading *Ivanhoe* (a southern favorite), "far from being inspired to knightly heroism, [I] grew infatuated with the monastic life, if it could be pursued in a cave opening on a desert" (57). At one stage, Will became so "intolerably religious" that he found himself going to early Mass "at the slightest provocation, racking my brain to find something to confess once a month, praying inordinately, and fasting on the sly." Although such behavior was puzzling to his family, he "just couldn't help it, it was a violent attack, perhaps I've never fully recovered. Indeed, painful as it was to the family, it was anguish and ecstasy, but mostly anguish, to me. I wanted so intensely to believe, to believe in God and miracles and the sacraments and the Church and everything. Also, I wanted to be completely and utterly a saint; heaven and hell didn't matter, but perfection did" (79). In fact, at the tender age of nine he informed his astonished mother that he wished to become a priest, a wish that she, though quite pious, firmly opposed.

But even at that early stage there was uncertainty in Will Percy's mind, as he immediately goes on to inform his readers:

Yet never, never for a moment, was my belief without doubt: the Satan of my disbelief was at my elbow scoffing, insinuating, arguing, day and night. I'm certain Shelley never sank upon the thorns of life and bled nearly so often as I did between ten and sixteen. To be at once intellectually honest and religious is a wrack on which I writhed dumbly, for I knew even then there were certain things which, like overwhelming physical pain, you must fight out alone, at the bottom of your own dark well, beyond ministration of assuagement or word of advice, incommunicado and leper-lonely. (79)

Subsequent exposure, while a student at the University of the South, to the sweet, melancholic unbelief of the Victorians, epitomized in Matthew Arnold's "Dover Beach" and Edward Fitzgerald's hedonistic translation of the *Rubaiyat,* led Percy to undergo a final crisis of faith that "altered the sunlight" from religion and was to affect the rest of his life.

Will Percy does not elaborate on the background to his crisis, but the references to Arnold and to "intellectual honesty" earlier suggest that his was the typical Victorian questioning of faith brought about by exposure to Darwin's theories and the higher criticism of the Bible.[12] The crisis came to a head one day when he went to confession at the local Catholic chapel that lay a short distance from his Episcopal college:

I knelt in the little Winchester church examining my conscience and preparing for confession. How it came about did not seem sudden or dramatic or anything but sad. As I started to the confessional I knew there was no use going, no priest could absolve me, no church could direct my life or my judgment, what most believed I could not believe. What belief remained there was no way of gauging yet. I only knew then there was an end, I could no longer pretend to myself or cry: "Mea culpa. Help thou mine unbelief." It was over, and forever.

Percy rode back to his college "mournful and unregretful," knowing that henceforth "I should breathe a starker and a colder air, with no place to go when I was tired. . . . From now on I would be living with my own self" (95).

Nevertheless, though Will Percy soon ceased being formally a Catholic, he

12. Percy mentions the contradictions in the Gospels in *Lanterns on the Levee,* but his tone is more that of David Hume than of the German higher critics.

continued to be associated with that communion and even judged on one occasion that he would have kept a teaching position at Sewanee "had not one or two dignitaries questioned my papist affiliations" (226). He remained on affectionate terms throughout his life with several nuns (his former teachers), who hoped— and even schemed rather elaborately—for his return to the faith. Indeed, the very fact that Percy recounts this detail in the pages of *Lanterns on the Levee* itself suggests a basic attunement to an essentially Catholic sensibility.

When William Alexander Percy abandoned Catholicism, he was left with that old staple of southern aristocrats, the teachings of Marcus Aurelius tempered by a commitment to a purely ethical Christianity. But he does not appear to have been so absolutely assured of his own choice that he was willing to impose it on others. Thus, in a chapter in *Lanterns* entitled "For the Younger Generation," Percy muses on his obligations toward the three brothers (Walker, LeRoy, and Phinizy) he had adopted in 1930, and there he makes some remarkable, and even contradictory, comments on the religious phenomenon. Acknowledging his own inability to guide them, he explains that he sent the boys to a variety of churches— they had all been baptized into their mother's Presbyterian faith—only to have them return "confused, resentful, and distressed" (313). They then came to him for guidance, and all that he could do was be "honest." Percy proceeds to explain his own minimal belief, criticizing conventional religion in passing because so often it does not lead to a general improvement in morals.

In his account, Percy recognizes first of all that man has always sought a god. He phrases the question very much in the semiromantic rhetoric of the period: "These blue and starred heavens with all their intricate beauty and with man riding the darkness like a god, how came they here? If no god coaxed them out of nothingness, how then were they born . . . why are they here? And why, why are we here?" (317). Then he attempts to answer his own question:

We know that thinking like ours could not have created even this paltry world of ours, yet we know equally that the injustice and horror of the world would not be tolerated by any good three-dimensional mind. We complain of the sorry scheme of things because against all reason and all evidence we assume the Schemer's mind to be dimensional like our own. We forget that the Master Schemer, worthy of our loyalty and able to conceive and make what our poor faculties perceive, must be possessed of faculties so far beyond our own that the pattern of their functioning, if explained, could not make sense to us. . . . To the mind that could dream and shape our beaconed universe, what is injustice to us may be unfathomable tenderness, and our horror only loveliness misunderstood. If we but knew, all we ask is that what we see and live in be not chance-built and accident directed. Our fear is to be participants in unplanned chaos. The rest doesn't matter. We need not assail the sorry scheme—the chaos we see is a hundredth-dimensional plan glimpsed by three-dimensional perceptions. (319)

Percy later suggests that our perceptions may one day expand so as to embrace such a being. At present, however, he is "unknowable and incomprehensible." So, in the meantime, we must be content with living in this world where "it is given to man to behold beauty and worship nobility. . . . These only are reality to his profoundest self; he needs no proof of them and no explanation. They are, he is, and over him there passes the shudder of recognition. These recognitions are brief moments we may live by for our lives." Percy claims that whoever gave us these perceptions "gave too, no doubt, the heavens' laws and conjured up creation" and that if one were to sit "in the Greek theater above Taormina with the wine-dark sea below and Aetna against the sunset, and if there he could meditate on Jesus and the Emperor [Marcus Aurelius], he would be assured a god had made earth and man" (320).

But as certain as William Alexander Percy is that there is a need for a rather generalized religious faith, he is just as sure that much of traditional religion is mere superstition. In his long poem "Enzio's Kingdom," he had attacked Catholic dogmatism.[13] Now he quotes a saying of his father's about the response to death encouraged by the official representatives of religion: "I've been pitying the thousands who have been sent across, terrified by the lies of priests in all the ages. There's nothing to fear" (314). When he recalls from his religious youth "dead phrases—salvation, washed in the blood of the Lamb, He descended into

---

13. William Alexander Percy, *Collected Poems*, 301–43. See also Lewis Baker's comment in *The Percys of Mississippi*, 125.

hell, the resurrection of the body, born of the Virgin Mary"—Percy asks, "Where lies the virtue in attempting to persuade honest young minds to entertain such outworn rubbish?" Indeed, it is religion's vain effort to keep such ideas alive, he asserts, rather than the attacks of the scientists, that will bring about its eventual demise. Thus again, in a terminology that Walker Percy will later pick up (but from an opposite point of view), Will Percy asserts: "Philosophical conceptions—the Trinity, the atonement, the fall, the redemption—cannot save this generation, for they speak a beautiful dead language." Yet Percy finally, and anxiously, stresses the need for some kind of religion, for "live words, tender with meaning and assurance. Without them the young drift through the world, aimless, unemployed, with no certainties in their heart to give them anchorage or peace" (315). Such faith is necessary to resist the belief in Race offered by Hitler, or Stalin's in the State, or even America's in the god of Mammon.

What, then, does William Alexander Percy propose as a practical solution to the problem? "There is left to each of us," he claims, "no matter how far defeat pierces, the unassailable wintry kingdom of Marcus Aurelius." Thus, "out of my own darkness, having first placed in their [Walker Percy and his brothers'] hands the Gospels and the *Meditations* of Marcus Aurelius, I try to point out to them the pale streak I see which may be a trail" (316). He philosophizes in a more general way: "All we can know is through the tidings brought us by our five inaccurate senses," and "We cannot smell what a dog or Helen Keller or an eagle smells" (317). But then we get a reiteration of the original criticisms of particularized religions and a seeming recourse to a medley of Stoic and Buddhist beliefs: "But we trouble our hearts with foolish doubts and unwise questionings—the fear of death, the hope of survival, forgiveness, heaven, hell. Rewards and punishments hereafter? What bribes we ask for our perfunctory righteousness?" (320):

As to our pathetic plea for personal survival with all the quirks and foibles that alone make personality identifiable—there is nothing to fret about here. We survive or we are annihilated, and all our anguish cannot undo our fate one way or the other. But we may assuage our vanity by listening to the Buddha's thought. Our dread and torment in this life we lead are its apartness, its eternal isolation. We try to rid us of ourselves by love, by prayers, by vice, by the Lethe of activity, and we never wholly succeed. Above all things we desire to be united and absorbed. . . . To become part of the creating essence and of all things created by it, in this alone might be found fulfillment, peace, ecstasy.

Percy finally dismisses such preoccupations as unnecessary: "Death, Heaven or Hell, Rewards or Punishment, Extinction or Survival, these are epic troubles for the Epic mind. Our cares are fitted to our powers. Our concern is here, and with the day so overcast and short, there's quite enough to do." He ends with a rather enigmatic hope that seems more in tune with Walker Percy's later writings than with his own: "So I counsel the poor children. But I long for the seer or saint who sees what I surmise—and he will come, even if he must walk through ruins" (321). In fact, at a convention of Mississippi newspaper editors in 1939, Will Percy had declared, "We need a Peter the Hermit, or a St. Francis. The right person, I believe, could kindle a great religious revival. Something of the kind must happen to the democracies, if they are to be saved." [14]

Although Walker Percy was much influenced by his cousin's Stoicism, in the end it was this that he found most objectionable in his inheritance, particularly when he himself became a Catholic, something, of course, that he might possibly never have done but for the fact that William Alexander Percy had been one. Thus Walker Percy's statement in an essay in the 1960s contrasting his position with his cousin's: "For it appears that what is upon us is not a twilight of the gods but a very real race between the powers of light and darkness, that time is short and the issue very much in doubt." Thus his view of the southern gentleman: "How like him to go into Chancellorsville or the Argonne with Epictetus in his pocket; how unlike him to have had the Psalms. It is true that he was raised on the Christian chivalry of Walter Scott, but it was a Christianity which was aestheticized by medieval trappings and a chivalry which was abstracted from its sacramental setting." [15] Thus, his overall view of the Stoic tradition: "Nor did it wish to survive. Its most characteristic mood was a poetic pessimism which took a

---

14. Baker, *The Percys of Mississippi,* 166.
15. Walker Percy, "Uncle Will," in *Signposts in a Strange Land,* ed. Patrick Samway (New York, 1991), 59; Percy, "Stoicism in the South," in *Signposts,* 85.

grim satisfaction in the dissolution of its values—because social decay confirmed one in his original choice of the wintry kingdom of self" (85). Thus his presentation of the alternative Christian point of view: "It must be otherwise with the Christian. The urban plebs is not the mass which is to be abandoned to its own barbaric devices, but the lump to be leavened. The Christian is optimistic precisely where the Stoic is pessimistic" (86). He concluded (in the light of the racial problems in the South), "The good pagan's answer is no longer good enough for the South" (88).

All these reactions were to come much later, of course; in the 1930s, Walker Percy was not yet fully aware of the inadequacy of his cousin's philosophy or that what was most important about William Alexander Percy's legacy was precisely that which Will had long since officially abandoned. In the meantime, it was science that seemed to be able to provide an answer to the questions of life for the young Percy, to respond to what his friend Shelby Foote described as the former's ever present need for authoritative solutions. And yet, already there was in the distant background the nagging question Walker Percy had about some Catholic neighbors in Greenville: "Why are they so sure of themselves?" [16] And it was possible that even his Uncle Will was not wholly secure in his own convictions and bore indirect witness to an institution of absolute authority and certainty: at one point in *Lanterns* when the local priest, Fr. Koestenbrock, is revisiting Greenville long after his retirement and is asked by Will Percy what he thinks about the Ku Klux Klan (then very active against not only blacks but also Jews and Catholics), he replies thus: "I do not think of it. The Church has been here a long time; it will be here a much longer time, after all these klans and foolish things are forgotten" (91).

16. Tolson, *Pilgrim in the Ruins,* 156.

2

SCIENCE, SICKNESS, AND SALVATION

✝

However much the philosophies of Stoicism and Catholicism may have nagged at Walker Percy from time to time during his Greenville days, his main interest was in science. In high school, he even wrote a poem entitled "Ode to Einstein." He was an avid reader of such popular scientific authors as H. G. Wells and Julian Huxley, a very ordinary and understandable interest, though one that suggests too an early tendency to see science as offering an answer to philosophical and theological questions that lay beyond its immediate expertise.[1] As has been noted again and again, Percy was searching for certainty. It is not surprising, therefore, that he chose to major in chemistry at the University of North Carolina in Chapel Hill when he went there in the fall of 1933. A more ominous quest for certainty, perhaps, and one aided by his minor in the language, was his 1934 visit to Hitler's Germany, during which he was enormously impressed by the dedication of that country's youth to a cause that seemed authoritative to them at the time, but one that would cause Percy many grim reflections on the subject in later years. The need for certainty also led him, on graduation, to enter Columbia's College of Physicians and Surgeons, though he would half-joke in interviews that he became a doctor because of an old southern tradition of males from families like his always having a profession.[2] In this case, however, Percy soon became disturbed by the "sloppiness" of most forms of medical practice because they dealt with the rather untidy matter of human beings, and, true to form, he decided to specialize in pathology "where it seemed medicine came closest to being the science it should be."[3] Thus we witness both his ongoing desire for finality and a hint at

1. Jay Tolson, *Pilgrim in the Ruins: A Life of Walker Percy* (New York, 1992), 97–98.
2. Lewis Baker, *The Percys of Mississippi: Politics and Literature in the New South* (Baton Rouge, 1983), 177. Percy was also influenced by Sinclair Lewis' 1925 novel, *Arrowsmith,* which deals with the idealisms and corruptions of the medical profession (see Lewis Lawson, *Following Percy: Essays on Walker Percy's Work* [Troy, N.Y., 1988], 164–77).
3. Walker Percy, *Signposts in a Strange Land,* ed. Patrick Samway (New York, 1991), 187.

what precisely he would later find unsatisfactory with the "solution" that science supposedly offered.

From the beginning, of course, Walker Percy must have been well aware of how imperfect human beings could be, for he came to New York bearing problems that had long troubled him from his family's traumatic history. But here, too, he sought the certainty of a "scientific" cure. While at Columbia, and on the advice of noted psychologist Harry Stack Sullivan, once a visitor at the Greenville household, Percy had daily sessions with psychiatrist Janet Rioch (a former associate of Erich Fromm) for a couple of years. After he had studied the works of Freud more deeply in 1939–1940, he switched to a certified psychoanalyst, Goddard Booth.[4] Such therapy does not appear to have been of much use, however, and his many references both to the theories of Fromm and to Freudian analysis in later years strongly suggest that he found these procedures problematic, if not altogether incapable of producing a successful outcome.[5] Still, it would take an even more intimate crisis to provoke Percy into a deeper self-questioning and the recognition that he needed to reconstruct his worldview in some more radical way.

Such a crisis arose when Percy became seriously ill with tuberculosis in 1941. He had unexpectedly contracted the disease while conducting autopsies on tubercular patients at New York's Bellevue Hospital. Years later, he explained how this "cataclysm" had intruded upon his fascination with the aesthetics of the scientific method:

> I found myself in the pathology laboratory at Bellevue, where it seemed medicine came closest to being the science it should be and farthest from the arts and crafts of the bedside manner. Under the microscope, in the test tube, in the colorimeter, one could actually see the beautiful theater of disease and even measure the effect of treatment on the disease process. Then came the cataclysm, brought to pass appropriately enough by one of

---

4. Tolson, *Pilgrim in the Ruins,* 137–42, 151.

5. William Rodney Allen, *Walker Percy: A Southern Wayfarer* (Jackson, Miss., 1986), 14. However, when in the 1970s psychiatrist Robert Coles stayed at Percy's home for a few days to get the background for his *New Yorker* essays on the author, Percy was quite disappointed that Coles made no apparent effort to psychoanalyze him (see Tolson, *Pilgrim in the Ruins,* 573–74).

these elegant agents of disease, the same scarlet tubercular bacillus I used to see lying crisscrossed like Chinese characters in the sputum and lymphoid tissue of the patients at Bellevue. Now I was one of them.[6]

Even though this crisis did not turn him away from his previous allegiance to the scientific method, it gave him a broader perspective and led him to question his earlier assumptions about modern science's all-sufficiency. Percy summed up the change that came over him in the following way: "After 12 years of a scientific education, I felt somewhat like the Danish philosopher Søren Kierkegaard when he finished reading Hegel. Hegel, said Kierkegaard, explained everything under the sun, except one small detail: what it means to be a man living in the world who must die" (188). Walker Percy was reentering the world of human—and humane—"sloppiness."

Sent to convalesce at a sanatorium in the Adirondacks at a time when the illness required a long period of confinement, exiled to his own "magic mountain" (Thomas Mann's novel about a tubercular patient would soon come to occupy his imagination and inspire imitation), he had both time and inclination to ponder the nature and destiny of man in a technological society. His illness not only strained his belief in the ultimate success of the scientific enterprise, but also strained his faith in the efficacy of an impersonal and detached Stoicism such as had been recommended by his Greenville cousin (which, he admitted on one occasion, he himself was too weak to adopt). Moreover, he now had the opportunity to shift his reading from the standard medical textbooks back to his broader intellectual interests from Greenville and Chapel Hill days, as well as to take up new ones (though Percy's associates at Columbia remarked on how often he was seen reading novels and magazines even then, and he was later attracted to one of his professors, Dr. William Carson von Glahn, because of the latter's wide-ranging humanistic pursuits).[7]

The usual account of what happened next—partly provided by Percy himself, who was often contradictory in the details of his memories—is that, challenged by this unexpected crisis in his own life to question whether it was satisfactory

---

6. Walker Percy, "From Facts to Fiction," in *Signposts,* 187–88.
7. Tolson, *Pilgrim in the Ruins,* 199, 136, 148–49.

to see *himself* as merely a specimen of a more general disease phenomenon, he turned to the writings of those novelists and philosophers (becoming popular at the time) who asserted the importance and freedom of the individual: Fyodor Dostoevsky, Albert Camus, Karl Jaspers, Gabriel Marcel, Martin Heidegger, Jean-Paul Sartre, Martin Buber, and, above all, Søren Kierkegaard. It seems, however, that matters took a somewhat less simple course, though the end result remained the same: religious conversion.

Percy did indeed spend much of the period of his illness reading novels by broadly "existentialist" writers such as Dostoevsky and Franz Kafka, but he also read widely in the philosophy of language, a discipline in exciting ferment in the 1930s and 1940s and one from which Percy experienced both hope and threat. In regard to his often-mentioned existentialist concerns, Percy has said on at least one occasion that he did not read Kierkegaard at this time and that his real interest in the existentialist philosophers came later and was a reaction against his original positivist pursuits.[8] Be that as it may, his main enthusiasm was for Scholastic philosophy, particularly that of St. Thomas Aquinas, whose *Summa Theologica*, the great medieval exposition of Christian theology on philosophical principles, Percy claimed to have read in its entirety. Initially, this undertaking gained much of its momentum from his efforts at refuting the doctrinal claims of a fellow tubercular patient, Arthur Fortugno, a Catholic. Directly encountering a system of Catholic thought that was certainly more intricate and vigorous than the rather anemic version that had been available to him from his Uncle Will's religious background, Walker Percy soon found himself losing the argument: by 1943, he and Fortugno were attending religious services together.

Whatever the exact sequence of his reading—and whenever he read Kierkegaard in particular—Percy has often claimed that what led him more than anything else to become a Catholic in 1947 was his encounter with Kierkegaard's "Of the Difference Between a Genius and an Apostle." First published a hundred

---

8. Percy told Bradley R. Dewey in a 1974 interview that he had not read Kierkegaard in the sanatorium. He then explained: "I was reading novels mostly, and linguistic philosophy, the philosophy of language. I was much more interested in Ernst Cassirer's philosophy of symbolic forms along with people like Susanne Langer and the logical positivists of the time. The existentialism came later. I guess it was a kind of reaction against the linguistic analytic philosophy of England and Austria" (Lewis A. Lawson and Victor A. Kramer, eds., *Conversations with Walker Percy* [Jackson, Miss., 1985], 106).

years earlier, the essay argues that what distinguishes an Apostle from a genius is not the content of his message or even his willingness to defend it with his life (though this may help) but the *authority* by which he proclaims the truth. Thus, contrasting St. Paul with Plato, Kierkegaard remarks, "What Plato says on immortality really is profound, reached after deep study; but then poor Plato has no authority whatsoever." [9] According to Kierkegaard (who has Hegel in mind), philosophy and theology have deceived Christianity into betraying itself: "They have simply forced back the sphere of paradox-religion into the sphere of aesthetics. . . . An Apostle becomes neither more nor less than a genius, and then—good night, Christianity! *Esprit* and the Spirit, revelation and originality, a call from God and genius, all end up by meaning more or less the same thing" (89). There is, then, a radical disjunction between the Christian message and the workings of ordinary philosophical-theological reasoning, since the authority of the former does not at all lie with the latter.

It is in this emphasis that he places on authority that Kierkegaard especially appealed to Percy. In his highly polemical introduction to Kierkegaard's essay, Walter Kaufmann stresses that the Danish philosopher held "that Christianity was from the start essentially authoritarian—not just that the Catholic Church was, or that Calvin was, or Luther, or, regrettably, most of the Christian churches, but that Christ was—and is" (27). Indeed, the Swiss theologian Karl Barth thought that Kierkegaard, had he lived longer, would have ended up a Roman Catholic, a follower of an institution with very precise directions, and for this reason Barth refused to place him among the great Protestant thinkers. This authoritarian element would play such an important role in Percy's understanding of the nature of Catholicism that he would oppose the kind of exploration and questioning of Church officials and doctrine that became pervasive even within the community of believers during the 1960s and afterwards.[10] In 1987, for example, referring back to the period of his conversion, Percy remarked, "If I should now discover, 40 years after entering the Church, that I now belong to a church consisting of a loose federation of flocks and bishops, my first reaction would be that I could have saved myself a lot of trouble if I had become a Methodist or an Episcopa-

---

9. Søren Kierkegaard, *The Present Age* (New York, 1962), 103.

10. Tolson, *Pilgrim in the Ruins,* 200, 367–68. Years later, Percy was troubled by a Benedictine friend who appeared much more skeptical about the Church than he could tolerate.

lian—no offense intended." [11] Thus, in a sense, one might say that Percy merely wished to exchange one "authority" for another, that of science for that of a highly dogmatic Roman Catholicism.

Reading Kierkegaard also led Percy eventually to engage with the more contemporary existentialists. Books, essays, and novels by Jean-Paul Sartre and Albert Camus at a relatively popular level, and by Martin Heidegger and Karl Jaspers at the more arcane reaches of the subject, promoted such a view of the world, one in which choice, made in *angst,* determined who one was, so that one was said to be totally responsible for one's own existence. Sartre and Heidegger were arguing for an existentialism that was basically atheistic in character: since there was no god, one had to create one's own values. But Gabriel Marcel offered a Christian version of this doctrine that was to have great appeal for Percy. Moreover, though the theories of the various existentialists differed considerably, they were all engaged in some form of humanistic program—Sartre entitled one of his most famous essays "Existentialism Is a Humanism"—and wary of scientific generalizations. [12] Again, the novels of Dostoevsky, included at the time in the existentialist camp because of the intensity with which he had expressed his convictions and his emphasis on man's alienation, were also coming to wider attention than heretofore and contributed to individualistic and religious preoccupations among his readers; Percy had, of course, read Dostoevsky earlier, but this new interest must have reinvigorated his own. As a result, Percy received intensive exposure to a series of personalistic philosophies that confirmed a view at which he himself had arrived independently.

Yet far too much can be made of Percy's interest in existentialist philosophy. In fact, the movement was under attack from the very beginning from Church authorities for its emphasis on the *irrational* aspect of religious choice. Roman Catholics did not see their invocation of an absolute mission as requiring a Kierkegaardian leap-of-faith for which there was no plausible explanation. On the contrary, they set high store by their detailed justifications for that authority. Oxford philosopher Elizabeth Anscombe, herself a Catholic, succinctly explains the situation that prevailed at the time: "To the educated laity and the clergy

11. Walker Percy, in "Symposium on Roman Catholicism and 'American Exceptionalism,'" *New Oxford Review,* LIV (March, 1987), 4–5.
12. Jean-Paul Sartre, *Existentialism and Humanism,* trans. Philip Mairet (London, 1948).

trained in those days, the word was that the Catholic Christian faith was *rational,* and a problem, to those able to feel it as a problem, was how it was *gratuitous*— a special gift of faith." [13] Kierkegaard had put emphasis on the latter, almost to the exclusion of the rational grounds for belief; Catholics tended to emphasize the rational without entirely forgetting the gift aspect of the matter.

In fact, in his 1950 encyclical *Humani Generis,* Pope Pius XII would issue a warning to Catholics against existentialism's possible subversions, forcing Gabriel Marcel and a number of prominent French Catholic theologians to clarify their positions in regard to it. While one would not want to overstate the importance of this encyclical, or to suggest that it was received without any skepticism by all those to whom it was addressed, *Humani Generis* does provide a useful insight into official—and widely accepted—Catholic thinking on several of Walker Percy's interests at the time of his conversion. Announcing that it is concerned with "Some False Opinions Which Threaten to Undermine the Foundations of Catholic Doctrine," the encyclical condemns the philosophy of existentialism in what might at first appear a strange context: that is, in the midst of an attack on a radical scientific evolutionism. Thus, with daunting rhetoric, it declares, "Some impudently and indiscreetly hold that evolution, which has not been fully proved even in the domain of natural sciences, explains the origin of all things, and audaciously support the monistic and pantheistic opinion that the world is in continual evolution. . . . Such fictitious tenets of evolution which repudiate all that is absolute, firm and immutable, have paved the way for the new erroneous philosophy which, rivaling idealism, immanentism and pragmatism, has assumed the name of existentialism, since it concerns itself only with the existence of individual things and neglects all consideration of their immutable essences." Existentialism is, of course, related to evolutionary theory in this way of looking at things (though, be it said that it is not a way that comes immediately to mind in regard to this particular philosophy) in that both presume a totally *natural,* or immanent, origin for human beings, one that allows for radical change and development without a teleological purpose. Later, the encyclical stresses the importance of human reason "to demonstrate with certainty the existence of God," reaffirms the Church's "demand" that "future priests be instructed in philosophy 'according to the

13. G. E. M. Anscombe, *Ethics, Religion, and Politics* (Minneapolis, 1981), 113.

method, doctrine, and principles of the Angelic Doctor [St. Thomas Aquinas],'"
and condemns those Catholic theologians who suggest otherwise:

> While scorning our philosophy, they extol other philosophies of all kinds,
> ancient and modern, oriental and occidental, by which they seem to imply
> that any kind of philosophy or theory, with a few additions and corrections
> if need be, can be reconciled with Catholic dogma. No Catholic can doubt
> how false this is, especially where there is question of those fictitious the-
> ories they call immanentism, or idealism, or materialism, whether historic
> or dialectic, or even existentialism, whether atheistic or simply the type that
> denies the validity of . . . reason in the field of metaphysics.[14]

A tour de force, certainly, and no doubt also both obscurantist and ominous to
those not in sympathy with its statements, but with its insistence on "absolute,
firm and immutable" truths, it provided a firm anchor for those in need of such
stability. Novelist Muriel Spark, for example, who converted in 1954, has said
that such Catholic doctrine "was the first philosophical integrity" she had ever
known because "it united a lot of disintegrating factors. It gave me a ground and
something to measure from—'the still point in the turning world,' as Eliot said." [15]

However, quite apart from such a papal admonition, as one trained in the
sciences, Percy himself was somewhat on guard against the emphasis on irration-
ality in the existentialist program. But he was most interested in the "elegant"
argumentation of St. Thomas Aquinas. In *Love in the Ruins,* Dr. Thomas More
observes that "Max the atheist sees things like Saint Thomas Aquinas, ranged,
orderly, connected up," a comment that well reflects Percy's own view.[16] Such
enthusiasm on Percy's part had resulted not only from his reading of St. Thomas

---

14. *Humani Generis,* in *The Papal Encyclicals, 1939–1958,* ed. Claudia Carlen (Raleigh, 1990),
175, 176, 180. James Collins refers briefly to the effect of the encyclical in *The Existentialists: A
Critical Study* (Chicago, 1951), xiv. The new *Catechism of the Catholic Church* published in 1994
reaffirms the teachings of *Humani Generis* on the creation of the soul: "The Church teaches that
every spiritual soul is created immediately by God—it is not 'produced' by the parents" (New Hope,
Ky., 1994, p. 93).

15. Quoted in Stephen Schiff, "Muriel Spark Between the Lines," *New Yorker,* May 24, 1993,
p. 40.

16. Walker Percy, *Love in the Ruins: The Adventures of a Bad Catholic at a Time near the End
of the World* (New York, 1971), 106.

himself, but also from acquaintance with the newly invigorated Thomism. Inspired by Pope Leo XIII in his 1879 encyclical *Aeterni Patris* and associated with Jacques Maritain, Etienne Gilson, and English autodidact Christopher Dawson, Thomism was then enjoying great success in the United States and Canada.[17] Indeed, both Maritain and Gilson had insisted that their version of Thomism was the true *existentialism.* Gilson even claimed (rather tendentiously) that "Thomism is the synthesis of Hegel and Kierkegaard."[18] In any case, if Kierkegaard was to make Percy aware of the need for decisive action in religious matters, Aquinas was to be his intellectual stimulus. Walker Percy's decision was by no means unique, however; his was simply one of a "tidal wave" of conversions among writers and intellectuals.

"In the late forties and fifties there was a tremendous spiritual awakening or hunger in this country and in the postwar generation," Walker Percy recalled in an interview late in his life.[19] To some, indeed, it must have seemed as if everyone of note was becoming Catholic. Among the converts were Heywood Broun, Henry Ford II, Clare Booth Luce, Jean Stafford, Robert Lowell, Thomas Merton, Avery Dulles, Frances Parkinson Keyes, Allen Tate, and Caroline Gordon. In 1949, Fr. John A. O'Brien edited *The Road to Damascus,* the first of a series of six volumes in which he collected conversion accounts by such notables as Luce, Keyes, Evelyn Waugh, and Alexis Carrel (Nobel laureate and author of *Man, the Unknown* in 1935). A year earlier, Merton's *Seven Storey Mountain,* an engaging report of the author's rather bohemian life (some of which was set in Columbia University at about the time Percy was there), his conversion, and subsequent entry into a

17. Modern Thomism (Neo-Thomism) is usually divided into two schools: (1) Transcendental Thomism, characterized by an adaptation of Thomism to Kantian thought and associated with such theologians as Joseph Maréchal (1878–1944), Karl Rahner, and Bernard Lonergan; (2) a form of Thomism more faithful to St. Thomas, usually identified with the names of Reginald Garrigou-Lagrange (1877–1964), Etienne Gilson, and Jacques Maritain. The distinction is by no means absolute, however: Rahner and Lonergan were critical of Kant, just as Maritain could not help being influenced by him; there are also independent philosophers—such as Anthony Kenny—who have used Thomist arguments in conjunction with linguistic analysis. See also Alasdair MacIntyre's "Too Many Thomisms?" in his *Three Rival Versions of Moral Enquiry: Encyclopaedia, Genealogy, and Tradition* (Notre Dame, 1990), 58–81.

18. Referred to in William Barrett and Henry D. Aiken, eds., *Philosophy in the Twentieth Century* (4 vols.; New York, 1962), III, 545.

19. Lawson and Kramer, eds., *Conversations,* 316.

Trappist monastery in Kentucky, had become a best-seller.[20] In England in the same year, Douglas Hyde, a prominent journalist in the British Communist party, had joined the long procession to the baptismal font and published his story, *I Believed,* to enthusiastic applause in 1950.[21] Moreover, some of the participants were known to Percy from his southern background: he had met Allen Tate, for example, in Sewanee and would one day send a draft of his first novel to him and his wife, Caroline Gordon, in large part because they shared the same faith. Tate was deeply interested in both Catholicism (though he would not convert until 1950) and Thomism (he was a close friend of Maritain's). He had influenced Robert Lowell to make such a move early in the 1940s, had written in 1930 that the South's cultural and political problems arose from the lack of traditional (Catholic) religion, and was engaged in defending the religious imagination against the attacks of the scientifically oriented philosophers.[22]

Then there was Monsignor Fulton Sheen, a philosophy professor at the Catholic University of America, who was emerging as one of the first major radio and television evangelists with his intellectually dramatic (some critics would say overdramatic) presentations about faith that were both informed by and critical of contemporary thought, especially that of the existentialists and Freud, while resting on a Thomist basis.[23] The future bishop was such a favorite of Percy's that he even wrote to Sheen requesting instruction. Listening to Sheen would have confirmed Percy's suspicions about the efficacy of psychoanalysis, though the priest was by no means entirely critical of the process. Indeed, some of his strictures today strangely echo those of Jeffrey Masson and seem less retrograde than they once did. Sheen suggested that psychoanalysis should be seen as a mere method, not as "a panacea applicable as widely as its more enthusiastic believers

---

20.   John A. O'Brien, ed., *The Road to Damascus* (New York, 1949); Thomas Merton, *The Seven Storey Mountain* (New York, 1948).

21.   Douglas Hyde, *I Believed* (New York, 1950). Apart from Roman Catholics who, naturally, were happy with Hyde's conversion, liberally agnostic critics in England and America such as Kingsley Martin, Stephen Spender, and Arthur Schlesinger, Jr., welcomed his change of loyalties. When Hyde came as a lecturer to Loyola University in New Orleans in 1960, Walker Percy joined him and others to celebrate the election of Roman Catholic Jack Kennedy as president (Tolson, *Pilgrim in the Ruins,* 289).

22.   Allen Tate, "Religion and the Old South," in *Essays of Four Decades* (Chicago, 1968), 569.

23.   For a brief but intimate portrayal of Sheen, see Wilfrid Sheed, *Frank and Maisie: A Memoir with Parents* (New York, 1985), 243–45.

claim." Moreover, "once psychoanalysis asserts that 'man is not a being different from the animals, or superior to them' [as Freud argued in his *Introductory Lectures in Psychoanalysis*] or that sin is a myth, religion an illusion, and God a 'father-image,' then it ceases to be a science or a method and begins to be a prejudice." [24] Most important of all, Sheen declared: "Even if the presuppositions of Freudian psychoanalysis were accepted—which they cannot well be—it is questionable whether this notion of the total inaccessibility of the 'unconscious' to our normal examination can be maintained. It is conceivable that the mind, when using the right approach, can achieve almost as much analysis alone as under the guidance of a third person" (70). Thus, the Catholic prelate spoke not only to Percy's hunger for doctrinal certainty but to his immediate psychological needs as well.

This wave of conversions in the 1940s took its remote stimulus from similar happenings in England and France in the nineteenth and early twentieth centuries. From England, there was the precedent of John Henry Newman and the Oxford Movement, of his disciple Gerard Manley Hopkins, more recently of G. K. Chesterton, Eric Gill, Evelyn Waugh, Ronald Knox, Graham Greene, and, subsequently, of Muriel Spark. From France, there was the influence of the Catholic revival (which involved conversions from other faiths to Catholicism, but more often a rediscovery of the Church by disaffected, anticlerical, and agnostic nominal Catholics) expressed in the works of Charles Péguy, Léon Bloy, Paul Claudel, Georges Bernanos, François Mauriac, Emmanuel Mounier, Gabriel Marcel, and, above all, in the neo-Thomism of Jacques Maritain and Etienne Gilson. It was a heady time indeed in America (sustained in part by the publishing house of Sheed and Ward), and even cradle Catholics who had never deviated from orthodoxy were affected, being renewed in their rather dull routines by this fresh wave of European enthusiasm. For example, Flannery O'Connor claimed that such writers led to her own discovery of the Church into which she had been born: "The French Catholic novelists were a help to me in this—Bloy, Bernanos, Mauriac. In philosophy, Gilson, Maritain and Gabriel Marcel, an Existentialist. They all seemed to be French for a while and then I discovered the Germans—Max Picard, Romano Guardini and Karl Adam. The Americans seem just to be producing

24. Fulton Sheen, *Peace of Soul* (New York, 1949), 67.

pamphlets for the back of the Church (to be avoided at all costs) and installing heating systems." [25]

Maritain, Gilson, and Christopher Dawson were especially prominent in American intellectual circles in the 1940s. T. S. Eliot had long sympathized with their thought, particularly with their nostalgia for the lost cultural and religious unity of the European Middle Ages, so much so in fact that John Middleton Murry recommended acidly in a review in 1926 that Eliot should "make a blind act of faith and join the Catholic Church: there he will find an authority and a tradition." [26] In the early part of the century, Maritain and his wife, Raïssa, revolting against the scientism then being indoctrinated in the Sorbonne, had made a pact to commit suicide should they fail to find the "truth" within a certain period of time. They were prevented from doing so by the intervention of Charles Péguy, and they subsequently converted to Catholicism. Persuaded to reside in America in the 1930s partly because his wife was Jewish, Maritain became a close friend of Allen Tate and Caroline Gordon, and with Raïssa he even translated the southern poet's "Ode to the Confederate Dead" into French. Maritain's influence on Percy was to be so profound that later Percy would send him one of his first philosophical essays and refer to him as his favorite living philosopher. [27] Indeed, Percy continued to invoke Maritain's version of the Thomist synthesis right up to the end of his life, even seeing Charles Sanders Peirce in this tradition.

It is necessary to explore the influence of neo-Thomism a little further, since it was so pervasive at the time. In *Faith, Sex, Mystery: A Memoir* (a book warmly commended by Walker Percy) Richard Gilman records how he, a Jew, was converted to Catholicism in the early 1940s by reading Gilson's *Spirit of Medieval Philosophy*. His account of the impact of that book provides a neat summary of how it, and Thomism, might have appeared to Percy also:

25. Flannery O'Connor added, however, that "there are a few good sources [in America] like *Thought,* a quarterly published at Fordham" (*The Habit of Being,* ed. Sally Fitzgerald [New York, 1979], 231). Walker Percy published his first philosophical essay in this journal in 1954.

26. Quoted in Peter Ackroyd, *T. S. Eliot: A Life* (New York, 1984), 155–56. It is interesting to note that a recent reissue of Christopher Dawson's 1950 work, *Religion and the Rise of Western Culture* (New York, 1991), carries a blurb from Dinesh D'Souza, a modern-day nostalgist for lost unity.

27. John M. Dunaway, ed., *Exiles and Fugitives: The Letters of Jacques and Raïssa Maritain, Allen Tate, and Caroline Gordon* (Baton Rouge, 1992), 36–39; Tolson, *Pilgrim in the Ruins,* 244.

It was as if what I had read during that day and a half had established an intellectual or philosophical world as solid and factual as the physical universe, as if the claims and arguments Gilson had made weren't claims and arguments at all but statements of what was actually so. I imagine that mathematicians and physicists have this extraordinary sense, when they've completed a proof or a demonstration, that something new exists now, not just in their minds but in reality. What now existed for me against all previous likelihood, all plausibility, was the Catholic religion, the arguments for whose truth had been made irrefutable for me during this long stretch of reading. Irrefutable, the way a rock is or the ocean. What hadn't existed for me before I read the book now did.[28]

Gilman's comment on the similarity to the experience of mathematicians and physicists suggests precisely what the attraction of Thomism may have been for Percy. Several converts at the time have recorded comparable experiences. Avery Dulles, for example, then an undergraduate at Harvard, found himself in complete agreement with what he thought was the central thesis of the book: "The patristic and medieval thinkers, profiting from the light of biblical revelation, were able to achieve greater consistency and rationality in their philosophical thought than the most brilliant minds of antiquity, including Plato and Aristotle." To Dulles, Gilson's book "triumphantly demonstrated the necessity, unicity, infinity, and immutability of God." And indeed, even now, looking over Gilson's prose, one can see what may have been the attraction for those raised in an intellectually confused or incoherent environment. In an earlier work, Gilson writes of St. Thomas' *Summa Theologica* as "the unbroken advance of reason constructing stone by stone this mighty edifice" and of his "demonstrations fashioned from clearly defined ideas, presented in perfectly precise statements, and placed in a carefully balanced arrangement."[29] It was indeed, as Percy observed, "elegant."

However, professional historians—most recently Norman Cantor in *Inventing the Middle Ages*—have cautioned that this was a typically Catholic way of view-

---

28. Richard Gilman, *Faith, Sex, Mystery: A Memoir* (New York, 1986), 52–53.

29. Avery Dulles, "The Medievalism of Etienne Gilson," in *New Oxford Review*, LIX (September, 1992), 13; Etienne Gilson, *The Christian Philosophy of St. Thomas Aquinas* (1956; rpr. New York, 1988), 376.

ing the thought of the period and that the supposed unity and coherence of the medieval mind is largely illusory.[30] It was a view, nevertheless, that received wide dissemination when Time-Life sponsored a popular version of Gilson's thesis. An additional comment by John Hellman on the phenomenon helps to establish historical perspective:

> In a higher culture in which Catholics were conspicuous by their absence, distinguished Europeans arrived [Maritain, Gilson, Dawson] with vast, complex, arcane intellectual baggage to fill the void. G. G. Coulton's charge that the heritage of Protestant unfairness to the Middle Ages led to an overcompensation in favor of the neo-Thomist revival may be supported by the relatively uncritical reception of Maritain, Dawson, and Gilson, at Princeton, Chicago, and Harvard, where — despite the nonconformity of their approaches — they remained relatively unchallenged champions of medieval culture. In Roman Catholic intellectual circles, such as they were, Gilson and Maritain were honored as living saints. Controversial and much less influential figures in their own country, they became "prophets" in the New World.[31]

Thomas Merton, Robert Lowell, Allen Tate — and Walker Percy — were among those most responsive to such prophecy.

In addition to the intellectual reasons for becoming a Catholic, there was a strong emotional attraction. The 1940s was a period in which much Catholic ritual was still shrouded in mystery, in which priests celebrated the Mass in Latin with their backs to their congregations, in which a silent faithful concentrated on private prayer and the inner life of the spirit and frequented darkened churches illuminated by red sanctuary lamps that witnessed the consolation of the divine presence. Whatever the liturgical and theological inadequacies of the system, its "dim religious light" had enormous appeal, one that many of the faithful have since

30. Norman F. Cantor, *Inventing the Middle Ages: The Lives, Works, and Ideas of the Great Medievalists of the Twentieth Century* (New York, 1991), 330–32. In a section entitled "Absolutizing the Middle Ages" (287–96), Cantor discusses how the Catholic church still sees the period as an area of contemporary, rather than merely historical, interest.

31. John Hellman, "The Humanism of Jacques Maritain," in *Understanding Maritain: Philosopher and Friend,* ed. Deal W. Hudson and Matthew J. Mancini (Macon, Ga., 1987), 128.

then sorely missed. The institution itself was presided over by Pope Pius XII, a figure remote, saintly, and seemingly absolutely confident of those divine truths of which he was the earthly representative.

But there was an even more obviously "supernatural" compulsion operating at the time when Walker Percy converted. In a 1987 foreword to *The New Catholics,* a collection of conversion narratives, Percy comments on the phenomenon: "More than one pilgrim finds himself standing at a strange rectory door, wondering how he got there, never having said two words to a priest—and here I have to smile, remembering how it felt." [32] The significant phrase is "wondering how he got there." Gilman gives an account of a related phenomenon which took place at an earlier stage in his conversion but which is typical of the time (and very similar to an incident in Thomas Merton's life also). During a visit to the New York Public Library, he was determined not to check out any books on Catholicism. But he seemed unable to resist Gilson's *Spirit of Medieval Philosophy:*

> So I put it back on the shelf, picked up the books I'd chosen before, turned around, found myself without any power to move, turned back again, took the Gilson book from the shelf once more, put it back, repeated the whole mad cycle three or four more times and then, besieged, light-headed as though I had a fever, nearly sick to my stomach, put the book with my others and, muttering to myself something to the effect of "if the only goddamned way I can get the hell out of this goddamned fucking place is to take out this fucking goddamned book, then I'll just have to do it," went over to the counter, checked out all the books and walked out of the library into the glaring sunlight. [33]

Other converts report similar incidents. They obviously appealed to Percy—who would later enthusiastically take his family to visit the Marian shrine at Lourdes famed for its miraculous cures—perhaps as almost palpable signs of divine intervention. [34]

32. Reprinted in Percy, *Signposts,* 345.
33. Gilman, *Faith, Sex, Mystery,* 49–50.
34. Converts at the time also tended to set great store by the "providential influence" of Cath-

At all events, for a variety of reasons—certainly natural, and by Percy's reckoning even genuinely supernatural—Walker Percy and his wife, after a period of reflection at the family cottage in Sewanee and instruction by a rather "plain" priest (Tolson refers to him as a "meat-and-potatoes parish priest"), were received into the Roman communion (with conditional baptism) at Holy Name Church in New Orleans in December, 1947. The only remotely intellectual question that Percy thought of asking when pressed was about the Church's position on evolution. Significantly, he was not troubled when the priest failed to give a satisfactory answer.[35] He had, after all, found the certainty he had so long been seeking.

It might legitimately be asked, of course, how Walker Percy could have embraced the faith that William Alexander Percy had so consciously rejected as "outworn rubbish"? When Walker Percy became a Roman Catholic, he must certainly have understood why his cousin had ceased to be one. It was probably in part his own experience of serious illness, as well as his response to the horrors of World War II—William Alexander Percy too had long been alarmed by Hitler's rise to power, a kind of subtheme to *Lanterns on the Levee,* but had not lived to see its disastrous outcome—that made Walker Percy conclude that Stoicism combined with a moral Christianity was insufficient to live a life in the twentieth century. After all, the Jesuit theologian Romano Guardini, a strong influence on Walker Percy, had argued that the secular world is more dependent on Christianity than it realizes:

olics they had come across earlier in their lives: in Percy's case, David Scott (a black neighbor in Greenville who had converted at age thirteen), the Catholic family he had known there also, roommates at Chapel Hill and Columbia, etc. See Gilman, *Faith, Sex, Mystery,* 86–98, for an extended illustration of this phenomenon. The providential exposure to particular texts was also considered important, as was indicated earlier in reference to Etienne Gilson's book. I would add to this even the effect on a spiritual seeker of a comment such as that made in William Alexander Percy's *Lanterns on the Levee* by Fr. Koestenbrock on revisiting Greenville (see end of Chapter 1).

35. Tolson, *Pilgrim in the Ruins,* 199–200. Catholic intellectuals (including Pope Pius XII) have reluctantly accepted the scientific evidence for evolution without pondering too much the problem that the theory poses for traditional religion: they simply insist that God infuses a soul at some point into each human being. In 1960, Jaroslav Pelikan referred to this as one of the Church's "complex rationalizations" on an issue about which it "theoretically maintains a historical exegesis of the first chapters of Genesis no less opposed to science than the fundamentalist exegesis is" (*The Riddle of Roman Catholicism: Its History, Its Beliefs, Its Future* [London, 1960], 63). Daniel C. Dennett also emphasizes this basic opposition in *Darwin's Dangerous Idea: Evolution and the Meanings of Life* (New York, 1995).

"In many cases, the nonChristian today cherishes the opinion that he can erase .
Christianity by seeking a new religious path, by returning to classical antiquity
from which he can make a new departure. He is mistaken. . . . When contemporary
man becomes a pagan he does so in a way other than that of the pre-Christian." [36]
But, in a deeper sense, Walker Percy seems to have been satisfied simply to accept
the truths of the Christian religion in a way that his Uncle Will was not. Perhaps
the difference can be explained by referring to a passage from an essay by
T. R. M. Creighton in which the author is drawing a distinction between Thomas
Hardy's crisis of *belief* and Gerard Manley Hopkins' crisis of *faith:*

> [Hardy] suffered what is commonly called "Victorian loss of faith," though
> the term is a misleading one and loss of *belief* describes the experience
> much better. Faith in its true sense is the feeling Hopkins had about the
> universe and Hardy and most other Victorians did not—a supra-rational,
> intuitive sense of a divine being which, whether you like to regard it as a
> particularly dotty delusion or a supreme insight into the nature of things
> vouchsafed to only a very few in any generation, is not lost through ac-
> quaintance with *The Origin of Species* and the rest, and is not vulnerable
> to logical arguments or emotional impressions which seem to contradict it.
> We know from various entries in the *Note-Books and Papers* and from the
> "Andromeda" sonnet that Hopkins was just as aware as his contemporary
> Hardy of the objections to Christian belief current in their time and that he
> had at least as fastidious and rigorous an intellect, but scientific facts had
> none of the relevance to his faith that they had to Hardy's belief and did
> nothing to shake it. The final upshot of his work, if one considers the last
> sonnets, is more tragic than that of all Hardy's multifarious dealings with
> religion, but the tragic conflict takes place on a different wavelength. [37]

There are problems with this kind of analysis, of course: it seems to place Hopkins
beyond the realm of judgment and to credit him with a necessarily unverifiable

36. Romano Guardini, *The End of the Modern World: A Search for Orientation* (New York,
1956), 172–73.
37. T. R. M. Creighton, "Some Thoughts on Hardy and Religion," in *Thomas Hardy After Fifty
Years,* ed. Lance St. John Butler (Totowa, N.J., 1977), 65–66.

insight, while Hardy is condemned to a lower order of existence. On the other hand, Creighton does point to a perceived difference between the two authors, a difference that is also apparent between Walker and William Alexander Percy. Perhaps another way of putting the matter would be to say that Walker Percy's conversion was such a cataclysmic event for him that, while he certainly felt the necessity to engage in polemics on its behalf, nothing could dislodge the truth of that moment.

The philosopher William Barrett makes a similar distinction between the agnosticism of Matthew Arnold in the nineteenth century and the religious faith of T. S. Eliot in the twentieth: Eliot is fully aware of Arnold's problems; according to Barrett, moreover, it is Eliot who is probably wrong; but the point is, Barrett concedes, that Eliot "expresses an attitude of mind or spirit that could not be arrived at earlier in history." [38] Indeed, Walker Percy himself may have been alluding indirectly to his cousin's case in a comment on Henry James's failure to take seriously the claims of the Church of Rome in spite of its frequent presence in his novels:

It [the period of James, and, implicitly, William Alexander Percy] was the Age of Unbelief, if ever there was one. It would have been absolutely unthinkable for any man, however knowing and intelligent, to see his way clear to conversion. It would have taken an heroic amount of grace. Of course there are obvious reasons for this: it was the Age of the Success of Science; the great Victorian edifice was still mighty and secure. But I believe that there is a dialectic of faith. . . . The dialectic is in our favor now; we are certainly coming into the Age of Faith. It is not so much Faith as the polarity of Faith-Unfaith. This alternative simply did not exist for our grandfathers or for James.[39]

It was in this spirit that Walker Percy replied to his own question in 1977 — "*How*

---

38. In Barrett and Aiken, eds., *Philosophy,* 541.

39. Excerpt from Walker Percy letter sent originally to Caroline Gordon and enclosed in her correspondence with Robert Lowell, n.d. [1951], bMS Am 1905 (513–522), by permission of the Houghton Library, Harvard University. I am grateful to Bertram Wyatt-Brown for supplying me with the full text of this letter.

is such a belief possible in this day and age?"—"What else is there?"[40] With the "unsuccess" of science in the twentieth century—in the sense that it has not provided the degree of human happiness anticipated, while certain of its technological products have caused untold misery to millions of human beings—the playing field is level again, and indeed religion looks like the attractive alternative.

Walker Percy's conversion to Rome in the late 1940s was not merely a matter of private concern. Shelby Foote's reaction when told about his best friend's religious intentions—that Percy's was "a mind in full intellectual retreat"—was an opinion shared by many at the time in regard to the whole phenomenon.[41] The topic had received attention in the pages of several journals, including the *Partisan Review,* where, in 1943, a series of articles appeared by Sidney Hook, Ernest Nagel, Ruth Benedict, and others, under the general heading "The New Failure of Nerve." These denounced what was happening and attacked in particular Reinhold Niebuhr, Jacques Maritain, and Aldous Huxley as causal influences. In the title essay, Hook drew on Gilbert Murray's *Four Stages of Greek Religion* for an explanation: "This failure of nerve [in the Greek period] exhibited itself in 'a rise of asceticism, of mysticism, in a sense, of pessimism; a loss of self-confidence, of hope in this life and of faith in normal human efforts; a despair of patient inquiry, a cry for infallible revelation: an indifference to the welfare of the state, a conversion of the soul to God.' "[42] Hook attributed part of this flight from reason at the present time to "the frenzy of Kierkegaard who frankly throws overboard his intelligence," whereas Ernest Nagel vigorously attacked the metaphysics of Gilson and Maritain as instances of "the unique mixture of pontifical dogmatism, oracular wisdom, and condescending obscurantism."[43]

Hook's was a version of the positivism that was in vogue among Anglo-American philosophers in the 1940s and that had been greatly reinforced by the influx

40. Walker Percy, "Questions They Never Asked Me," in *Signposts,* 416.

41. Tolson, *Pilgrim in the Ruins,* 191. Percy was spending time in Santa Fe, New Mexico, where Foote came to visit him. He had explained to Foote: "If you take the claims of Christianity seriously, then it seems to me that Catholicism is where you have to end up" (190).

42. Reprinted from *Partisan Review* (1943) in Sidney Hook, *The Quest for Being and Other Studies in Naturalism and Humanism* (Westport, Conn., 1971), 73.

43. *Ibid.,* 76; Ernest Nagel, "Malicious Philosophies of Science," *Partisan Review* (January-February, 1943), 49.

of members of the famous Vienna Circle fleeing Hitler's armies. The latter included Rudolf Carnap and Otto Neurath, who were now publishing a series of pamphlets entitled *The International Encyclopedia of Unified Science* from the University of Chicago, a series that many people engaged in both religion and the arts found alarming. Its individual essays—by Neurath and Carnap and by such American philosophers as John Dewey and Charles Morris—argued against the validity of any statement that lacked a verifiable content and were notoriously hostile to all forms of metaphysics.[44] Hook, Dewey, Morris, and the others in turn came under attack from Allen Tate (who complained that the *Partisan Review* would only allow his refutations to be printed in the pages of its letters section), and would soon receive the criticisms of Walker Percy also. "As an old anti-positivist," Tate wrote, "I cannot do less than to point out a standard objection to the positivist program, reminding its adherents that our supposed 'failure of nerve' might actually turn out to be the positivists' failure to allow for all that our nerve ends are capable of taking in." [45] Tate hammered this point home, over and over: "If [a man] is told that mere 'operational techniques' will see him through, whether these are put to work in society, or in the laboratory, or in industry, or in the arts, he may believe it for a while, and try to realize it; but like a child after the game is over and the fingers are uncrossed, he will return to the real world, unprepared and soon to be overwhelmed by it because he has been told that the real world does not exist" (122). Percy, whose illness had made him even more directly convinced of the limits of science, would argue in the same vein in subsequent years.[46]

That Allen Tate and other converts were slowly winning some degree of respectability among the intelligentsia can be seen from the fact that, in 1950, the same *Partisan Review* that in 1943 had presented a small number of relatively hostile essays on "The New Failure of Nerve" now devoted part of each of four issues to a symposium on "Religion and the Intellectuals." A much wider variety

44. See Otto Neurath, Rudolf Carnap, and Charles Morris, eds., *Foundations of the Unity of Science* (Chicago, 1969). The original pamphlets began appearing in 1938.

45. Allen Tate, "The Hovering Fly," in *Essays of Four Decades,* 115.

46. In 1952, Maritain wrote to a Mgr. Fontenelle in Rome requesting that Tate be granted a private audience with Pope Pius XII (and with Mgr. Montini, the future Pope Paul VI) on the grounds that "he has accomplished over the past twenty years a significant oeuvre in his country, *by opposing positivistic trends*" (my emphasis) (John Dunaway, ed., *Exiles and Fugitives,* 104).

of notables contributed: W. H. Auden, John Dewey, I. A. Richards, A. J. Ayer, Sidney Hook, Alfred Kazin, Allen Tate, Paul Tillich, Jacques Maritain, and William Barrett among others. Sounding a note of regret, the "Editorial Statement" recognizes that the first decades of the century had been characterized by a "triumphant naturalism" but that now there is a "conversion and return." [47] This being the case, the statement continues, what is needed is a more serious discussion of what is happening than can be found in the popular press "with its noisy publicity for the latest conversion of one or another prominent personality" (215). Nevertheless, when it comes to posing the relevant question for the contributors, there is still much of the old antireligious bias: "Assuming that in the past religions nourished certain vital human values, can these values now be maintained without a widespread belief in the supernatural?" (217). In the responses that follow, it soon becomes obvious that for many of the religious writers this is not what is at issue at all.

A. J. Ayer, then a fervent logical positivist, and Sidney Hook are the most dismissive of the new religious phenomenon. For Ayer, religion provides us with no verifiable knowledge about the world, nor does one need to believe in an afterlife for our present existence to be worthwhile. What has happened recently, he thinks, is that our understanding of science has become much more problematic, so that some people—but not the scientists themselves, he cautions—are frustrated in their search for what they perceive as "necessary truths" (219). Hook, meanwhile, is dismayed that what seemed in 1943 to be "a strong current" of conversions has become "a tidal wave." Moreover, these new converts "can no longer make distinctions and regard all social philosophies which are not theocentric as different roads to the culture of *1984*" (225). Most of all, it troubles him that they are attracted to a mystical rather than a rational theology, to subjectivity rather than objectivity, to the "tormented inner experience of Augustine, Pascal, Kierkegaard" rather than "the clear, if defective, arguments of Aquinas." Converts are seeking comfort rather than truth, and they "accept optimism on the vastest scale imaginable" (229).

Although not conventionally religious, Alfred Kazin is more sympathetic (and specifically in line with what will turn out to be Walker Percy's views) in finding

47. "Editorial Statement," *Partisan Review,* XVII (February, 1950), 103.

"more understanding, among religious writers, of what the human situation is about, of what man is like, than from positivists, laboratory psychologists, instrumentalists, etc." (233). He believes, "It is impossible to *explain,* however easier it may be to uphold, democracy without reference to those cardinal conceptions of the sanctity of individual life and the brotherhood of man that come to us from the prophetic tradition [of Judaism and Christianity]" (234).

The arguments offered by Tillich, Auden, Tate, and Maritain are, of course, generally more positive in their attitude toward religion. Tillich begins by reversing the way in which the original question has been posed, arguing—in the manner of Romano Guardini in *The End of the Modern World*—that "this development [the many conversions] is not a 'failure of nerve' but it is the courage to see what a favorable historical constellation had covered for almost a century that could not be hidden any longer, the dark underground of the personal and social life" (254). Still, like John Dewey, he rejects the supernatural, God as *a* being, religious statements as offering knowledge, or that self-surrender to religious authority is called for.

W. H. Auden abandoned his long romance with Marxism to return to High Anglicanism in 1940, and shortly thereafter published some of the poems related to his homecoming in the *Southern Review*. Later still, in his apartment in Gramercy Park, he avidly devoured Kierkegaard's writings on the three stages of existence (a sacred text for the early Percy). He claims not surprisingly, therefore, that "no religion is credible today which lacks an existentialist aspect" (124–25). Like Kazin, he finds it "easier for an artist to see the inadequacies of naturalism because in his professional work he is occupied with the personal and the existential" (126). Allen Tate, however, seems more anxious to defend religion by attacking the revival of interest in myth. He blames Ernst Cassirer for being "a naturalist whose 'supernaturalism' was a little like the shell game at the county fair: it was a trick of the eye" (253). Walker Percy will prove a good deal more sympathetic with Cassirer, though not with the new theories of myth as such.

Maritain's essay is the most trenchant of all. He begins by rejecting the premise of the debate, arguing that the question should be "why human beings are *not* always and everywhere intent on the word of God." The bombs in the recent war, he asserts, have done away with "*salvation through science,*" while "atheistic radicalism" leads to totalitarianism, and "democracy can only live on Christianity." The reason for the spate of religious conversions is that "the question has essentially been a question of personal relationship between their [the converts] own selves and the divine Self" (323, 324). More important (and troubling) is his claim: "As concerns the pluralist principle, I think that it must apply in the body politic, since, as a matter of fact (a fact which in itself is a misfortune), men are religiously divided." But he adds: "To regard pluralism as a good in itself in the very realm of religious belief would be nonsense, since in this realm what matters is truth about God; and there is only one truth." Man needs definite beliefs, not the kinds of religion proposed by thinkers such as Dewey, or Kazin, or even Tillich, all of which are "not worth considering" (325). Belief in the existence of God is natural; lacking revelation, religions other than the Roman Catholic are a "mess" (326). Although Maritain's essay is almost a textbook example of Catholic triumphalism, it does convey that religion's confidence in its own authority at the time when Walker Percy converted to it.

What is significant, then, about Walker Percy's conversion beyond the simple fact of its taking place is that the *kind* of Catholic Percy became was largely determined by the philosophical and theological thinking of the period in which the decision was made. Not only was the Church seen as a secure anchor in a time of turbulence, but following Maritain in particular, there was a received sense that Western intellectual life had been off course since at least the time of Descartes. Thus, in a text that directly influenced Percy, Maritain's *Dream of Descartes,* the French philosopher claimed that "St. Thomas brings together, [while] Descartes cleaves and separates." [48] Even such a liberal contemporary Thomist as Bernard Lonergan expressed the matter in the following way in 1957: "Galilean [*i.e.,* from Galileo] methodology is penetrated with philosophic assumptions about reality and objectivity and, unfortunately, those assumptions are not too happy. Their influence is evident in Descartes. Their ambiguities appear in Hobbes and Locke, Berkeley and Hume. Their final inadequacy becomes clear in Kant, where the real and objective bodies of Galilean thought prove to constitute no more than a phenomenal world." [49] While Lonergan is simply making an epistemological crit-

---

48. Jacques Maritain, *The Dream of Descartes* (London, 1946), 132.
49. Quoted in Eric O. Hanson, *The Catholic Church in World Politics* (Princeton, 1987), 355.

icism of Galileo, in the light of the Church's actual treatment of the famous astronomer (whose original condemnation was not revoked by the pope until 1993), such language is troubling. But all of this is a way of saying that the Church—Percy's church—in spite of its emphasis on the importance of reason, has never accepted the thought of the European Enlightenment and has always looked back to an earlier age for its ideal of human society.

To present the point from a slightly different angle: in 1966, at the beginning of his second novel, Percy uses as his epigraph a quotation from Romano Guardini's *End of the Modern World*. In it, the author writes poignantly about the (existential) loneliness of faith in the modern secular age but how, nevertheless, Christians will survive to live in a world "open and clean" and unencumbered by past traditions. Guardini's argument, however, also has less humble overtones, ones that reflect a desire to create a new unity of faith similar to that of the Middle Ages (and not really different from Gilson and Maritain)—the kind of view that Percy seems to have adopted in later life:

The cultural deposit preserved by the Church thus far will not be able to endure against the general decay of tradition. Even when it does endure it will be shaken and threatened on all sides. Dogma in its very nature, how-ever, surmounts the march of time because it is rooted in eternity, and we can surmise that the character and conduct of coming Christian life will reveal itself especially through its old dogmatic roots. Christianity will once again need to prove itself deliberately as a faith which is not self-evident; it will be forced to distinguish itself more sharply from a dominantly non-Christian ethos. At that juncture the theological significance of dogma will begin a fresh advance; similarly will its practical and existential significance increase. I need not say that I imply no "modernization" here, no weak-ening of the content or of the effectiveness of Christian dogma; rather I emphasize its absoluteness, its unconditional demands and affirmations. These will be accentuated. The absolute experiencing of dogma will, I be-lieve, make men feel more sharply the direction of life and the meaning of existence itself.[50]

50. Guardini, *The End of the Modern World*, 175–76, 130.

The emphasis placed here on the unchanging nature of an ahistorical Church dogma is remarkable. It is an emphasis that will be called into question in subsequent decades even among Catholic theologians. But it is only fair to say that it is an emphasis that never lost its appeal for Walker Percy, since it was what had attracted him to the Church in the first place. Indeed, the controversies within the Church from the late sixties onwards over issues of what constituted basic Christian morality — in the areas of sexuality, gender roles, and abortion, for example — and the desire of many to come closer to a secular understanding of these matters, must have appeared to Percy as a situation that had already been foreseen by Guardini and for the solution of which he had provided a clear guideline: dogma's "absoluteness, its unconditional demands and affirmations" would need to be "accentuated" rather than compromised. Furthermore, while Guardini is not too clear on the details of the new world that will emerge in the age of mass man, the sketch that he outlines is not only troubling to a secular consciousness but seems not too unlike that proposed by the rabid protagonist of Percy's 1977 novel, *Lancelot* (a character with whom he himself explicitly identified): "Christianity will arm itself for an illiberal stand directed unconditionally toward Him Who is Unconditioned. Its illiberalism will differ from every form of violence, however, because it will be an act of freedom, an unconditional obedience to God" (130).

Walker Percy's conversion, then, was not the end of the religious road for him. Although he would later claim on several occasions that his own belief remained tranquil for the most part — and there is no reason to doubt this — there were still internal and external demons to battle. To defend his recently acquired belief and to persuade others of its liberating truth — both of which he wished fervently to do — he would have to engage not only with those thinkers who supported his position but also with those who opposed it. In short, he would have to master the complexities of Thomisitic, existentialist, and positivist thought. Or he might attempt to write novels about fellow religious seekers . . .

3
NOVELIST OR PHILOSOPHER?

✝

Walker Percy's illness, and a subsequent relapse, had left him more or less unable to return to his former profession; at the very least, the occasion conveniently provided him with an excuse to opt out of medicine. Income from the portion of his Uncle Will's estate left to him in 1942, meanwhile, enabled the recent convert to pursue his interests in philosophy and religion and to fulfill a long-standing desire to write fiction. The two pursuits sometimes alternated, sometimes were united. In both enterprises, however, Percy saw himself as engaged in a quasi-missionary effort on behalf of his newfound beliefs.

Much of the incentive to write fiction at all came from the example of the existentialists. Kierkegaard, Marcel, Sartre, and Camus had all been in one way or another philosopher-storytellers. As Percy was to explain later, his model came from French rather than from English or American writers because "the French always had this notion of [the] union of philosophy and literature, of using art forms to either express ideas or to discover ideas, to explore reality." [1] Percy also had the example of Dostoevsky and Thomas Mann with their novels in which ideas were presented at a length and an intensity not to be found in recent Anglo-American literature. And besides, novel writing promised to provide a way of working out some of the tensions left over from Percy's family history, especially those involving his father's suicide and his own highly ambivalent attraction for William Alexander Percy's Stoic view of life.

Accepting all of the above motivations, it is easy to see that there were serious problems with the venture from the start. Given Percy's philosophical bent, there was the danger that the fiction would be too cerebral; indeed, Percy would subsequently comment on the excessive influence that theories seemed to have on French writers. Gabriel Marcel, who once referred to his own writing of plays as

---

1. Lewis A. Lawson and Victor A. Kramer, eds., *Conversations with Walker Percy* (Jackson, Miss., 1985), 31.

"a way out of the labyrinth into which I had been led by my abstract thinking," had nevertheless frequently been accused of composing works that were themselves overly abstract. Sartre and Camus were more successful in adapting to the fictional mode, but that may have been because they were less set in their ideas to begin with. And Percy himself, in spite of his censure of overintellectualized fiction, has declared his lack of interest in the short story precisely because he considered it to be a form in which artistic conception rather than intellectual concern predominated.[2] There would always be a tension in Percy's work between the idea he wished to convey and a reluctance to give it adequate artistic expression, something that constantly troubled the more art-conscious, if less aesthetically accomplished, Shelby Foote.

Then, as Jay Tolson has noted, "The whole impetus behind Percy's attempt to write fiction was to express something quite mysterious: the journey that led to his accepting a transcendent order and purpose."[3] Even though Percy was never to become a "fire-breathing Catholic" in the manner of Robert Lowell, this religious motivation had its obvious problems. Since Percy wanted in some way to tell the story of his conversion so that others too might see the light, there was the danger that his fiction writing would be too dogmatically Catholic. After all, if Percy himself had arrived at a strong but relatively tranquil (unlike Lowell) belief in the teachings of the Catholic church during the 1940s and had grounded himself in their philosophical underpinnings, one might wonder whether his novels would turn out to be simply vehicles of religious propaganda, or whether they would reflect continuing efforts at spiritual exploration in a new mode. And since Percy had worked out his philosophical and religious positions in such great detail *before* beginning his fiction writing—a detail quite uncommon even among intellectual converts—it is hard to see how he could still be regarded as a "wayfarer," for in an important sense he had already "arrived." Of course, it is standard theological teaching that the Christian must always be uncertain of his own religious adequacy, and in that sense he will always be a "wayfarer," but such un-

---

2. Walker Percy, in Donald Barthelme, William Gass, Grace Paley, and Walker Percy, "A Symposium on Fiction," *Shenandoah,* XXVII (Winter, 1976), 9; Gabriel Marcel, quoted in Martin Luschei, *The Sovereign Wayfarer: Walker Percy's Diagnosis of the Malaise* (Baton Rouge, 1972), 14.; Lawson and Kramer, eds., *Conversations,* 31–32.

3. Tolson, *Pilgrim in the Ruins: A Life of Walker Percy* (New York, 1992), 212.

certainty is quite different from the kind of doubt about the ultimate goal itself that is so common in the twentieth century. One might make a comparison with the T. S. Eliot who published *The Waste Land* in 1922: though we now know that the original poem was more Christian in emphasis than appeared to be the case after Ezra Pound's editing, *The Waste Land* nevertheless conveys a sense of a searching Eliot who will not come "home" until his 1927 conversion and the poems of *Four Quartets*. Not so with Walker Percy, since his conversion precedes his fiction writing.[4]

There is even a sense in which Percy's work could never be truly existentialist or exploratory: Kierkegaard believed in the propositions of Christianity as "impossible" and "absurd" and hence requiring a dramatic and always precarious commitment to them in a way that even a sympathetic Percy could not quite agree with—he has said that while his sympathies were with Kierkegaard, his intellect was with Aquinas. Sartre moved on to become a Marxist, so that his novel about existential alienation, *Nausea,* is a representation of his thought as he was on his way elsewhere. Camus remained a pilgrim uncertain of his ultimate philosophical beliefs. Percy much more resembles Flannery O'Connor, who was always very certain in her religious commitment, but then she did not set out to write about wayfarers as Walker Percy was to do, and, besides, he was sometimes critical of the amount of informed belief it took to understand the operation of "grace" in her stories. He would be more explicit, or at least not as covert.

Yet Percy also believed deeply that it was the Christian who would make the best novelist—Cardinal Newman's observations to the contrary notwithstanding—since it was he alone who best understood the nature of man. Indeed, according to Maritain, "only a Christian, nay a mystic, because he has some idea of *what there is in man,* can be a complete novelist." In a 1971 interview with John Carr, Percy would remark that to him "the Catholic view of man as pilgrim, in transit, in journey, is very compatible with the vocation of a novelist because a novelist is writing about man in transit, man as pilgrim."[5] So if there was to be

---

4. When Peggy Castex noted in an interview in 1983 that Percy was a convert, he replied instantly, "Yes, but I've been a Catholic ever since I've been writing, so the whole framework is, I suppose, Catholic" (in Lewis A. Lawson and Victor A. Kramer, eds., *More Conversations with Walker Percy* [Jackson, Miss., 1993], 56).

5. Jacques Maritain, *Art and Scholasticism with Other Essays,* trans. J. F. Scanlan (1929; rpr. New York, 1971), 171; Lawson and Kramer, eds., *Conversations,* 63.

a tension between the writer as moralist and as artist—and Percy never denied such—that tension was not irresolvable.

In practice, certainly, Percy began his fiction writing with an excessively propagandistic approach. Significantly—though he claimed that she was the only novelist he knew—he sent the draft of his first completed effort, *The Charterhouse,* a novel set in a Birmingham country club with a former seminarian (who eventually returns to his religious vocation) as one of its protagonists, to the southern writer Caroline Gordon, who was herself soon to become a Catholic convert.[6] She quickly recognized the Catholicism implicit in it—even interrupting her thirty-page single-spaced commentary at one point to make the pious recommendation that "here we ought to stop and say a few prayers of thanksgiving for the fact that you are a Catholic and therefore have some notion of what it's all about" (221). But in spite of her growing religious interest, she was too much a disciple of Henry James and a protégé of Ford Madox Ford to wholly commend Percy's diatribe. Her husband, Allen Tate, liked the novel but appended a note saying that the story desperately needed more action. When Shelby Foote read it, he regretted Percy's having gone into the Church: "There is something terribly cowardly (at least spiritually) about the risks to which you wont [*sic*] expose your soul. . . . I seriously think that no good practicing Catholic can ever be a great artist; art is by definition a product of doubt." [7]

Percy's next attempt, begun in 1953, was a novel about the rather unpromising subject of baptism in which he sought to present his protagonist as someone in need of the Good News—though Percy had at least read Henry James in the meantime, probably on Gordon's advice.[8] But, typically, in *The Gramercy Winner,* which was partly an imitation of Mann's *Magic Mountain,* Percy took the German novelist's somewhat humorous exploration of life in a tubercular sanatorium and turned it into a much more pointed religious tract. In Percy's story, the protagonist, after being presented with a variety of possible attitudes toward human existence, is finally won over to Roman Catholicism. Like Jamie Vaught in *The Last Gentleman,* he is baptized shortly before his death. In other words, whereas Mann rather playfully explores the strengths and weaknesses of a rationalist humanism

6. Details of the novel are to be found in Tolson, *Pilgrim in the Ruins,* 212–16.
7. *Ibid.,* 222, 215.
8. *Ibid.,* 234.

as against those of a mystical fideism in the characters of Ludovico Settembrini and Leo Naphta, respectively—and seems to opt for a middle course between them—Percy's effort is distinctly in favor of a Catholic solution to its protagonist's problems; he sides with the answer offered by the Naphta-like character. Of course, since *The Gramercy Winner* is also highly autobiographical, Percy's decision to present things in such a way is not surprising.[9]

It is hardly surprising, either, that Percy should have failed in the fiction he attempted between 1948 and 1954. As Tolson observes, "At times, Percy exhibited an almost puritanical contempt for the artifice of art, and in that state of mind he would crave a more direct medium for expressing what he had to say" (233). So, for a convert as anxious to pass on the truth to others as Percy was, it was time to begin composing philosophical arguments on its behalf.

Even during the years when he was attempting to write fiction, Walker Percy had, of course, been deeply engaged with philosophy. Understandably, perhaps, at thirty-one he was not prepared to return to the university to study for an advanced degree in the subject. This meant, however, that he would always remain an autodidact in this discipline (as also in linguistics), a circumstance in which he himself tended to take pride at times when castigating the supposed "experts," but one also that severely limited his ability to contribute seriously to the subject. It may well be that the discourse that is carried on by academic professionals in their respective fields is often narrowly self-referential, out of touch with the issues as they are being debated or even perceived in the world at large, and unwisely dismissive of the ideas of those not affiliated with recognized institutions of higher learning. On the other hand, such academic exchanges are subject to peer correction and modification in a way that is not true of the amateur contributor who tends, if lucky enough to have an audience at all, simply to encounter even less instructed enthusiasts who happen to share his point of view on the particular issue at hand. Be that as it may, Percy did read extensively in the Scholastics both ancient and modern (including Maritain's *Art and Scholasticism* and *The Dream of Descartes*), in the existentialism of Sartre, Camus, Marcel, and Heidegger with James Collins' *The Existentialists* providing an overview of the subject from a

9. See Gary M. Ciuba's *Walker Percy: Books of Revelations* (Athens, Ga., 1991), 30–55.

Catholic and Thomistic perspective, and among the philosophers of language, Ernst Cassirer, Susanne Langer, Bertrand Russell, Ernst Mach, Moritz Schlick, Ludwig Wittgenstein, Rudolf Carnap, Alfred Tarski, and Charles Morris. Moreover, his comments and notes suggest that he frequently read his sources in their original languages. And, while delving into such a diversity of approaches, he claimed that it was Aquinas and Maritain who gave order and purpose in guiding him through his eclectic choice of authors.[10]

Percy's undertaking was not as individual as it might at first appear; indeed, in its catholic eclecticism, it was very typically Catholic. The interest in Thomism, of course, went without saying, and some sense of that movement's revival was given earlier. But it was also common for Catholic intellectuals to pay close attention to the reigning philosophies of the day, which in the 1940s and later meant existentialism and some version of the philosophy of language. Much of this effort involved the refutation of errors, or the desire to show how Aquinas had anticipated arguments found in the moderns. It could also represent a genuine appreciation for more recent thought—as, for example, in Frederick Copleston's *Contemporary Philosophy,* which treats existentialism and logical positivism with surprising sympathy.[11] In general, Catholics firmly believed that they possessed the essential "truth" about the nature of reality and the destiny of man, and so any additional "truth" discovered by others—provided, of course, it was genuine—could not in itself contradict what they claimed. Even in the case of astronomy, the Vatican has long had its own observatory (now located in the Arizona desert) in the belief that knowledge about the origins of the universe is just as relevant to it as to secular scientists.[12] Thus, in spite of papal condemnations now and then, there was a certain openness to examining alternative positions. Those with religious interests (not merely Catholics) were likely to have some familiarity with both contemporary philosophical schools, whereas among professional philosophers themselves, analytic philosophers tended to think that the existentialists

10. Tolson, *Pilgrim in the Ruins,* 241.

11. Frederick C. Copleston, *Contemporary Philosophy: Studies of Logical Positivism and Existentialism* (Westminster, Md., 1956).

12. See Jack Hitt, "Would You Baptize an Extraterrestrial?" *New York Times Magazine,* May 29, 1994, pp. 36–39. First established in 1935, the observatory was moved from its original location outside Rome to rural Arizona in 1993 to escape air pollution problems. Its new location, however, has since caused difficulties with the local Native American population.

were simply talking nonsense. Existentialists, in turn, accused analytic philosophers of having an altogether too narrow range of investigation.

Nevertheless, in professional philosophical discourse—in contrast with the situation that obtained in university history and literature departments, for example—in America and England, neo-Thomism, eclectic or otherwise, was not generally held in high esteem. "If the importance of a philosophy be estimated by the number of its professional adherents," John Passmore remarks in an unsympathetic, but relatively accurate, survey of the scene in the 1960s, "neo-Thomism has no serious rival except dialectical materialism."[13] Passmore is referring, of course, rather contemptuously to the large numbers of Catholic seminarians who were required to be indoctrinated in the subject much as members of the Communist party in the Soviet Union imbibed Marxism—and with the same implications. Moreover, not only was much Thomism dispensed badly in inadequate textbooks, but even in the universities in Rome to which reputedly the brightest students for the priesthood were sent, the teaching style was sadly unphilosophical: Anthony Kenny, for example, himself a student at the Jesuit-run Gregorian in the 1950s, notes that "instruction . . . was in Latin lectures delivered through a microphone to classes of hundreds of students packed into tiered benches."[14] In all, then, Walker Percy identified with a group that, though numerous, was no longer considered to be on the cutting edge of philosophy, but rather on the defensive in the hostile environment of various forms of post-Kantian critical thought, more eager to propagate dogmatic truths than to engage in Socratic dialectic.

Then there was the additional problem that even within this limited realm Percy was not a professional philosopher. Ralph McInerny, a Thomist at Notre Dame, has noted the similarity in the way that the academic philosophical community, suffering from what he considers to be "indolent obscurantism," regards both Percy and Mortimer Adler, the philosopher associated with the *Encyclopedia Brittanica* and Great Books projects (and a frequent guest on William F. Buckley's

---

13. John Passmore, *A Hundred Years of Philosophy* (New York, 1968), 317.

14. Anthony Kenny, *A Path from Rome* (New York, 1986), 45. The Latin textbooks that the present author (KQ) used in the late 1960s as a seminarian were faithful to St. Thomas, with only an occasional footnote (also in Latin) to refute the various errors of "recent" philosophers such as Descartes, Kant, and Sartre (considered *very* contemporary!).

Firing Line) and long influenced by Aristotle and St. Thomas (but not a convert to Christianity until 1984). According to McInerny, the professionals have not allowed Adler to bring "order" to the discipline (also the goal of Percy in following the guidance of Aquinas and Maritain). They have preferred instead the skepticism of Bertrand Russell and Thomas Nagel (a staunch critic of Percy's philosophical knowledge). It is thus interesting in this regard that British analytic philosopher Anthony Quinton acknowledges that Adler would generally be regarded "as at best a denizen of the twilight zone" *because* he has been identified with "orthodox Catholic Christianity and political conservatism": "The Great Books programme . . . served the interests of traditional Christian philosophy, more specifically Catholic scholasticism, and involved a rejection of the social and educational ideals of the American version of secular rationalism, which is roughly to say John Dewey." [15]

One of the further reasons for the low esteem in which the philosophy of Aquinas tended to be held was that it was common for all "intellectual" converts at the time to be overeager to apply their newly discovered Thomism well beyond the range of either its application or their competence: Allen Tate, with no philosophical training, became such a staunch antipositivist that, in 1952, Maritain wrote to Rome requesting that he be granted a private audience with the pope on the basis of his accomplishments in this area. Thomas Merton had tried to show that his mentor at Columbia, Mark Van Doren, had really—albeit unknowingly—been operating along Thomistic lines. Caroline Gordon saw her mission as being to "disarm criticism from the Logical Positivists with which every campus swarms." Walker Percy's criticisms of Shelby Foote's early efforts at fiction were very much couched in "Thomistic categories." [16] It is the occasional opposition to the movement from among even some of those more sympathetic with an aesthetic approach to reality that shows just how pervasive the Thomist trend was. Thus, for example, John Crowe Ransom roundly criticized Robert Lowell in 1943 when Lowell tried to convert him to Catholicism using Thomistic arguments:

15. See Mortimer J. Adler, *A Second Look in the Rearview Mirror* (New York, 1992), 259–60; Anthony Quinton, "Mortimer Adler," in *Thoughts and Thinkers* (New York, 1982), 341.

16. John M. Dunaway, ed., *Exiles and Fugitives: The Letters of Jacques and Raïssa Maritain, Allen Tate, and Caroline Gordon* (Baton Rouge, 1992), 104, 50; Garry Wills, *Bare Ruined Choirs: Doubt, Prophecy, and Radical Religion* (Garden City, N.Y., 1972), 46; Tolson, *Pilgrim in the Ruins*, 216.

I think you argue that Thomism makes for human happiness, and I'm aware that it does, with *many minds*; with others it doesn't work. Thomism is philosophy as well as recorded "revelation"; as philosophy it's exposed to the liabilities of philosophy, and is countered by other philosophy. You are too easy about that, saying that "by guaranteeing certain demonstrable but arduous truths, Christian Revelation did actually confirm and liberate philosophy." But how can somebody else (was it the Pope, about 1870?) guarantee a truth to us? In what manner will compensation be made if it's found to be falsity rather than truth? And what were the specific arduous truths? You tend to want a kind of philosophy that subordinates itself, and quits applying its method, at a certain point; but that's not philosophy in my estimation.[17]

As time went on, Walker Percy tended to be less evangelical and more nuanced in his application of Thomistic doctrine, but he was operating from the same premises as his more ardent fellow-converts and doing so in the face of the same intellectual disdain.

Given the questionable esteem in which the Thomist approach was held by the Anglo-American secular academic world at large, which tended to operate in the empiricist-positivist mode, it is understandable that Catholics should have found more common cause with the European existentialists: in spite of the professed atheism of many of them—especially of Heidegger (who had begun, however, as a Jesuit novice and was afterwards a promising Catholic philosopher in the Thomist tradition) and Sartre—they also included several believers (Kierkegaard, Buber, Marcel), and their emphasis on the need to act in order to discover the truth of existence (an Augustinian notion) was congenial to Catholic sensibilities. Moreover, they acknowledged that without God, in his absence, man was in a situation of lacking something essential, alienated from himself, certainly not resting in some bland hedonistic contentment.

The reigning secular school in America, the philosophers of language—into which can be lumped for practical purposes those engaged in the philosophy of

17. Thomas Daniel Young and George Core, eds., *Selected Letters of John Crowe Ransom* (Baton Rouge, 1985), 308.

science, linguistic analysis, some forms of pragmatism, naturalism, logical positivism, logical empiricism, behaviorism, and semiotics—obviously posed a rather more serious problem and tended to be seen as the natural enemy. Originating in the empiricism of John Locke, David Hume, and Auguste Comte, and with various subsequent refinements based on advances in logic and in the physical sciences, this strain of thought was uniformly antimetaphysical. Of course, over the years many religious philosophers would adapt its techniques to their own needs (whether successfully or not remains a matter of debate), and the antimetaphysicians themselves would constantly have to broaden their criteria of acceptance so as not to exclude arbitrarily propositions that seemed intuitively to have meaning. But on the face of it—and keeping in mind many exceptions—they were hostile both toward religion and toward the arts, seeing both as repositories of metaphysical statements that could in no way be verified by empirical means, and so needed to be shown to be false, unsubstantiated, or misconceived. Moreover, with the recent addition of several members of the Vienna Circle and the founding of the *International Encyclopedia of Unified Science* at the University of Chicago to propagate their views, the movement was more aggressive than ever.

Typical of the time, at the *Kenyon Review,* Allen Tate's mentor, John Crowe Ransom, hoped to temper this positivistic influence by inviting naturalist philosophers such as Ernest Nagel and Charles Morris to contribute to a debate on the arts in his journal.[18] Interestingly, after an initial opposition to the new movement, Ransom himself opted cautiously in its favor and decried any assertions of either art or religion that flew in the face of scientific fact.[19] But Ransom's assistant, Philip Blair Rice, was troubled by both the authoritarianism of the "neo-orthodox" religionists (*i.e.,* the Thomists and others) and the narrowness of those advocating use of the "scientific-method" exclusively. Rice recommended attention to "the writings of Santayana, Cassirer, and . . . Mrs. Langer" as an alternative to the two extremes, a recommendation to which Walker Percy attended in full measure.[20] In any event, since it was never Percy's intention merely to study

18. Charles Morris, "Science, Art, and Technology," *Kenyon Review,* I (Autumn, 1939), 416–22; Ernest Nagel, "Recent Philosophies of Science," *Kenyon Review,* III (Summer, 1941), 303–19; Bertrand Russell, "Non-Materialistic Naturalism," *Kenyon Review,* IV (Autumn, 1942), 363–64.

19. See also my *John Crowe Ransom's Secular Faith* (Baton Rouge, 1989), 71.

20. Philip Blair Rice, "Thomas Mann and the Religious Revival," *Kenyon Review,* VII (Summer, 1945), 358, 360.

philosophy, but rather to persuade others through public argument of the truth of his convictions, it was in such a contentious philosophical climate that he would have to begin if he hoped to "convert" people as intelligent and as scientifically trained as himself.

Between 1954 and 1961, then, Walker Percy published several philosophical essays in academic journals in the field. He also attempted a book about the philosophy of language "which the publisher didn't even bother to return and I didn't ask for." [21] Only three of these essays, "The Man on the Train," "The Loss of the Creature," and possibly "The Message in the Bottle" itself, suggest the kinds of themes that were to appear in his earliest published fiction. The others are all highly professional attempts at bridging the gap between the Thomists, the quasi-scientific methods of the linguistic semioticians (the philosophers of language), and the more intuitive ponderings of the existentialists in their study of the nature of man. When the Jesuit periodical *Thought* was celebrating its sixty-fifth anniversary in 1990, it reprinted thirteen distinguished pieces, all supportive of a broadly Christian humanism and among which was Walker Percy's first formal philosophical essay, "Symbol as Need." In the anniversary volume it appeared with articles by other important names in Catholic intellectual life of the twentieth century—Karl Rahner, Jacques Maritain, Hans Urs Von Balthasar, and James Collins among them—a grouping very reflective indeed of the thrust of Percy's thought after his conversion: in other words, in philosophy at least, he would always be first and foremost a Catholic apologist.

"Symbol as Need" is a typical example of the kind of integration Percy was seeking between Thomism, positivism, and existentialism. Here he combines the revisionary positivism of Susanne Langer with the Thomistic metaphysics of Jacques Maritain and the existentialist personalism of Gabriel Marcel. Percy's 1954 essay, overtly a review of Langer's 1953 *Feeling and Form: A Theory of Art,* establishes his basic themes, especially his insistence on the distinction be-

---

21. Walker Percy, *Signposts in a Strange Land,* ed. Patrick Samway (New York, 1991), 189. The manuscript was entitled *Symbol and Existence* and contained an essay that Maritain had commended, "Symbol and Magic Cognition," as an application of his own work. The material here would, however, prove to be the basis for Percy's subsequent essays, collected in *The Message in the Bottle* in 1975 (see Tolson, *Pilgrim in the Ruins,* 244).

tween symbol and sign. That he is operating from a Thomist basis is clear throughout: he begins, for example, by noting the similarities between Langer's position—even at the level of phrasing—and that of Maritain in spite of the fact that Langer is not at all familiar with the French philosopher's writings. Later, Percy makes the rather typical Thomist assertion that "it is apparently Saint Thomas and not Mrs. Langer or Cassirer who had the first inkling of the mysterious analogy between the form of beauty and the pattern of the inner life." [22] In fact, she has had a more difficult time arriving at her quasi-Thomist position since she, according to Percy, has been hampered by her empiricist premises. Nevertheless, Percy praises her (a one-time logical positivist) for having finally come to realize that the art *symbol* "conveys its own appropriate meaning, a meaning inaccessible to the discursive form" and that it is therefore different from an ordinary *sign* (288).

It is our ability to use symbols, according to Percy, that makes us distinct from the other animals because they are confined to using signs; hence the positivistic attempt to equate symbols with signs is part of an effort to reduce human beings totally to the level of the other animals. Here Percy shows that he is equally critical of I. A. Richards' psychologism (rejected also by Tate), the behaviorists (B. F. Skinner in particular), and others who practice such reductions. Percy believes that Langer has provided an alternative to this tendency in her previous book, *Philosophy in a New Key:* "The new key in philosophy—and a truly exciting idea it is—is the universal symbolific function of the human mind. . . . Any science which assumes that the symbolic transformation is but a genetic extension of the function of signification [in animals] must omit precisely that which is peculiar to human semiotic" (292). It is noteworthy that the position against which Percy is objecting here did not trouble other humanistic writers who were also engaged in the debate: they simply felt that the account of symbolic action was incomplete because it did not show the unique qualities of the poetic imagination. They were not opposed in principle, however, to the most thoroughgoing natu-

22. Walker Percy, *The Message in the Bottle: How Queer Man Is, How Queer Language Is, and What One Has to Do with the Other* (New York, 1975), 290. Percy's many quotations from Maritain point to a weakness at this point in his development for rather obscure statements: thus, for example, according to Maritain, the art symbol is "a sign—both a *direct* sign of secrets perceived in things, of some irrecusable truth of nature of adventure caught in the great universe, and a *reversed sign* of the subjective universe of the poet, of his substantial *Self* obscurely revealed" (290). Yes, indeed!

ralistic explanation of human behavior. Percy's point, in contrast, seems to be that human behavior simply *cannot* be explained naturalistically, that Langer—after a long experience as a positivist—has finally come to accept this conclusion, and that therefore there must be a nonnaturalistic explanation for the existence of such a symbolific capacity.

The example most frequently used by Percy to refute such positivistic semioticians as Charles Morris is similar to that employed by Allen Tate in "Literature as Knowledge" under similar circumstances: "Signs announce their objects. Thunder announces rain. The bell announces food to Pavlov's dog. When I say James to a dog, he *looks* for James; when I say James to you, you say, 'What about him?'—you *think* about James. A symbol is the vehicle for the conception of an object and as such is a distinctively human product" (292–93).[23] Percy will not allow at this stage, as even Langer does, that the evolutionists, positivists, and Freudian analysts have helped us to understand the development of symbolic behavior. He notes slyly that the anthropologists and geneticists "have had a bad time of it in their attempts to fit man's manifold follies into a plausible evolutionary scheme. It is as if he had not proven worthy of a decent evolutionary past" (293). Finally, Percy turns to Gabriel Marcel for support of the idea that humans have a desire to know the names of things (a point that will be developed in subsequent essays), not just their function or composition, which after all might be dictated by simple biological necessity.

Thus, that man uses symbols and has a desire for them has been established. A problem arises, however, when Langer goes on to explain—or, in Percy's view, to nonexplain—the origins of such symbolic behavior as resulting from a "need" in human beings, that it is an " 'elementary need' of the new cerebral cortex" (295). Percy counters: "Simply to call the symbolic transformation a need and let it go at that is to set up an autonomous faculty which serves its own ends, the equivalent of saying that bees store honey because there is in bees a need of storing honey" (296). He finds this to be a "terrible disjunction," acceptable neither to materialists, idealists, or realists. But then when Percy himself attempts to answer the question, he replaces Langer's supposedly unsatisfactory explana-

23. Allen Tate, "Literature as Knowledge," in *Essays of Four Decades* (Chicago, 1968), 72–105.

tion with some of his own that are unconvincing because of their obscurity and the outdated metaphysical terminology in which they are expressed, the language of then-current Thomism. If it is accepted that the art symbol is a "means of *knowing*," Percy writes, then "the consequences are serious indeed":

> For it will be a knowledge, not in the sense of possessing "facts" but in the Thomist and existential sense of identification of the knower with the object known. Is it not possible that this startling semantic insight, that by the word I *have* the thing, fix it, and rescue it from the flux of Becoming around me, might not confirm and illuminate the mysterious Thomist notion of the interior word, of knowing something by becoming something? that the "basic need of symbolization" is nothing more or less than the first ascent in the hierarchy of knowledge, . . . and that therefore the activity of knowing cannot be evaluated according to the "degree to which it fills a biological need," nor according to the "degree to which the symbol is articulated," but by nothing short of Truth itself? (296–97)

This is a full-blown Thomism indeed, a version of what Bishop Fulton Sheen once referred to in a revealing moment as "supernatural biology," enough to cause even the most sympathetic positivist to withdraw from the debate, at least temporarily, in despair.

Percy had wanted to publish his first essay in a journal with a religious orientation. Now that he had succeeded in this venture, he was ready to launch out into the world of a more secular kind of philosophy where his presuppositions would not necessarily be those of his audience. Moreover, in choosing to comment on Langer and her mentor, Ernst Cassirer, in his first essay, he had picked on sympathetic figures who were not at the forefront of current empiricist thought and who indeed were often regarded as historians of philosophy rather than strict philosophers as such. In "Symbol as Hermeneutic in Existentialism," which appeared in *Philosophy and Phenomenological Research* two years later, Percy again attempts to reconcile Anglo-American empiricism with the existentialist program, but this time he is ready to tackle a more hostile form of that empiricism.

Even so, Percy, as one might expect, is from the beginning much more sympathetic with the existentialists than with the empiricists, since the former make a better effort toward giving an account of *all* realities. Empiricists, in contrast, tend to dismiss existentialists for their "exhortatory" approach, so that "such notions as dread, *Dasein,* boredom, and the dichotomies authenticity-unauthenticity . . . will appear as *reducibles*" to them (277). Percy notes that there are several faults with the empirical approach, however: the empiricist sciences cannot agree on what man should be reduced to; existential activities are smuggled in the descriptions of deterministic disciplines—*choice,* for example, is allowed in a Freudian analysis that theoretically ought to exclude it; there is the "uncritical taking for granted or the equally uncritical ignoring of consciousness and intersubjectivity" (278). What is wrong here, Percy claims (invoking Christopher Dawson), is that the empiricists are in the grip of their own *religious* presuppositions, which cause them to propose a much truncated version of a more comprehensive and thus "truer" empiricism.

But the existentialists have their problems, too: they confuse psychological with ontological phenomena, for instance, and thus provoke their opponents. They need, as James Collins put it, "to take account of Kierkegaard without surrendering to Kant." In other words, they need to recognize the importance of the human subject without being committed to Kant's notion of a transcendental subjectivity. Thus Percy reaches the general conclusion that the empirical sciences of man are in need of "an insight, a proper empirical finding" that will take account of the "reality of existential traits," so that if these "cannot be reduced to supposed prime elements or verified by measurement, [they] can at least be validated experientially" (279). Whatever work is to be done, then, has to be undertaken from "below."

Language is the "necessary bridge" on which empiricism and existentialism "intersect" (279–80). So far so good. But now Percy, returning to the theme of the previous essay that signs and symbols are essentially different, is ready to make several further claims for symbols. He insists that a symbol "is the vehicle for the conception of an object and not a term in a reflex schema which directs the organism to a referent," which presumably a sign is. Again, referring to the act of naming things, Percy asserts, "The relationship between symbol and conception is generically and irreducibly different from the purely causal order of signal-significatum," a fact borne out by the "unwitting testimony" of Helen Keller (an example that he will use again and again, and at greater length, in subsequent essays) (290). Our human need for symbols rather than signs is shown by the fact that, without them, objects in the world either irritate or unnerve us, since we don't "know" what they are.

Furthermore, symbolization also involves an "I" and a "You"—"If there were only one person in the world, symbolization could not conceivably occur (but signification could)" (281). Elaborating on this last point, Percy claims that a proper understanding of symbolization affects the understanding of the nature of the self and "rectifies existential theories about the nature of consciousness" (282). Since consciousness is intentional and not just for itself in Sartre's sense, or an isolated ego as Descartes implied, both empiricists and existentialists (except Marcel) are wrong about it. Thus, the "decisive stroke against the myth of the autonomous Kantian subject is the intersubjective constitution of consciousness. There is a mutuality between the I and the Thou and the object which is in itself prime and irreducible" (283). Percy illustrates the case in language that sounds almost more mystical than empirical: in an I looking at a Thou, "I know one thing about him—he is an existent. However successfully I may have been able to objectize him, when he looks at me, *his being escapes through his eyes* [my emphasis]. As Marcel says, it is of the nature of the other that he *exists*" (286).

As will be seen in the next chapter, there has been much criticism of the approach to language that Percy takes here: his self-training has not provided him with an awareness of what the contemporary issues are, and his knowledge of what has been achieved to date is sometimes spotty. Moreover, he tends to run together several areas of knowledge that are generally regarded as disparate. Having admitted as much, however, one might want to argue that Percy has rather different objectives in mind than being up to date, or strictly abiding by the usual disciplinary compartmentalizations, though, of course, he is also very anxious to show that his assertions have an empirical basis. Thus, for him, man is necessarily distinct from other animals (Maritain too accepted evolution as long as it allowed that a soul had been infused into humans) and the sign/symbol gap is simply where Percy chooses to locate this difference. Again, that man does not exist as an isolated consciousness is fundamental: human subjects act in community, intersubjectively. Both of these notions are necessary for a Christian understanding of human existence, and by reducing human beings merely to the status of the other animals in the world, the new empiricists are therefore outside the fold, as is Sartre with his negative interpretation of the existence of the other.[24] It may be, of course, that Percy's points could have been established in more contemporary ways. For now, however, he was content to continue the philosophical explorations with which, unlike his fiction, he had achieved at least the success of respectable publication.

24. Sidney Hook had earlier responded to the criticism that naturalism doesn't deal with alienation by pointing out that this philosophy "has never been so far removed from the crudities of reductive naturalism as to-day" (*Partisan Review* [March, 1950], 229).

4

PHILOSOPHER

"For many years Walker Percy has been writing in little-known magazines about language and meaning and existence" runs the blurb on the back cover of *The Message in the Bottle,* in which were collected his philosophical essays in 1975, several years after he had become well known as a novelist.[1] Although an academic reader might question whether the *Southern Review* and the *Partisan Review* were "little-known magazines," with a circulation of less than 10,000 copies each their impact on the general reading public cannot have been great. Even more marginal were the essays that appeared in both Thomist and more general philosophical periodicals such as the *New Scholasticism,* the *Modern Schoolman,* and the *Journal of Philosophy,* with titles like "Symbol as Hermeneutic in Existentialism," "Symbol, Consciousness, and Intersubjectivity," and "Culture: The Antinomy of the Scientific Method." Yet these form a significant part of Percy's *oeuvre,* one that he thought was of critical importance, and one of which he was proud even if he never quite penetrated such an exalted bastion of the analytic establishment as *Mind.*

Percy's major point in the essays of the 1950s (which are really expansions of his first two articles, and which I will deal with here collectively since their arguments generally overlap) is always that "a purely empirical enquiry into the symbol function, an inquiry free of the dogmatic limitations of positivism, may provide fresh access to a philosophy of being," by which he means a traditional metaphysics (246). He is always opposed to "the usual version of the nature of language . . . [which] turns upon the assumption that human language is a marvelous development of a type of behavior found in lower animals." For him, the ability to symbolize rather than merely signify makes humans "qualitatively" different from the other animals. "Naming is *generically* different from what the

---

1. Walker Percy, *The Message in the Bottle: How Queer Man Is, How Queer Language Is, and What One Has to Do with the Other* (New York, 1975).

other animals do," he argues (154); through it, a human being "no longer coincides with what he is biologically. Henceforth, he must exist either authentically or inauthentically" (134).

Percy is opposed to logical empiricism because, he claims, it has ended up either in the solipsism of Mach, Wittgenstein, and the early Carnap (*i.e.,* in a theoretical uncertainty about the existence of other minds — a tendency vigorously opposed, it should be noted, by the later Wittgenstein), or the physicalism of the later Carnap and the American behaviorists (*i.e.,* all statements about mental acts can be reduced to their physical correlates). These philosophers are not interested "in how words get applied to things" or in the problem of knowing (248). Percy even suggests that semioticians may be avoiding an analysis of symbols and symbolization because it would bring them into confrontation with metaphysics.

Percy is opposed, more specifically, to the *Encyclopedia of Unified Science* project at the University of Chicago and to those associated with it: Otto Neurath, Morris, Carnap, and others. He notes their failure to find a unified language in which to describe the achievements of the different sciences, their "methodological negation of mental entities," and he cannot understand why Morris and semioticians like him are not puzzled by the fact that humans alone have developed symbolic logic (244). In essence, Percy disputes the idea that there can be a unified science unless one collapses symbols into signs (which one cannot do, of course).

What is wrong with reducing symbols to signs is that the move fails to take account of what is going on in the very human practice of denotation. Denotation, Percy claims, "is in reality a most mysterious act, one which is quite unprecedented in animal behavior and imponderable in its consequences." The use of the word *mysterious* here, of course, closely followed by *imponderable,* tends to undermine Percy's argument in the eyes of his positivist opponents, though he himself believes strongly that this "mysterious act" *can* be studied by a discipline such as experimental psychology. In any case, the question for him is as follows: "Can denotation be derived by a refinement of behavioral reaction, or is it something altogether different?" (254). The distinction between signification and symbolization (or denotation) is proven, Percy thinks, by the fact that children are interested in objects beyond a need gratification (they want to know the *names* of things, not merely use them). It is also proven by the example of "Victor, the wild boy of Aveyron, who discovered the symbol *despite* every attempt of his positivist teacher to present it as a sign of a want." Reinforcing the point that this symbolizing or denoting or naming process is something beyond animal need, Percy asks rhetorically if Helen Keller's joy in her breakthrough into language was a "'hallucinatory need-satisfaction'" or "a purely cognitive joy oriented toward being and its validation through the symbol" (260).

The crux of the matter is that empiricists, positivists, and semanticists will not allow that there is a *real* relation between word and thing, that the person experiences "cognitive joy" because of the real knowledge of the world that symbols provide, whereas those in the Scholastic or Thomist tradition will grant this. Thus Percy, borrowing from the seventeenth-century religious philosopher John of St. Thomas, uses Scholastic terminology to describe this pairing of word and thing: "the symbol has the peculiar property of containing within itself *in alio esse,* in another mode of existence, that which is symbolized" (261). In taking this course, Percy is rejecting the notion of Kant, and even of Cassirer, that we only know the symbols or words and not the things in themselves. In the Scholastic view, in contrast, *in* knowing the symbol, we thereby know the thing in itself. Thus, our access to the world is immediate.

While an empiricist might grudgingly admit, for argument's sake, the Scholastic theory of what is involved in the act of knowing, he would be unlikely to accept Percy's next move in which profounder dimensions are associated with naming. In one of his more celebrated essays, "Metaphor as Mistake," Percy presents a series of errors in naming objects, or in interpreting their names, and argues that from such mistakes "we somehow know [the object] better, conceive it in a more plenary fashion, have more immediate access to it, than under its descriptive title" (68). Indeed, Percy goes on to suggest—using the example of a blue darter hawk which some blacks in the South mistakenly call a blue-*dollar* hawk—that the name (as long as it has authority and obscurity behind it) satisfies an ontological need rather than a psychological one and that the mistaken name embraces a truth about the bird that the correct and descriptive one misses: "Blue-dollar is not applicable as a modifier at all, for it refers to *something else* besides the bird, a something which occupies the same ontological status as the bird" (71). This suggests that a mistaken name gives an "inscape" into a thing which the correct name does not! To the objection that his praise for "wrongness" may lead to all kinds of license, Percy invokes "the authority of the Namer" as a natural corrective (76–77).

But furthermore, Percy insists (invoking a number of thinkers of controversial repute), in the original act of naming a thing, we go beyond our ordinary apprehension of it:

> Cassirer, following Usener and Spieth, emphasized the situation in which the primitive comes face to face with something which is entirely new to him and strikingly distinctive, so distinctive that it might be said to have a *presence*—an oddly shaped termite mound, a particular body of water, a particular abandoned road. And it is in the two ways in which this tensional encounter is resolved that the Urphenomenon is said to beget metaphor and myth. The Tro or momentary god is born of the sense of unformulated presence of the thing; the metaphor arises from the symbolic act in which the emotional cry of the beholder becomes the vehicle by which the thing is conceived, the name of the thing. (69)

Percy asks whether this encounter is ontological rather than instrumental and, rejecting both Cassirer and the need-satisfaction empiricists, replies: "In this primitive encounter which is at the basis of man's cognitive orientation in the world, either we are trafficking in psychological satisfactions or we are dealing with the unique joy which marks man's ordainment to being and the knowing of it" (70–71).[2] What one senses here, of course, is a radical shift in the style of inquiry, a switch from scientific empiricism to metaphysical speculation. Each of the two approaches may have its own validity, but their combination at this point jars the average reader and tends to make him suspicious of Percy's proclaimed objectivity.[3]

In addition, Percy asserts that symbolization is different from signification because it always implies two people, the namer and the person for whom something is named. "There has occurred a sudden cointending of the object under the auspices of the symbol, a relation which of its very nature cannot be construed

2. In a footnote on p. 79 of *Message in the Bottle,* Percy argues for a "mysterious connection" between word and thing: he offers as example the fact that variations of *sta* and *plu* are used in all indo-European language for similar or related purposes.

3. See Robert Scholes, *Textual Power: Literary Theory and the Teaching of English* (New Haven, 1985), 105–10, for a more mundane account of the naming process using theories from W. V. O. Quine and Wittgenstein.

in causal language" (257). Thus an empirical analysis of the symbolizing phenomenon leads to an understanding of what Gabriel Marcel and others mean by "intersubjectivity." It reveals intersubjectivity as "a very real, if mysterious, relation." According to Percy, "The 'organisms' no longer exist exclusively in a causal nexus but are united by a new and noncausal bond, the relation of intersubjectivity" (258).

The existence of intersubjectivity calls into question the procedures of those philosophers who think only in terms of an "aboriginal ego-consciousness," something impossible in Percy's view since it is inconceivable that a person raised alone would ever discover symbolization (275). On the other side, the empiricists do not so much deny the existence of intersubjectivity (though they dislike the term) as take it for granted, leaving its metaphysical implications unexplored. Against this position, Percy contends:

> It is something of a fool's errand to attempt to derive intersubjectivity by theorizing about interactions among organisms, responses to responses. Physico-causal theory is formed entirely within the intersubjective milieu and cannot of its very nature transcend it. A physical function, $a = f(b)$, is a saying of one scientist to another, an I to a Thou, that such and such a quantifiable relation obtains among the data before them. It does not say anything about the behavior of the scientists themselves because they are practicing intersubjectivity in their uttering and understanding of their causal function. They are co-knowers and co-affirmers of the function $a = f(b)$, but their co-knowing and co-affirming cannot itself be grasped by this particular instrument which they have devised between them. If we wish to study the knowers themselves, the I-Thou relation, we must use some other instrument, speak some other language, perhaps an ontological one rather than a physico-causal.

Intersubjectivity, then, transcends "the physico-causal relations obtaining among data" (271). That it is a phenomenon with profound metaphysical implications is an assertion, however, that remains in question more than Percy supposes.

At one point in "Semiotic and a Theory of Knowledge," Percy neatly summarizes the general argument of his essays:

The symbol meaning relation may be defined as not merely an intentional but as a cointentional relation of identity. The thing is intended through its symbol which you say and I can repeat, and it is only through this quasi identification that it can be conceived at all. Thus it is, I believe, that an empirical and semiotical approach to meaning illumines and confirms in an unexpected manner the realist doctrine of the union of the knower and the thing known. The metaphysical implications of semiotic are clear enough. Knowing is not a causal sequence but an immaterial union. It is a union, however, which is mediated through material entities, the symbol and its object. Nor is it a private phenomenon—rather is it an exercise in inter-subjectivity in which the Thou serves as an indispensable colleague. Both the relation of intersubjectivity and the intentional relation of identity are real yet immaterial bonds. (264)[4]

Here again, the advance to mentioning "immaterial bonds" tends to call into question at least Percy's claim that "an impartial empirical analysis of the extraordinary act of symbolization will bridge the gap" between the behaviorists and the existentialists (272).[5]

Nevertheless, Percy presses his point, arguing that certain antinomies (or at least contradictions of some kind) have arisen in the physical and social sciences as presently conceived because of a fundamental flaw in their respective constitutions. For example, the statements and assertions of the various sciences are not

4. Percy attacks Polish thinker Alfred Korzybski for objecting to the use of the copula and for seemingly blaming human beings for this error, though Percy acknowledges that the problem doesn't arise with some other languages. In Percy's view, some kind of *pairing* of word with object is always going on, for without such a pairing we could not speak at all. Percy explains: "This is not an unprecedented happening; it is also, as the semanticists have noted, scandalous. A is clearly not B. But were it not for this cosmic blunder, man would not be man" (158). However, it does seem that some of Korzybski's followers have since learned to speak with ease while avoiding all forms of the verb "to be" (see Cullen Murphy, " 'To Be' in their Bonnets," *Atlantic,* CCLXVIII [February, 1992], 18–24).

5. Here Percy is referring specifically to the theory of social behaviorist George Herbert Mead rather than to B. F. Skinner (272). Mead resembled the later Wittgenstein in laying stress on the social and interpersonal construction of meaning. His work has also been compared to "the sociology of daily life" found in Sartre's *Being and Nothingness* (see Annie Cohen-Solal, *Sartre: A Life* [New York, 1987], 276–77), though Percy tended to view the French philosopher as solipsistic, Mead as interpersonal.

themselves space-time events. Brain events, Percy contends, are not the same as assertory events. This is not to claim anything mystical, however, Percy reassures us: "Certainly an assertion is a real event in the world albeit not a space-time event; it is also a natural, not a supernatural, event." The "antinomy of science," then, is that science cannot account for its own assertions: "Here, as in the other antinomies, it is the assertory act itself which is refractory to the scientific method" (234).[6] Assertion is an "immaterial act," pointing to the fact that science needs to reexamine its own premises and admit that it is more involved with metaphysics than it currently acknowledges.

Again, very relevant to the topic of the present study, Percy argues that the social scientists (he uses the term more generously than one might wish), in allowing only a functional validity to the propositions of religious faith, fail entirely to account for the actual phenomenon itself:

> The decree requires that a belief be labeled as a myth and at the same time certified as valid as a cultural function. . . . Thus C. J. Jung "accepts" the Catholic dogma of the Assumption because it validates the anima archetype, while at the same time he denies its claim to literal truth. Jung's approach, once the total competence of the functional method is accepted, seems reasonable. I am not interested in the truth or falsity of religion, says Jung, but only in the structure of the human psyche. Yet such a neutrality is warranted only if the neutrality is consistent. It is not consistent when ideological belief is assigned first to the category of myth, then made to do duty as a neutral term in an objective culturology. (226)

Although Percy's last statement here is somewhat obscure, the argument is, I think, that Jung distorts the true nature of religious belief in such a way that, at least from the point of view of the believer, his "explanatory" schema no longer

6. Percy's critic, philosopher Thomas Nagel, makes a related point when he remarks that an objective science needs to deal with subjective consciousness (and never satisfactorily does so): "The subjectivity of consciousness is an irreducible feature of reality—without which we couldn't do physics or anything else—and it must occupy as fundamental a place in any credible world view as matter, energy, space, time, and numbers" (*The View from Nowhere* [New York, 1986], 7–8).

validly "explains" anything (hence there is a fundamental flaw in the construction of his "science").

When Percy finally presents an overview of the problem, he offers the following: "The functional method of the sciences is a nonradical method of knowing because, while it recognizes only functional linkages, it presupposes other kinds of reality, the intersubjectivity of scientists and their assertions, neither of which are space-time linkages and neither of which can be grasped by the functional method. Therefore, when the functional method is elevated to a total organon of reality and other cognitive claims denied, the consequence must be an antinomy, for a nonradical instrument is being required to construe the more radical reality which it presupposes but does not understand" (240). This kind of relativism, Percy claims, ends in "nonsense" because it ultimately implies that its own investigations are relative, too. He concludes that the social scientists also need to reexamine the premises of their methods and recognize "that there is a metascientific, metacultural reality, an order of being apart from the scientific and cultural symbols with which it is grasped and expressed." The need for such "derives not merely from metaphysical and religious argument but also from the antinomy into which a nonradical science falls in dealing with man" (242).

A much more general, but absolutely fundamental, consequence that Percy draws from all this is that an understanding of the nature of language will "reveal the ordinary secular concept of man held in the West as not merely inadequate but quite simply mistaken," since man is not "in direct continuity with rocks, soil, fungi, protozoa, and mammals." Moreover, in a statement that echoes those of Maritain and Lonergan when criticizing the direction of Western thought since the time of Galileo, Percy claims that the Enlightenment belief in the comprehensiveness of an "objective-explanatory-causal science" will be shattered. Even more portentous, perhaps, is his conclusion that man "is, in Heidegger's words, that being in the world whose calling it is to find a name for Being, to give testimony to it, and to provide for it a clearing" (158). Although, with some early exceptions, Percy is not generally given to quoting such transcendentalist rhetoric, preferring instead more empirically grounded descriptions, in its openness toward a wider horizon than that allowed for by the empiricists, Heidegger's sentiment here is certainly true to this American Catholic author's way of thinking.

Up to now, Percy has been presenting a minimal empirical view of man. But, of course, his ultimate goal is always religious conversion, and hence his philosophical essays have been broadly preparatory for this. "The Message in the Bottle" was published in 1959 in the Jesuit journal *Thought,* where Percy had essentially begun his public philosophical career five years earlier. Though basically an argument for the validity and importance of the Christian message, and precisely in its Roman Catholic version, "Message" follows directly from Percy's previous attempts to formulate a new and more radical anthropology. By far the most significant of Percy's essays, it is full of traditional philosophical references to positivism, analytic and synthetic judgments, and so forth. Percy has been arguing up until now that the antinomies of science arise because an improper division of knowledge was made to begin with (the point asserted by Maritain, Guardini, and Lonergan also)—or at least because lots of kinds of "knowing" have been rendered supposedly invalid by the various sciences as presently conceived. Moreover, there has been a failure by the scientist to see himself and his activities as part of a larger whole. Percy therefore is here attempting to look at the world in quite a different way to show how false the usual scientific view is. In this context, the fact that he finally argues for a specifically Catholic solution is *very* logical since a vague, generalized Christianity would not do at all. Indeed, Percy's epigraph juxtaposes a quotation from Aquinas which claims that "the act of faith consists essentially in knowledge" with one from Kierkegaard stating that "faith is not a form of knowledge" (119). While he plays these formulations off one another throughout the essay, Percy finally comes down on the side of Aquinas, that is, on the side of a *rational* faith, and he is severely critical of Kierkegaard.

Percy wants us to imagine a castaway washed up on an island who does not know where he comes from but, in time, adapts to his new environment. Should such a person find bottles with messages in them as he wanders along the shore, his classification of their information would be quite different from that of present-day scientists (Percy playfully imagines some messages arriving from Rudolf Carnap). Percy's point here is to show that the scientific classificatory system fails to find a place for *news*—information relevant to a person in a predicament—a failure that in a crisis situation could be fatal; this is so because its whole interest is in *knowledge* as obtained by a disinterested observer. But "to the castaway it seems obvious that a radical classification of the sentences [in the bottles] cannot abstract from the concrete situation in which one finds oneself [though] he is as interested as the scientist in arriving at a rigorous and valid classification" (124).

Percy's castaway, it soon becomes clear, is a man who is conscious that he doesn't know whence he came and is awaiting the Christian message to provide him with this information. Thus, argues Percy, when such news comes, it cannot be examined in a detached way. Just as when a responsible person at a meeting cries out that there is a fire in the auditorium, the hearers do not proceed to examine his statement with skeptical detachment, it is likewise, Percy asserts, with the news that is relevant to our salvation: we cannot presume to examine it in the cold light of reason (though, as we shall see, there are checks that one can make). But "once a piece of news is subject to the verification procedures of a piece of knowledge, it simply ceases to be news" (133). Again, Percy makes the troubling claim: "The news is not delivered to be confirmed—for then it would not be a piece of news but a piece of knowledge" (137).

Percy stresses the point that news "is a knowledge which cannot possibly be arrived at by any effort of experimentation or reflection or artistic insight" (126). One may, of course, mistake knowledge for news and look to science to solve one's feeling of homelessness. Or, as is the case with many eclectic thinkers, one might accept Christianity as knowledge in a universe of complex probabilities; or again, as Whitehead, Huxley, and Toynbee did, one might presume that Christianity claims to be some kind of eternal *knowledge*. All of these solutions are wrong, according to Percy. Rather, Christianity is based on an *event*—it is not an esoteric philosophy such as Buddhism—and thus as event, as news, it must have an outside source.

Percy's claim that his purpose in this essay is not apologetic seems a little disingenuous: "We are not here concerned with the truth of the Christian gospel or with the career in time of that unique Thing, the Jewish-People-Jesus-Christ-Catholic-Church. An apologetic would deal with the evidence of God's entry into history through His covenant with the Jews, through His own incarnation, and through His institution of the Catholic Church as the means of man's salvation. It would also deal with philosophical approaches to God's existence and nature. My purpose is rather the investigation of news as a category of communication" (141). And indeed, Percy immediately goes on to say that—in spite of his previous statement—he hopes to clear up some confusions about understanding Christianity.[7]

How, then, does the castaway know that he is homesick? Percy answers, "He knows for the simple reason that in his heart of hearts he can never forget who he is" (143). The castaway is waiting for news from across the sea and "faith of a sort is the organ for dealing with" such news (144). But it is not quite the faith that Kierkegaard described. "The fact is that Kierkegaard, despite his passionate dialectic, laid himself open to his enemies. For his categories of faith, inwardness, subjectivity, and Absolute Paradox seem to the objective-minded man to confirm the worst of what he had thought all along of the Christian news" (145). Rather, it is the faith described by Aquinas: "The classification [of the messages] of the castaway would correspond roughly to the two knowledges of Saint Thomas: (1) scientific knowledge, in which assent is achieved by reason, (2) knowledge of faith, in which scientific knowledge and assent are undertaken simultaneously." [8]

Percy acknowledges that some safeguard procedures are necessary *before* one accepts such news. First of all, the news must be relevant to one's predicament. The "reputation" and "mien" of the newsbearer are also important. Thus "a certain drunkenness of spirit—enthusiasm in the old sense of the word—is enough to disqualify him and lead me to suspect that he is concerned not with my predicament but only with his own drunkenness" (Percy gives as example the Jehovah's Witnesses).[9] In a footnote, Percy commends sober deliverance of the message and criticizes a "sonorous pulpit voice or . . . a pitch calculated to stimulate the emotions. But emotional stimuli are not news. The emotions can be stimulated on any island and at any time" (135). The important point is that "*a piece of news requires that there be a newsbearer,*" and thus there being in existence a stranger who delivers the news "is reason enough to heed the news"

7. Percy is, of course, correct in saying that his essay is not a detailed defense of the particularities of the Christian message, but rather a general preparation for its possibility.

8. Kierkegaard was overimpressed by Hegel's system and not confident enough in the value of religious knowledge. Shortly afterwards, Percy states: "Kierkegaard may have turned his dialectic against the Hegelian system, but he continued to appraise the gospel from the posture of the Hegelian scientist" (147).

9. Monsignor Ronald Knox famously criticized this aspect of the religious tradition in his 1950 book, *Enthusiasm: A Chapter in the History of Religion,* a study most recently acclaimed by Harold Bloom in *The American Religion: The Emergence of the Post-Christian Nation* (New York, 1992), 47.

(136). Since the Christian news has been prophesized for centuries beforehand, one would be a fool not to pay attention to it when it finally arrived, Percy asserts.

To sum up: the hearer of the news is not a scientist but rather a man in a predicament, and the news cannot be verified "because this would mean that God and the apostle must wait in the porter's lodge while the learned upstairs settle the matter" (146). Yet, Percy again asks how we can know that this news is genuine:

> Since everyone is saying "Come!" now in the fashion of apostles—Communists and Jehovah's Witnesses as well as advertisers—the uniqueness of the original "Come!" from across the seas is apt to be overlooked. The apostolic character of Christianity is unique among religions. No one else has ever left or will ever leave his island to say "Come!" to other islanders for reasons which have nothing to do with the dissemination of knowledge *sub specie aeternitatis* and nothing to do with his own needs. The Communist is disseminating what he believes to be knowledge *sub specie aeternitatis*—and so is the Rockefeller scientist. The Jehovah's Witness and the Holy Roller are bearing island news to make themselves and other islanders happy. But what if a man receives the commission to bring news across the seas to the castaway and does so in perfect sobriety and with good faith and perseverance to the point of martyrdom? And what if the news the newsbearer bears is the very news the castaway has been waiting for, news of where he came from and who he is and what he must do, and what if the newsbearer brought with him the means by which the castaway may do what he must do? Well then, the castaway will, by the grace of God, believe him. (148–49)

It is hard to imagine that Percy was unaware of the difficulties of this kind of argument: whether or not the Christian message is the only one for which a person has journeyed from his own island (the Incarnation? St. Paul?) is certainly open to question, nor does sober delivery appear always to have been the method by which even the most orthodox Christianity has been presented. More fundamentally, one must ask how the recipient is to judge between the competing messages without some resort to verificatory procedures. Hence Percy's essay should probably be seen more as a novel approach in Christian apologetics than as an attempt at a persuasive *philosophical* argument. But one can certainly assume from "The Message in the Bottle" that Percy himself was convinced of the truth of the Christian proclamation and that it was the terminus of his long philosophical inquiry, offering him Aquinas' "knowledge of faith, in which scientific knowledge and assent are undertaken simultaneously."

By the time that "The Message in the Bottle" appeared, Walker Percy had exhausted—for the moment at least—his philosophical themes. Indeed, the style and content of the essay itself suggest that he was moving in a narrative direction. Besides, he was writing other pieces also that were near to the concerns of his fiction. In any event, troubled by the seeming lack of an audience for his philosophical writings ("Who reads these things anyway?" he asked at the time), and without an academic position to make publication in them professionally rewarding, Percy had concluded, "I wasn't equipped as a philosopher to express my ideas. My essays on the subject were amateurish, but this, novel writing, seemed to be a wonderful way to explore it." [10] The message would remain the same, however; only its bottling would change.

There were others who would eventually conclude that Percy was an amateur in philosophy. While Percy had received no comment on his essays on their first appearance, this situation changed in 1975 with their publication (with additional pieces) as *The Message in the Bottle: How Queer Man Is, How Queer Language Is, and What One Has to Do with the Other*. A general criticism then was that Percy raised interesting questions but was not up-to-date in either philosophy or semiotics. Thomas Nagel, then a philosopher at Princeton, observed that it was unlikely that recent research on language would change our lives—the hope of what he referred to as the "spiritually ambitious." He put the matter bluntly: "Percy is unaware of much of the work pertinent to their [the problems he raises] solution, he doesn't seem to understand half of what he has read, and contributes very little to what has already been written." Linguist Frank Parker, citing numerous omissions and confusions, made similar criticisms of Percy's knowledge

10. Lewis A. Lawson and Victor A. Kramer, eds., *Conversations with Walker Percy* (Jackson, Miss., 1985), 301.

of his subject. Critic Walter Michaels noted, "In the context of contemporary semiotics, this fascination with the relation between word and thing seems at best atavistic, at worst reactionary." Michaels added that Percy was still fighting battles long resolved (*e.g.,* that with the empiricists) and failing to engage with the issues as they presented themselves. All of this was certainly the case, but it was such again precisely because of the tradition of religious apologetics from which Percy had recently come.[11]

11. Thomas Nagel, "Sin and Significance," *New York Review of Books,* September 18, 1975, pp. 54–56; Frank Parker, "Walker Percy's Theory of Language: A Linguist's Assessment," in *Delta,* XIII (November, 1981), 145–67; Walter Michaels, *Georgia Review,* XXIX (Winter, 1975), 972–75.

5

The Existentialist

When Walker Percy ceased for the moment writing "obscure articles for obscure journals" and returned to fiction, his purpose was to continue as a "polemicist and moralist" and so essentially to say in his novels what he had already said in the essays.[1] In addition to "The Message in the Bottle," two slightly earlier pieces had in part prepared the way for this return. "The Man on the Train: Three Existential Modes," appearing in the *Partisan Review* in 1956, had a less specialized audience in mind from that of his more philosophical articles. Here Percy uses a relatively accessible existentialist vocabulary—especially the notions of alienation, rotation, and repetition (the latter two being "deliverances" from the former)—rather than one borrowed from either Thomism or linguistic philosophy. Still, his purpose remains the same: to show how there are experiences in life that are simply not accounted for by the conventional empirical mode of examination, though these experiences are in a broader sense quite empirical in that they are observable after some fashion or other.

Percy's central point is that alienation is one such experience not accounted for by objective-empirical categories (he does not consider either the sociological or Marxist accounts of the phenomenon, and indeed his examples tend to be quite different from theirs): a person can have all his needs satisfied and yet feel a certain malaise. Alienation is in this sense actually a "reversal" of the objective-empirical. Thus, for example (examples that will become staples of Percy's novels), people are not afraid, as one might suppose, of the Bomb falling but rather that it will not fall; bored commuters on a train long for, rather than dread, a disaster that will break down the barriers between them; contrary to expectation, guides to mental hygiene and the improvement of one's life leave one more de-

---

1. Jay Tolson, *Pilgrim in the Ruins: A Life of Walker Percy* (New York, 1992), 93, 89.

pressed and alienated than ever. In all, alienation (of whatever kind and degree) is a fact of life that cannot be ignored even by philosophers.

Literature and, to a lesser extent, movies can, according to Percy, cancel out alienation. This is in part because they make the readers or viewers feel that they are not alone in their isolation; in part it is because they transmit the Kierkegaardian modes of rotation and repetition. But neither rotation nor repetition is guaranteed to cure alienation. Indeed, rotation—the encounter with the unexpected—as presented in movies, especially Westerns, can leave one more alienated than ever because there is a gap between the perfected action that one sees on the screen and our everyday lives; instead of being healed, one is caught up by "a spiral of despair whose only term is suicide or total self-loss" (95). Furthermore, since the perfect form of rotation is amnesia in which everything is always new, the forgetting would eventually have to be so progressive "that every corner turned, every face seen, is a rotation" (92). Repetition, meanwhile, rather than encountering the new, seeks escape from alienation in a return to, and a kind of Proustian savoring of, the past. But it too is an uncertain deliverance from "everydayness" and stands in danger of being perverted by the objective-empirical. Thus, in *The Moviegoer,* in which Percy uses these categories explicitly, it quickly becomes clear that the rotations and repetitions that movies offer present the hero with no lasting escape from his existential malaise. Nevertheless, however unhopeful Percy may be about either rotation or repetition curing alienation, the main purpose of the essay is to assert the sheer existence of the condition itself in the face of an objective-empirical mind-set that, in Percy's view, would conveniently wish to ignore it.

The second essay, "The Loss of the Creature," one of Percy's most interesting pieces, appeared in 1958 in the University of Houston's *Forum,* then edited by Donald Barthelme. Although the article may seem at first to be a departure from the author's previous work, the argument in fact derives directly from it. Percy points out that a person now has to rediscover the world because all too often it is encountered in highly packaged forms—in photos of the Grand Canyon, designated ways of seeing, pat presentations of all manner of experiences. It is only when a person stumbles unexpectedly upon a place such as the Grand Canyon that it can really be seen for what it is, Percy claims. Such an occurrence would be, in Kierkegaard's terminology (though Percy never uses the word in the essay), a true rotatory experience. What has happened, Percy contends, is that we have surrendered our sovereign view of things to the expert. The *theory* of the thing has replaced the thing itself, as Alfred North Whitehead warned (or, as Walter Benjamin noted, in this age of "mechanical reproduction" objects have lost their "aura").[2] Once more, Percy is bringing to the reader's attention an important circumstance, or problem, that tends to be omitted from straightforward analyses of experiences as simply fulfilling need-satisfactions (even as he himself is omitting discussion of the fact that *all* perception is mediated through signs of one kind or another). He is also referring back to his discovery during his illness that he was an individual who would have to face his own mortality, not a mere specimen of tubercular disease. In other words, this is a further illustration of the point that life as lived has complexities that are ignored in objective-empirical accounts of perception.

It is clear from a review of these essays that by now Walker Percy wanted to engage a wider audience and even change the way that audience perceived the world; he also wanted to earn money, if possible, instead of offprints. In any case, Percy was to be quite definite about his purpose in writing fiction: "It's hard for me to imagine any novelist not being motivated by some desire to approach some kind of truth or what he thinks to be the truth. If I didn't think that I don't think I'd bother to set pen to paper."[3] Thus, in a significant way, the novels would be

2. This, of course, is a version of the "defamiliarization" proposed by Viktor Shklovsky (cited subsequently by Percy) and others among the Russian Formalists. It presupposes, however, that there is an unmediated way of "seeing," something that later theorists question. Walter Benjamin, "The Work of Art in the Age of Mechanical Reproduction": objects lose their "aura" because of the masses "bent toward overcoming the uniqueness of every reality by accepting its reproduction." Benjamin, however, proposes a political rather than a religious solution to this crisis (in *Illuminations* [New York, 1968], 223).

3. Donald Barthelme, William Gass, Grace Paley, and Walker Percy, "A Symposium on Fiction," *Shenandoah,* XXVII (Winter, 1976), 9. Percy has also said that "nothing would be worse than a so-called philosophical or religious novel which simply used a story and a plot and characters in order to get over a certain idea" (Lewis A. Lawson and Victor A. Kramer, eds., *Conversations with Walker Percy* [Jackson, Miss., 1985], 89). But the emphasis here is on *simply*. Obviously, in so far as Percy is a successful novelist, there is a real tension between the artist and the propagandist in him. My argument is that the propagandist is present more than has been generally acknowledged to date and that what Lewis Lawson has referred to as his "indirect communications" are, in fact, relatively "direct," at least in the years after Percy has become successful and is no longer under the exacting editorial eye of Stanley Kauffmann (see Lawson, *Following Percy: Essays on Walker Percy's Work* [Troy, N.Y., 1988], 4–40).

designed to fulfill the role that the essays previously had: to make a persuasive argument for a particular (religious) point of view. Later, when Percy received a congratulatory note from Caroline Gordon following the publication of *The Moviegoer*, he confessed: "Actually I do not consider myself a novelist but a moralist or a propagandist. My spiritual father is Pascal (and/or Kierkegaard). And if I also kneel before the altar of Lawrence and Joyce and Flaubert, it is not because I wish to do what they did, even if I could. What I really want to do is to tell people *what they must do and what they must believe if they want to live*" (Percy's emphasis).[4]

But, of course, there were reasons other than what might be referred to as the "proselytizing" that persuaded Percy to return to novel writing in the late 1950s. Such an exercise, for one thing, allowed for a kind of exploration of the human consciousness that he now knew was not available to the philosophical essay. "My primary concern is not in telling a story and putting characters together so that something is going to happen, but in using the fictional situation, a man in a concrete situation, exploring reality in a way which cannot be done any other way. It cannot be done with science, a microscope, or with sociology or psychology, however refined it is." The drift of Percy's meditations in a narrative direction this time was a repetition of the experience of Kierkegaard, Marcel, Sartre, and Camus, but in a much more complex sense than when Percy attempted fiction in the late 1940s. Years afterwards, he would explain his alternations between writing philosophical essays and novels as "the fruit of twenty years' off-and-on thinking about the subject [of man], of coming at it from one direction, followed by failure and depression and giving up, followed by making up novels to raise my spirits, followed by a new try from a different direction but at a different level, followed by failure, followed by making up another novel, and so on."[5]

Writing the kind of fiction Walker Percy had in mind would also allow him to examine further his family and personal sagas: after all, *The Gramercy Winner* had dealt with only a small part of his life, Percy's period in the sanatorium and

---

4. Tolson, *Pilgrim in the Ruins,* 300.
5. Lawson and Kramer, eds., *Conversations,* 27; Walker Percy, *The Message in the Bottle: How Queer Man Is, How Queer Language Is, and What One Has to Do with the Other* (New York, 1975), 10.

his religious conversion. Thus Binx Bolling of *The Moviegoer* and Will Barrett of *The Last Gentleman* will be preoccupied with their dead fathers in a way that there is good reason to believe is based on Walker Percy's own experience. Thus the character of Aunt Emily with her "terrible gray eyes" in *The Moviegoer* will be modeled on William Alexander Percy. At a related and even more intimately personal level, Will Barrett's analytic sessions in *The Last Gentleman* would seem to have their remote origin in Percy's early psychiatric treatment in New York. At the end of it all, Percy would know more about himself than he had found out from his strictly philosophical inquiries.

If the novels can be seen as Walker Percy's coming to terms with certain problems from his past, then they are not simply pronouncements on a priori religious or philosophical commitments—although, as before, Percy was convinced that the Christian, because he saw man as essentially a pilgrim en route to his proper destination, would make the most "complete" novelist. Nevertheless, Percy still had the problem of avoiding the merely hortatory. It is not surprising, therefore, that even by the time he had written the first draft of what was to become *The Moviegoer,* his editor at Knopf, Stanley Kauffmann, found that the manuscript had "only forty good pages and a rather evangelical Catholic ending." [6] What especially troubled Kauffmann was that Percy had used the death of the protagonist's uncle and a subsequent conversation with a priest to bring about the hero's transformation. "It is as if someone had suddenly switched on a lot of rosy lights," Kauffmann complained.[7] In view of Percy's overall "program," Kauffmann felt that the manuscript needed more on the search aspect of the main character's life. So, while Percy may indeed have believed that in writing a novel "you don't have a thesis and then illustrate it. What you do is put a man in a certain situation and see what happens," a version of thesis illustration seems to have been what resulted, initially at least.[8]

Yet the final version of *The Moviegoer* was to be a great artistic success. The novel offers such a wonderful rendering of landscape, character, dialogue, and

6. Alfred Kazin, "The Pilgrimage of Walker Percy," *Harper's,* CCXLII (June, 1971), 81.

7. Quoted in Tolson, *Pilgrim in the Ruins,* 282. In an earlier draft, Binx is told that his father had wanted to become a Catholic: "I think he wanted the security of dogmas and creeds" (MS of *The Moviegoer,* Walker Percy Papers, in the Southern Historical Collection, University of North Carolina Library, Chapel Hill).

8. Lawson and Kramer, eds., *Conversations,* 61.

mood that its "message" is hidden and diffuse, though not in any way undermined by the narration. Percy has said of it that he drew on Dostoevsky for the sense of people obsessed, in a predicament; on Camus for precision and style; on Sartre for the sense of outsiderness; and on Twain for Americanness. Readers familiar with Percy's essays—and there probably weren't many such people at the time— could readily have seen, of course, how several of the same philosophical themes and examples are included and even interrupt the narrative at times and how the actual wording is sometimes similar. But, though there are indeed set pieces (all longer than the three sentences recommended by Gordon and Tate as a convincing length for one person speaking in a dialogue), this is not at all to say that the novel contains material that is excessively didactic in nature—what Reynolds Price has referred to in regard to Percy's subsequent novels as "occasional lumps of unprocessed Franco-American metaphysics." Rather, as Lewis Lawson aptly observes, while Percy has succeeded "in filtering through Binx's consciousness a considerable amount of existentialist . . . statement," he has done so in a manner that is in keeping with the protagonist's fictional character.[9] To a degree, in the final text of *The Moviegoer* Percy achieved his purpose in the terms that he would use to describe it in 1966:

When I sat down to write *The Moviegoer,* I was very much aware of dis-carding the conventional notions of a plot and a set of characters, discarded because the traditional concept of plot-and-character itself reflects a view of reality which has been called into question. Rather would I begin with a *man* who finds himself in a *world,* a very concrete man who is located in a very concrete place and time. Such a man might be represented as *coming to himself* in somewhat the same sense as Robinson Crusoe came to himself on his island after his shipwreck, with the same wonder and curiosity.[10]

The idea of beginning "from the subjective"—which, according to Sartre, both

9. *Ibid.,* 275; Caroline Gordon and Allen Tate, eds., *The House of Fiction* (New York, 1950), 457–58; Reynolds Price, Review of Walker Percy's *Lancelot,* in *Washington Post Book World,* February 27, 1977, p. E7; Lewis Lawson, "Walker Percy's Indirect Communications," in *Following Percy,* 10.
10. Percy, *Signposts in a Strange Land,* ed. Patrick Samway (New York, 1991), 190.

Christian and atheist existentialists have in common—rather than from a position associated with some dogma or other is quite evident in this quotation.

And yet again, the above statement is not altogether as open as it appears at first glance. It clearly echoes the "Message in the Bottle" essay, for example, with all the presuppositions which that implies about the *way* in which a man might come to himself or *what* he would find when he had arrived at that destination. In fact, Walker Percy himself was troubled when many reviewers saw Binx Bolling mainly as having psychological problems, an antihero in the manner of John Updike's contemporaneous Rabbit Angstrom rather than a pilgrim quester. He used several occasions in subsequent years to try to state what the novel was *really* about as though he wished to restore the message that Kauffmann had edited out or at least muted. He claimed that *The Moviegoer* is concerned with "a hidden ideological conflict involving, on the one hand, what I call Southern stoicism. . . . The other ideology is Christian Catholic." The purpose, he said, was that "the reader is supposed to recognize the outsider in himself, and to identify with the alienated values of these characters."[11] Accepting the National Book Award in 1961, he described *The Moviegoer* in the following terms: "Its posture is the posture of the pathologist with his suspicion that something is wrong. . . . The pathology in this case has to do with the loss of individuality and the loss of identity at the very time when words like the 'dignity of the individual' and 'self-realization' are being heard more frequently than ever." Echoing his philosophical essays, Percy went on: "In short, the book attempts a modest restatement of the Judeo-Christian notion that man is more than an organism in an environment, more than an integrated personality, more even than a mature and creative individual, as the phrase goes. He is a wayfarer and a pilgrim."[12]

In truth, then, a Percy novel will turn out to have an agenda—more or less explicit—and be intended to lead to a definite conclusion every bit as much as one of his philosophical essays. Although this pattern only becomes clear after

11. *Ibid.,* 72, 281. See also Percy's statement in *Conversations* that he "was not interested in the New Orleans part" but rather in "having a conflict, a confrontation of two cultures—the Greco-Roman Stoicism of Binx's father's family and the Roman Catholicism of Binx's mother's family—and seeing what happened when these two met" (219).

12. Percy, *Signposts,* 246.

The Moviegoer (in which it is present *in obscuro*), the overall plan tends to work thus: in the essays, as we have seen, Percy generally combines insights from modern, scientifically oriented semiotics with elements of a rather outdated Catholic Thomism and with existentialist philosophy, all in the service of some kind of affirmation of faith, usually of questionable philosophical merit. The essays begin with a genuinely existentialist dilemma, but then proceed by a kind of Scholastic examination of several possible solutions, only to end in the Aquinian resolution characteristic of that thinker's *Summa Theologica*.[13] Likewise, in the novels, a character finds himself in a situation for which existentialist philosophy has provided a descriptive vocabulary of words such as *alienation, everydayness, malaise,* and so on; he must then work out his salvation between the poles of a scientific analysis of the human condition and some other form of belief—usually several varieties of Stoicism and Christianity. Percy has described his own procedure thus: "I . . . ask, What are the options for characters living in a deranged world in which the Church is no longer regnant, no longer even terribly important in many places? I find it very useful to array the possible options, the different ways of human existence." [14] Finally, the protagonist comes to accept the Christian message in a way that, as Percy has admitted, all too often takes the reader by surprise and strains his credulity.[15]

How is the aforementioned pattern actually embedded in *The Moviegoer*? To what extent is it evident, to what extent hidden? Binx Bolling, the protagonist and narrator of the story, is certainly suffering from existentialist unease at the beginning of the novel. In spite of being a successful stockbroker from an important family in New Orleans, he feels himself submerged in the "everydayness" of the world around him, and he is suffering from the presence of what he calls the

13. In the late 1980s when Percy was contemplating writing a new philosophical book, a title he had in mind was St. Thomas' *Contra Gentiles*. On that occasion he also noted that "there are certain resemblances between what St. Thomas was doing in the 13th century and what I'm doing" (Lewis A. Lawson and Victor A. Kramer, eds., *More Conversations with Walker Percy* [Jackson, Miss., 1993], 222).

14. *Ibid.,* 233.

15. A kind of skeleton of a Percy plot is offered in *The Second Coming* (New York, 1980) when Percy lists briefly the various beliefs of his characters (184). Such an approach is, of course, in danger of reducing characters to mere "frames of mind," a fault of which Percy has been accused on more than one occasion.

"malaise," a sense of loss and alienation. He has long since exhausted the illusory satisfactions of science, for they failed to address him as a unique human being rather than as a mere specimen of humanity. During the years of his scientific pursuits, Binx explains, "I stood outside the universe and sought to understand it." This phase of his search ended "one night when I sat in a hotel room in Birmingham and read a book called *The Chemistry of Life*. When I finished it, it seemed to me that the main goals of my search were reached or were in principle reachable. . . . The only difficulty was that though the universe had been disposed of, I myself was left over." [16] As a result of this experience—which echoes Kierkegaard's response to Hegel as well as Percy's account of his own reaction in 1941 to being told that he had tuberculosis—Binx now approaches the problem from an altogether different angle. Still suffering from the malaise, he finds a temporary solution to it by immersing himself in the concreteness of the world around him rather than in abstract speculation about it.

Thus Binx tries to escape being an "anyone anywhere" by successfully achieving Kierkegaardian "repetitions" and "rotations," both of which states were themes of "The Man on the Train" essay. Repetition results when one revisits a scene after years of absence or rereads a book: the experience is of a heightened sense of awareness of the intervening time. Rotation likewise leads to a heightened awareness of reality. Binx defines it now as "the awareness of the new beyond the expectation of the experience of the new. For example, taking one's first trip to Taxco would not be a rotation, or no more than a very ordinary rotation; but getting lost on the way and discovering a hidden valley would be" (144). Binx's more usual kinds of repetitions and rotations are achieved, however, by attending the movies (where he becomes friendly with the owners and box office ladies of the theaters in order to make the experience more real) or by engaging in affairs with a succession of his secretaries.

It is now, however, the eve of Binx's thirtieth birthday, and he is becoming uneasily aware that even rotatory and repetitionary experiences get used up and fail to guard against the impingement of everydayness. Pressured by Aunt Emily to make a decision about the direction of his life, and by his own inner needs to renew his search for meaning, he is being forced "to array the possible options,

16.   Walker Percy, *The Moviegoer* (New York, 1961), 69–70.

the different ways of human existence." [17] Unfortunately, he cannot have recourse either to the romantic Stoicism of his father's family or to the stolid Catholicism of his mother's because neither of these beliefs is intelligible to him. Surprisingly, however, he reports their respective convictions with great clarity, a clarity that draws attention to the author's philosophical agenda as much as it does to Binx's actual dilemma.

The attitude of his father's side is represented by Aunt Emily, a patrician who lives in the Garden District and who explains that she doesn't "quite know what we're doing on this insignificant cinder spinning away in a dark corner of the universe." Nevertheless, she believes strongly that "a man must live by his lights and do what little he can and do it as best he can." Binx's response to this option—in effect, William Alexander Percy's "wintry kingdom of Marcus Aurelius"—is to say that she is right "even though I do not really know what she is talking about" (54). In fact, Binx perceives the inadequacy of Aunt Emily's Stoicism in the way in which she handles both him and her stepdaughter, Kate, who is suffering from severe disorientation and is under medical and psychiatric care. Aunt Emily appeals to principles that are no longer readily understood by the younger generation. When Binx returns from a trip to Chicago on which he has taken Kate shortly after a presumed suicide attempt on her part and during which "intimacy" is assayed between them—and all without her stepmother's knowledge—Aunt Emily chastises him with a long reassertion of Stoic principles. She concludes:

> I did my best for you, son. I gave you all I had. More than anything I wanted to pass on to you the one heritage of the men of our family, a certain quality of spirit, a gaiety, a sense of duty, a nobility worn lightly, a sweetness, a gentleness with women—the only good things the South ever had and the only things that really matter in this life. Ah well. Still you can tell me one thing. I know you're not a bad boy—I wish you were. But how did it happen that none of this ever meant anything to you? Clearly it did not. Would you please tell me? I am genuinely curious. (224)

Binx, however, while not in agreement with her view of the matter, is unable to offer a satisfactory explanation for his behavior.

17. Lawson and Kramer, eds., *More Conversations,* 233.

The other embodiments of philosophical Stoicism with which he has to deal are his dead father and Sam Yerger, a family friend. Binx comes to see the hollowness of the narcissistic romanticism that led his father to find an escape in going to war and in being killed above the wine-dark sea of Crete. It is a solution that fails to come to terms with the actual world of the here and now. Sam Yerger's brand of Stoicism, on the other hand, is initially attractive. He has lived an interesting life with great enthusiasm and has written several successful books, including *The Honored and Dishonored,* which "dealt, according to the dust jacket, 'with the problem of evil and the essential loneliness of man' " (168). But it is clear from the way in which Binx describes Sam's life (including the reference to the blurb on the dust jacket) and the somewhat modish solution that he has proposed for the cure of Kate's neurosis that his is not now (if it ever was) considered to be a desirable form of existence.[18]

Binx—at this stage—is also opposed to his mother's Catholicism. Though far from being a propagandist in the manner of Aunt Emily, she herself, unlike some of the members of her new family, tries assiduously to avoid all occasions on which an intimate discussion of religious matters might take place. Nevertheless, both she and the others are interested in Binx's predicament:

> My mother's family think I have lost my faith and they pray for me to recover it. I don't know what they're talking about. Other people, so I have read, are pious as children and later become skeptical (or, as they say on This I Believe: "in time I outgrew the creeds and dogmas of organized religion"). Not I. My unbelief was invincible from the beginning. I could never make head or tail of God. The proofs of God's existence may have been true for all I know, but it didn't make the slightest difference. If God himself had appeared to me, it would have changed nothing. In fact, I have only to hear the word God and a curtain comes down in my head. (145)

The only thing that Binx—still in existentialist mode—understands, then, is that a search must be undertaken if he is to escape from the grip of everydayness and

18. In "The Man on the Train," Percy lamented the alienation implied in a similar blurb on the dust jacket of a novel by Elio Vittorini (*The Message in the Bottle,* 96).

that "while it no longer avails to start with creatures and prove God," neither is it possible "to rule God out." He begins with what he calls "the strangest fact of all": "the strange fact of one's own invincible apathy—that if the proofs were proved and God presented himself, nothing would be changed" (146). It is remarkable both how interested he is in religion and, at the same time, how little he expects from it.

The Catholics in the novel include Binx's stolid mother, her children, Uncle Jules (Aunt Emily's husband), and Harold Graebner, the man who saved Binx's life when they were soldiers together in Korea. On the trip to Chicago, Binx finds that Harold is equally suffering from the malaise and trying to relive his past achievement—and hence his Catholicism is of little comfort. Uncle Jules, meanwhile, is "an exemplary Catholic," but Binx wonders why he takes the trouble, for "the world he lives in, the City of Man, is so pleasant that the City of God must hold little in store for him" (31).

Thus far, Binx is still the natural existentialist, more aware of the absence of God than hopeful of finding a religious solution to the meaning of life. But then Lonnie, Binx's crippled stepbrother, seems to inspire the protagonist to undertake a religious search or at least to keep such an option open. In spite of his maladies, Lonnie remains a devout believer, especially in the rather pious consolations of popular Catholicism which he somehow manages to make striking and novel. He is by no means perfect, however: he confesses to Binx that he was envious of the academic success of his dead brother, and he listens to his transistor radio with a kind of frenzied need for stimulation that seems to undercut the adequacy of his religious convictions. Nevertheless, Binx's conversations with him on the matter of religion are to be taken—because of the honesty and lack of circumlocution in the dialogue—less as polite indulgences than as genuine prophetic encounters. Moreover—and here one is certainly leaving the realm of the "evident" for that of the "hidden" message—there is reason to believe that the Eucharist Lonnie offers up for Binx is instrumental in Binx's subsequent (and presumed) conversion. This circumstance poses the kind of difficulty that David Lodge found in writing about Graham Greene, whose "*données* are often based on Catholic dogma and belief, on such assumptions as that there is such a thing as 'mortal sin,' that Christ is 'really and truly' present in the Eucharist, that miracles can occur in the twentieth century. The fictional endorsement of such ideas in the context of a pluralist and largely secular culture presents very real artistic problems."[19] Nevertheless, it would be quite remarkable if a believing Catholic like Percy did not consider this event of major significance (in fact, the Eucharist plays an explicit part in some of his later fiction), much as critic Jane Tompkins has argued that the death of little Eva in *Uncle Tom's Cabin* must be understood in its cultural context as a victory (an "access of power" in heaven to help those on earth) rather than a tragedy.[20] In other words, for the purely secular reader, the encounter with Lonnie can hardly be seen to have the significance that a believer would, in all sincerity, attach to it.

Much of the novel is devoted to portraying—unobtrusively to all those not familiar with the essays—the various philosophies from which Binx must make his choice. (Science and scientific humanism—one of his father's enthusiasms—are less prominent here than in Percy's subsequent fiction.) It is only toward the end of the story that he can be seen to advance from Kierkegaard's stage of aestheticism (in which he is mainly interested in experiencing the concreteness of the world) to that of morality.[21] The neurotic Kate can be said to be the "disaster" that awakens him to a sense of moral responsibility, which he exercises in choosing to marry and take care of her. In Marcel's terms, his is a progression from self-consciousness to its opposite, intersubjectivity.

So far so good (excepting the problem of the Eucharist, of course). Most critics have interpreted the novel somewhat in the fashion described above, though not perhaps as mechanically as I have done here. But, on a closer reading, one is surprised at how strong the Catholic subtext of the novel is (the many references

19. Quoted in Donald Greene, "Graham Greene and Evelyn Waugh: 'Catholic Novelists,' " in *Graham Greene: A Revaluation,* ed. Jeffrey Meyers (New York, 1990), 41. Terrye Newkirk develops this idea in her *"Via Negativa* and the Little Way: The Hidden God of *The Moviegoer" (Renascence,* XLIV [Spring, 1992], 183–202), though her main argument that Binx is actually a "religious contemplative" following the traditional mystical path to God is unconvincing. What her essay shows, however, is that even Percy's first novel, which is the least overtly Catholic of all of them, can be given a much more religious reading than anything I have attempted in this study.

20. Jane Tompkins, *Sensational Designs: The Cultural Work of American Fiction, 1790–1860* (New York, 1985), 127–34.

21. Percy has said that "in the end Binx jumps from the esthetic clear across the ethical to the religious. He has no ethical sphere at all" (Lawson and Kramer, eds., *Conversations,* 66). This seems to make light of Binx's commitment to Kate, though it does strengthen the argument for the importance of religion in the novel. But Percy has also claimed on another occasion that, at the end, Binx is both ethical and religious (Lawson and Kramer, eds., *More Conversations,* 163).

to the Mass, for instance), and at the frequency of its apocalyptic allusions. Clearly, more is going on than immediately meets the eye. And, in fact, Percy has claimed much more significance for the final scene of the novel than almost anyone had realized. Here, according to Percy, Binx makes a leap of faith to Kierkegaard's religious stage. On Ash Wednesday, a year before Lonnie dies, Binx can look at a prosperous Negro who has just emerged from a church and wonder whether or not the indistinct mark on his forehead represents the action of God's grace. When the boy dies, however, the ever truthful Binx tells his young stepsiblings that their dead brother will rise again on the last day, a statement intended by Percy to be an affirmation of faith even if the text itself remains unclear on the issue. "The implication is . . . you see," Percy explained in a 1971 interview, "in *The Brothers Karamazov,* Alyosha does the same thing with those kids. One of the kids says, 'Is it true we're all going to rise up on the last day and be together?' A little boy named Kolya had just died. And Aloysha said, 'Yeah, that's true. We're really going to be there.' And the kids say, 'Hurrah for Karamazov!' And so this was a salute to Dostoevsky." [22] What such an explanation—intertextual certainly, but rather obscurely so—suggests is that to a degree an ending consistent with Percy's own philosophical and theological views has been imposed upon the narrative rather than allowed to arise naturally from it. Again, without this endorsement, to the ordinary secular reader it would appear that the ever ironic Binx has overcome the malaise by committing himself to the neurotic Kate and by partly going along with Aunt Emily's modified hopes for him.

Walker Percy's reference to Dostoevsky helps, perhaps, to clarify what is being enacted in *The Moviegoer.* Recent interpretations of the Russian novelist have focused interest on the tension between that author's well-known Christian dogmatism and what is actually achieved in his great novels. Mikhail Bakhtin acknowledges Dostoevsky's ideological position, but he argues that it is partly subverted in the polyphonic texts of the novels: "But what unfolds on the level of his novels is not a polyphony of reconciled voices but a polyphony of battling and internally divided voices. These latter voices were no longer present on the level of Dostoevsky's narrowly ideological aspirations but were present in the

22. Lawson and Kramer, eds., *Conversations,* 66.

actual reality of his time. The social and religious utopia inherent in his ideological views did not swallow up or dissolve in itself his objectively artistic vision." This is true also of Percy (as Michael Kobre has sensitively shown)—but to a limited extent.[23] Binx is certainly not a fixed character from the beginning; he develops and learns to separate his own voice "from another voice with which it has inseparably merged" (239). A conflict *is* present. And even Percy himself has an entry in his notebook for 1951 that supports this dialogical interpretation: "Dostoievski's way of creating characters from his own complexity. The Brothers. He is all three. Priest, atheist, worldling." [24] But it is clear that Percy also falls into the camp of those who, according to Bakhtin, show "the tendency to monologize Dostoevsky's novel" which "remains to this day so strong." Bakhtin continues: "It is expressed in a striving, through analysis, to give finalizing definitions to the heroes, to find without fail a definite monologic authorial idea, to seek everywhere a superficial real-life verisimilitude, and so forth. The rigorous unfinalizability and dialogic openness of Dostoevsky's artistic world, that is, its very essence, is ignored or rejected." [25] Percy's case is by no means as extreme as that condemned here, and yet, without the strong demands of a Stanley Kauffmann editing a first novel, the result might have been much more monological than Percy's sympathizers (though not Percy himself) like to imagine.

Walker Percy's first published fiction represents a journey from unbelief to belief, from apathy to commitment, from a secular to a sacred universe. What has provoked the final stage of the pilgrimage remains unspoken in the actual text of *The Moviegoer,* though it is explainable in terms of the traditional economy of grace which the author arguably presupposes. Indeed, it would be difficult to see how he could tell the kind of story he has in mind without having recourse to the reality of the metaphysical and religious doctrines he is affirming. In any case, the latent Catholicism of the novel, muted in the revisions he was required to make by his editor at Knopf, is reasserted and brought to light in Percy's subsequent comments on his first successful work. From now on, however, his agenda

23. Mikhail Bakhtin, *Problems of Dostoevsky's Poetics,* trans. Caryl Emerson (Minneapolis, 1984), 249–50; Michael Kobre, "The Consolations of Fiction: Walker Percy's Dialogic Art," *New Orleans Review,* XVIII (Winter, 1989), 45–53.
24. Quoted in Tolson, *Pilgrim in the Ruins,* 269.
25. Bakhtin, *Problems in Dostoevsky's Poetics,* 271–72.

will be much less hidden. As Tolson has noted: "The end of art was knowledge, which to Percy was knowledge of the Christian message" (301). The ironic voice that pervades the novel had prevented critics from giving it a religious interpretation; Percy intended that his next production would be less ambiguous, an exercise rather in "ass-kicking for Jesus' sake." [26]

26. Quoted in Tolson, *Pilgrim in the Ruins,* 301.

6

HOMO VIATOR

Whatever the critical and even popular success of *The Moviegoer,* Walker Percy felt deeply that its religious motivation had not been sufficiently recognized, and, as Jay Tolson has noted, "the philosopher in him did not want to accept the kind of ambiguity necessary for a novelist." It was now his intention therefore, to rectify this situation with his next novel by being a good deal more explicit. He described the plot to his publisher as consisting of an "odyssey" that would lead the "troubled protagonist to a vision of possible salvation in the act of baptism." [1] Something similar, of course, had been the broad theme of the aborted *Gramercy Winner.* Percy's intent is shown also in the fact that the new novel seems to have focused originally on Sutter Vaught, a psychiatrist become pathologist become pornographer, who is nevertheless more explicitly concerned with religious matters than the eventual protagonist, Will Barrett, who is basically an onlooker. Percy describes the plot as follows: "In the course of an ordeal, a suicide attempt, he [Sutter] recovers himself and experiences a conversion to a belief in God and His entry into space-time via Jews, Christ and Church, the supreme scandal to the transcending posture of abstraction. There remains only the artistic problem of whether his suicide should succeed and he should die or whether he should return to psychiatry and 'lead a useful and productive life' " (326). If Percy was to modify his plan later on so that even *The Last Gentleman* has an "open"—though hardly "ambiguous"—ending, this was done to achieve his purpose more effectively rather than to mute it merely for artistic reasons.

In the late 1950s when *The Moviegoer* was being written, the Catholic church

---

1. Jay Tolson, *Pilgrim in the Ruins* (New York, 1992), 302, 304. Even the latter part of Thomas Merton's laudatory comment on *The Moviegoer* may have troubled Percy: "You are right all the time, not just sometimes. . . . It is not that what you say is true. It is neither true nor false, it points in the right direction, where there is something that has not been said and *you know enough not to say it*" (my emphasis). Tolson suggests, however, that here Merton has noticed the dialogic or Bakhtinian aspects of Percy's novel (315).

was not yet undergoing the *aggiornamento,* much less the turmoil, that would begin with the Second Vatican Council in the next decade. *The Moviegoer* is essentially a novel of consciousness that focuses on the interior life and faith (or lack of it) of Binx Bolling. The external structures of religion remain intact, supportive, and even quietly triumphal: after all, there were the numerous converts who had recently seen its light, the first Roman Catholic American president had just been elected (and theologian John Courtney Murray had shown that being Catholic, far from standing in opposition to the essence of the American political ideal, was in fact wholly consistent with it), and the first stirrings of liturgical and theological renewal held great promise for future development.[2]

Much the same is true in *The Last Gentleman* in regard to its presentation of the religious situation (notwithstanding the epigraph from Romano Guardini on the loneliness of faith toward the end of the modern world, the initial changes brought about by the Second Vatican Council, or even the assassination of President Kennedy that so deeply troubled Percy as to cause major restructuring of his book).[3] On the other hand, the *social* fabric of the country has begun to dissolve. Thus, one of the serious considerations of *The Last Gentleman* is the matter of race, which was now coming into sharp focus as the civil rights movement intensified in the South, provoking violent reactions in several places there, including Percy's native Birmingham, Alabama, and the campus of the University of Mississippi. But what is especially interesting about Percy is that his own shift from southern moderate on the race issue to reformer clearly resulted from his religious conversion and did not spring from any emergent liberal bias. An article entitled "The Failure and the Hope," which appeared in *Katallagete* (described as the "Journal of the Committee of Southern Churchmen") in December, 1965, makes this fact abundantly clear: Percy offers a strong Christian statement on the evils of southern racism and on the peculiar alliance between Stoicism and cultural Christianity that caused a resistance to the just demands of blacks.

2. The renewal of the Catholic liturgy was in large part due to the work of Romano Guardini. John Courtney Murray's ideas on religious freedom had a major impact on the deliberations of the Second Vatican Council, liberalizing the Roman Church's understanding of church-state relations (see Murray, *We Hold These Truths: Catholic Reflections on the American Proposition* [New York, 1960]).

3. Guardini has in mind a world in which there are fewer believers—hence those who do believe are lonely—rather than a world in which the Church itself has become confused about its mission. The latter was what happened in the late 1960s and 1970s.

While the South is a region "where the public and secular consciousness is still to a degree informed by theological habits of thought, the old notions of sin, of heaven and hell, of God's providence," Percy notes, Christians there have been cruel to the Negro, failing to see him as "a member of the same Mystical Body, freed and dignified by the same covenant which frees and dignifies us." [4] The old southern morality that tried to treat the Negro decently "was paternalistic and Stoic in character and . . . derived little or none of its energies from Christian theology" (332). Now, however, Percy argues that in the South "the ultimate basis for racial reconciliation must be theological rather than legal and sociological" (330). However much it has failed in the past, only Christianity has "the interior resources of renewal" to cope with the problem. The old Stoicism has failed and the new liberalism cannot successfully replace it, since the "middle-class society from which have come so many of the earnest young revolutionaries is itself marked by the malaise and anomie and other symptoms of the new sickness" (338).

Percy's use of this material in *The Last Gentleman* is engagingly complex. His own sense of the race issue can often be identified with that of Will Barrett, who is a moderate in this regard. Will is amused by a white man who tries to become black (a "pseudo-Negro") to see what the experience is like—an obvious comic commentary on fellow-Catholic John Howard Griffin and his famous account of such a self-transformation, *Black like Me*. But there is an implied criticism of Will, too, since he can only act in the right way in extreme circumstances, as when he strikes the good ol' boy racist sheriff: "for once things became as clear as they used to be in the old honorable days." [5] Will is bound, and limited, by the Stoic ethic in regard to race. It is Val, the rather unattractive southern nun driven to work with deprived blacks only because of her Christian conversion, who is intended by Percy to represent the kind of person who recognizes that all races are one in the Mystical Body of Christ, Percy's own aspiration.

Again, the nature of Percy's religious commitment is shown in the critical view of psychiatry he takes in his new novel. In "The Coming Crisis in Psychiatry," which had appeared in *America* in 1957, Percy made important comments on the

4. Walker Percy, *Signposts in a Strange Land,* ed. Patrick Samway (New York, 1991), 327–29.
5. John Howard Griffin, *Black like Me* (New York, 1962); Walker Percy, *The Last Gentleman* (New York, 1966), 312.

inadequacies of Erich Fromm's "humanistic psychoanalysis," supposedly a corrective to Freud's (also, of course, attacked here). He joins with those who are calling Freudianism into question at every level, pointing out that it "has nothing to say" about existentialist themes, while he also rejects Fromm's Marxist explanation of alienation. A clue to what has gone wrong is, perhaps, "to be found in Fromm's ambiguous treatment of transcendence. If there is any one feature which all existentialists agree upon as an inveterate trait of human existence, it is transcendence. Some, like Gabriel Marcel, may regard it as the true motion of man toward God; others, like Jean-Paul Sartre, may regard it as an absurd striving, the 'useless passion.' But, atheistic or theistic, they would all agree that transcendence is the one distinguishing mark of human existence." [6] The trouble with Fromm is that what he wants is that "transcendence should not be transcendent" (261).[7] In a more general sense, of course, Percy has always objected to those who look to psychiatry as a kind of religion.[8] Transferred to *The Last Gentleman,* Percy offers a subtle critique of psychiatry as he describes Will Barrett's analysis in New York. Undoubtedly, Will *is* sick and does need help. But Dr. Gamow is no match for his wiles and, more important, he fails to see the real cause of his patient's illness.[9]

As if to indicate at the outset an advance from the existentialist ethos of his first novel to the more openly Catholic ambiance of his second, Walker Percy begins as before with a quotation from Kierkegaard ("If a man cannot forget, he will never amount to much"), but this time he adds another from the Jesuit theologian

6. Percy, *Signposts,* 260–61.

7. Tolson criticizes Percy for being unfair to the Freudians. He also suggests that Percy's "reluctance to look at any of the historical dimensions of the therapeutic culture revealed his own limitation as a culture critic and even as a philosopher. This limitation would remain a weakness of his theoretical and critical writing, and was tied, one suspects, to his own difficulty in confronting the past except through the indirect means of fiction" (*Pilgrim in the Ruins,* 267).

8. Lewis A. Lawson and Victor A. Kramer, eds., *Conversations with Walker Percy* (Jackson, Miss., 1985), 94. Percy believes in grace and, as Tolson notes, his fiction offers "a sustained argument against assorted notions of 'psychological man.' " Indeed, Percy has remarked, "In my own experience the most valuable lesson of psychoanalysis was learning what it could not do" (quoted in Tolson, *Pilgrim in the Ruins,* 333).

9. It is only very slowly that Dr. Gamow becomes aware that he is being *entertained* by Will's descriptions of his illness, that they are mere "trophies to put him off the scent while the patient got clean away" (*The Last Gentleman,* 31). One often suspects that Percy himself is engaged in the same strategy.

Romano Guardini's 1956 book, *The End of the Modern World:* "We know now that the modern world is coming to an end . . . at the same time the unbeliever will emerge from the fogs of secularism. He will cease to reap benefit from the values and forces developed by the very Revelation he denies. . . . Loneliness in faith will be terrible, love will disappear from the face of the public world, but the more precious will be that love which flows from one lonely person to another . . . the world to come will be filled with animosity and danger, but it will be a world open and clean." Earlier we saw how this very lyrical and appealing quotation yet implies the reemergence of a Christian world in a way that many people today would find unacceptable. Moreover, the claim that the "modern world is coming to an end" also implies, quite intentionally, a kind of religious apocalypse. Thus, the Catholic religion will figure prominently and explicitly in the new novel, though the main character is not fully aware of its significance, since being the "last gentleman" serves to prevent him from understanding how dire the situation really is. Rather it is the newly converted Val Vaught and her degenerate brother, Sutter, who come nearest to intuiting Guardini's analysis. At one point, Sutter describes his sister, who works among linguistically retarded blacks in rural Alabama:

> Val had a dream of what the Church should come to. (And I agree! Absolutely!) For example, she did not mind at all if Christendom should be done for, stove in, kaput, screwed up once and all. She did not mind that the Christers were like everybody else, if not worse. She did not even mind that God shall be gone, absent, not present, A.W.O.L., and that no one noticed or cared, not even the believers. Because she wanted us to go the route . . . to leave God out of it and be happy or miserable, as the case might be. She believes that then, if we go the route and run out of Christendom, that the air would be cleared and even that God might give us a sign.[10]

One might even suppose that religion appears gratuitously in this novel— Barrett is frequently puzzled and embarrassed when the other characters bring the matter up—were it not for the fact that his incomprehension of the situation

10. *Ibid.,* 362–63.

is precisely the point that Percy is trying to get across. In fact, this time Percy includes much of the wording of his most "religious" essay, "The Message in the Bottle," in the very text of his fictional creation. In *The Moviegoer* the polemical nature of the long philosophical passages may have gone unnoticed so natural did they seem to the characters espousing them (Binx and Aunt Emily). Now, however, the preaching note in Percy will be more obvious, casting a new light on even his previous work.

Will Barrett bears some resemblance to Binx Bolling — both come from upper-class southern families and, more important, both are seekers who always tell the truth. Binx claimed that Aunt Emily's "sweet sad piping of the nineteenth century, good as it can be . . . [is] not good enough" (48); for Will, similarly, Brahms's Great Horn Theme is "the very sound of the ruined gorgeousness of the nineteenth century, the worst of times" (96). Both are plagued by "ravenous particles," a kind of fallout from a destructive age. But for the most part the differences between them are what impress one. Will, five years younger than Binx, knows less — he still retains a belief in the possibilities of science — and so has more to discover. Unlike Binx, he seems satisfied at times "to want to make a contribution." Will's personal situation is again far more critical than Binx's was: his father committed suicide when he was fifteen and he himself is variously described as being mentally ill, having a defective ego structure, and suffering from fugue states. For five years he has been attending daily psychiatric sessions in an attempt to cure himself. The author puts the matter thus: "Much of the time he was like a man who has just crawled out of a bombed building. Everything looked strange." But, Percy adds, "Such a predicament . . . is not altogether a bad thing. Like the sole survivor of a bombed building, he had no secondhand opinions and he could see things afresh" (11). In fact, Percy intended that Will should be identified with the similarly handicapped Prince Myshkin in Dostoevsky's *Idiot,* and he even instructed Peter Handke to use that title for the German translation of his novel.[11] Finally, unlike Binx, Will is not only not a Catholic (though he has a couple of aunts who are), but he has a Protestant resistance to what he deems that church's manipulative strategies. Yet, in Percy's view, it is precisely because

11. See Cecile Cazort Zorach, "Peter Handke as Translator of Walker Percy," *South Atlantic Review,* LII (January, 1992), 69–83.

the gap between Will and religious belief is so wide that it will be easier this time for the reader to see the specific contours of that belief.

A part of Will's problem is that, in the tradition of Faulkner's Quentin Compson, he is the last gentleman, the last of a line of increasingly problematic forebears (the Percy Stoics) of overrefined sensibility, born into an age that is later than the ones he seems made for. (For a long time he is very concerned with the battles of the Civil War.) Percy sounds the theme beautifully early on and repeats it at regular intervals throughout the narrative:

> Over the years his family had turned ironical and lost its gift for action. It was an honorable and violent family, but gradually the violence had been deflected and turned inward. The great grandfather knew what was what and said so and acted accordingly and did not care what anyone thought. He even wore a pistol in a holster like a Western hero and once met the Grand Wizard of the Ku Klux Klan in a barbershop and invited him then and there to shoot it out in the street. The next generation, the grandfather, seemed to know what was what but was not really so sure. He was brave but he gave much thought to the business of being brave. He too would have shot it out with the Grand Wizard if only he could have made certain it was the thing to do. The father was a brave man too, and he said he didn't care what others thought, but he did care. More than anything else, he wished to act with honor and be thought well of by other men. So living for him was a strain. He became ironical. For him it was not a small thing to walk down the street on an ordinary September morning. In the end he was killed by his own irony and sadness and by the strain of living out an ordinary day in a perfect dance of honor.

Will himself is described as not knowing what to think and as therefore having become a listener and a watcher of other people's behavior. When he was a boy he witnessed the insanity of a neighbor, and it seemed to him "that if he could figure out what was wrong with the man he would learn the great secret of life" (9–10).

The novel opens with Will living in New York. He is a Princeton dropout working as a humidification engineer at Macy's and undergoing analysis for his recurring amnesiacal fugues. He is a man ready, however—in typical Percy mode—to receive a "sign," and so now his life is about to take a definite direction. Using the telescope he has just purchased to see things more clearly, to "recover" them, he spies a beautiful young woman (Kitty Vaught) in Central Park. She is, he thinks, the "sign" he has been waiting for. Will soon becomes involved with her southern family, who are in New York to take home their son Jamie, who is dying of leukemia. Thus Will's "search" is conducted through a return from "ground zero" in New York to the South (where he hopes to discover his identity) with Jamie and his sister. He abruptly terminates the analysis which he has been undergoing and in true existentialist fashion prepares to act out the reality of his life. The analysis itself is described in ways that suggest its own futility and inappropriateness.

On the journey Will encounters a number of possibilities for living and is thus provided with tentative solutions as to what life is all about. In fact, Will is explicitly identified with the hero of *The Magic Mountain,* and so his various encounters have an affinity with those offered to Hans Castorp by Settembrini, Naphta, Frau Chauchat, and Peeperkorn. Will's search, however, is initially conducted from a technical, detached stance: "I shall engineer the future of my life according to the scientific principles and the self-knowledge I have so arduously gained from five years of analysis" (40). This detachment will remain his constant problem in finding a solution, for Will's very posture is "self-defeating." Much later in the novel Sutter Vaught observes this of him:

Let us say you [Val] were right: that man is a wayfarer (i.e., not transcending being nor immanent being but wayfarer) who therefore stands in the way of hearing a piece of news which is of the utmost importance to him (i.e., his salvation) and which he had better attend to. So you say to him: Look, Barrett, your trouble is due not to a disorder of your organism but to the human condition, that you do well to be afraid and you do well to forget everything which does not pertain to your salvation. That is to say, your amnesia is not a symptom. So you say: Here is the piece of news you have been waiting for, and you tell him. What does Barrett do? He attends in that eager flattering way of his and at the end he might even say *yes!* But he will receive the news from his high seat of transcendence as one more item of psychology, throw it into his immanent meatgrinder, and wait to see if he feels better. He told me he's in favor of the World's Great Religions. What are you going to do about that? (339)

Will's attitude makes it impossible for him to respond genuinely to a message that is beyond rational judgment—at least in the manner described in "The Message in the Bottle." His stance, moreover, in being open to the "World's Great Religions" is very similar to Carl Jung's stance, which Percy had so strongly criticized earlier.

The origin of Will's discontent lies in part in his father's suicide. In the course of his journey southward, this repressed memory surfaces at intervals and allows him to contemplate Barrett senior's philosophy. Will's memory of his father—a lawyer who defended blacks (and Catholics) in a rather patronizing way—is presented in terms that are reminiscent of Aunt Emily of the previous novel: as a man who would "speak of the galaxies and of the expanding universe and take pleasure in the insignificance of man in the great lonely universe." He would recite Arnold's "Dover Beach" (*the* great poem about loss of faith) "or else speak of the grandfather and the days of the great deeds" (297). But this attitude proved insufficient for his father, who felt (in William Alexander Percy fashion—and in a certain parallel with Sutter) that the old way of life had been defeated, that the present was an age of petty fornication, and so took his own life to escape from the impending degradation. Will learns that he does not have to go the same way:

I think he [Will's father] was wrong and that he was looking in the wrong place. No, not he but the times. The times were wrong and one looked in the wrong place. It wasn't even his fault because that was the way he was and the way the times were, and there was no other place a man could look. It was the worst of times, a time of fake beauty and fake victory. *Wait.* He had missed it! It was not in the Brahms that one looked and not in the solitariness and not in the old sad poetry but—he wrung out his ear—but here, under your nose, here in the very curiousness and drollness and exactness of the iron and the bark that—he shook his head—that . . . (318–19)

The kind of romanticism, then, that would "take pleasure in the insignificance of man in the great lonely universe" must be escaped from, and here-and-now reality embraced—in a way similar, though opposite, to Sartre's Roquentin, who was disgusted by the sheer existence (the "drollness and exactness of the iron and the bark") of things. By the end of *The Last Gentleman* it is clear that Barrett is no longer willing to accept suicide as an appropriate response to the trials of the times.

In addition to his father's "solution," the other immediate possibility that offers itself to Will is that of settling down with Kitty and leading an ordinary life, living as an Episcopalian in a rather noncommitted way. He tries on several occasions to realize this possibility (and it may even be present still at the very end of the novel), but always there is a gnawing fear that this is simply not enough, that to do so would be to be lost in Binx Bolling's everydayness, that this kind of happiness will eventually "drive him wild with despair." Percy presents the matter with malicious irony when he has Will ask Kitty if she means to live in an upscale new housing development while he, meanwhile, is "looking around at the ferny Episcopal woods and the doleful view and thinking of feeding the chickadees for the next forty years" (274). Throughout, Kitty is presented in such a way that it is obvious that she is no solution to Will's search, though this is done rather cruelly (and in sexist terms): "She had a woman's knack of cutting loose from the ache, putting it out to graze. She knew how to moon away the time; she could doze" (155–56).

Jamie, in his innocence, is kin to Lonnie of the previous novel. Indeed, in a narrative that might be said to be about his quest for baptism—though he long resists the sacrament—he eventually functions as a catalyst for Will's potential (but never realized) religious transformation. Initially, however, though Will is certainly drawn to this sixteen-year-old—they are described as fellow engineers—Jamie's "philosophy" does not seem to interest him greatly. Jamie is mainly concerned with abstract ideas, with reading Wittgenstein's *Tractatus Logico-Philosophicus* and a book on the theory of numbers, whereas Will tends to ponder "the mystery of the singularity of things" (179). "The difference between him and me," Will notes, "is that I could not permit myself to be so diverted (but diverted from what?). How can one take seriously the Theory of Large Numbers, living in this queer . . . place?" (231). Again, Jamie reads Kahlil Gibran (mocked in *The Moviegoer*), "a bad sign even in healthy people," as Val remarks (286). It is only with Jamie's baptism (in which Will is reluctantly instrumental) prior to his death that his life has some significance for Barrett, and then merely in that Barrett realizes that something has happened (similar to the way in which Lonnie's death functioned for his siblings in *The Moviegoer*).

Rita, Sutter's estranged wife, is described as having some of the same attitudes as Will's father (but she is also dishonest). She is intelligent and generous in her way. Kitty admires her for her dedication to the American Indians—she is interested in the Ahaiyute myths and helps a young Zuni to get into Harvard—and for the help she has given to the family in her real concern for Jamie. But, again, it is clear from the way in which she is presented that she offers no solution to things: she is the quintessential Percy caricature of the liberal conscience. She opposes Jamie's baptism as a rite to be performed by "a rather stupid Irishman in a black skirt" who will utter "atrocious ecclesiastical Latin" (223), and she reads Erich Fromm's *Art of Loving,* a work previously condemned by Percy and even here leading to Will's disappointment with her (263).

So, finally, the "religious" option is presented to Will in the person of Val Vaught, the nun, and in her lecherous doctor brother, Sutter. In Will's first encounter with Val (who has heard his father speak "on the subject of *noblesse oblige* and our duty to the Negro" but who does not agree with his "reasons" [199, 201]), she asks him to see that Jamie is baptized: "I don't want him to die without knowing why he came here, what he is doing here, and why he is leaving" (201). Will refuses her request, however, because of his latent Protestantism: "Perhaps we are true Protestants despite ourselves, he mused, or perhaps it is just that the protest is all that is left of it. For it is in our stern protest against Catholic monkey business that we feel ourselves most ourselves." When he asks her how she feels she can make such requests of people, Val replies in terms that echo "The Message in the Bottle"—that it is "extraordinary how you can ask the most unlikely people" to do something important "and how often they will just look startled and go ahead and do it" (204).

When Will meets Val later at her school for retarded black children in Alabama, she explains how she received her vocation and she recites her inadequacies as a nun. She believes in the whole Catholic thing. "But try as I might, I couldn't remember the five proofs of God's existence or the difference between a substance and an accident." Indeed, she presents a rather unattractive picture of the faith: "That's what I don't understand you know: that I believe the whole business: God, the Jews, Christ, the Church, grace, and the forgiveness of sins—and that I'm meaner than ever. Christ is my Lord and I love him but I'm a good hater and you know what he said about that. I still hope my enemies fry in hell. What to do about that? Will God forgive me?" (289). Will's response to this rhetorical query—he claims that he cannot really "see" her—is evasive. After she has told him about her interest in linguistics and how language can free the children in wonderful ways, Will finally categorizes her and thus dismisses the need for a decision: "She struck him as an enthusiast of a certain sort who becomes wry as a counter-measure to her own outlandishness. . . . He understood this. And was it not also the case that her offhandedness was a tactic and that she had *her* hooks out for *him?* He didn't mind if she had, and was even prepared to put on a thoughtful expression as much as to say: you do give me pause, Sister; that is something to think about" (289–90). The fact, however, that Val is engaged in teaching language to retarded children gives her a positive status in Percy's philosophical hierarchy. And again, as is seen more clearly at the end of the novel, the messenger of faith does not have to be an outwardly attractive person. It is Will's detached scientific stance together with his Stoic gentlemanliness that prevent him from being challenged by Val's commitment.[12]

Val brings religion into the narrative somewhat gratuitously. Even so, since she *is* a nun, her interests and arguments can be justified within terms of her character. Dr. Sutter Vaught, on the other hand—the negative witness to faith, so to speak— intrudes his peculiar ideas in a way that the reader may find less convincing, though it must be granted that, since his sister has recently become a nun, her

---

12. W. L. Godshalk's comment that "Jamie's baptism, an elaborate comedy, is a biting commentary on the inadequacy of Val's Catholicism" seems to me to miss the point of Percy's *intention* at least: Val's commission is entirely in keeping with the message of "The Message in the Bottle" (see "The Engineer, Then and Now; or, Barrett's Choice," in *Walker Percy: Novelist and Philosopher,* ed. Jan Nordby Gretlund and Karl-Heinz Westarp [Jackson, Miss., 1991], 35). As John Edward Hardy notes caustically: "One must wonder how it is that the earlier examples of Joyce, Greene, O'Connor *et al.,* have failed to prepare Percy's critics for this kind of Catholic fiction" (*The Fiction of Walker Percy* [Urbana, 1987], 99). Percy himself obviously agreed: "The doctrine of the church is that the sacraments are transmitted regardless of the character of the priest" (Lewis A. Lawson and Victor A. Kramer, eds., *More Conversations with Walker Percy* [Jackson, Miss., 1993], 6). Percy goes on to confirm the relationship with Greene's whiskey priest in *The Power and the Glory* (7).

decision—that is, the Christian solution—would naturally be present to him as a possibility. In any case, though by no means a Catholic, Sutter is concerned with the interconnection between transcendence and immanence and sees sexuality as a possible mode of their resolution. Will hears about him early on from Jamie when one of Sutter's "scientific" articles is mentioned: "It was titled *The Incidence of Post-orgasmic Suicide in Male University Graduate Students,* and divided into two sections, the first subtitled 'Genital Sexuality as the Sole Surviving Communication Channel between Transcending-Immanent Subjects,' and the second, 'The Failure of Coitus as a Mode of Reentry into the Sphere of Immanence from the Sphere of Transcendence' " (62). Not surprisingly, the engineer cannot make head or tail of the business.

Still, from his first encounter with the doctor, Will feels that Sutter knows something that he himself does not know. When Will tells him that he is troubled because he feels so bad while some of his fellow fraternity brothers feel good, Sutter responds with a story about a perfectly contented man who broke out screaming and was cured by being placed in a terminal ward. Sutter gives no explanation why this treatment worked, but the implication clearly is that ordinary life can lead to screaming (Will himself had admitted as much earlier) and that everydayness can be overcome by confrontation with the possibility of death. But when Will seeks direction from Sutter, Sutter refuses to give it to him, though it is he who asks Will some fundamental questions about his religious beliefs. Afterwards, when Sutter leaves secretly with Jamie, Will follows them to Santa Fe, into the desert. Intermittently along the way, Will reads accounts of the doctor's philosophical attitudes in the notes in Sutter's abandoned steno pad. This rather contrived device on Percy's part—one with which he himself was not altogether happy—provides comments on religion for at least the last third of the novel.

The entries are really meditations on a succession of autopsies that Sutter has conducted. The first deals with a white male optician, a family man, who was found dead at a brothel. The note is a not altogether intelligible analysis of what such a person's condition implies. In essence it says that lewdness, "skin to skin," is all that is left to man in the modern world, since the "real" has been absorbed by theory. In an aside to his sister, Sutter claims: "I do not deny, Val, that a revival of your sacramental system is an alternative to lewdness (the only other alternative is the forgetting of the old sacrament), for lewdness is itself a kind of sacrament (devilish, if you like). The difference is that my sacrament is operational and yours is not" (270). Sutter's conclusion is that the only difference between himself and Val is "that you think that purity and life can only come from eating the body and drinking the blood of Christ. I don't know where it comes from" (271).

Later, following an account of an autopsy on a young black girl killed in an explosion (possibly a reference to the infamous Birmingham church bombing of 1963), Sutter launches into an attack on Val's beliefs. He begins by praising her:

> You opted for the Scandalous Thing, the Wrinkle in Time, the Jew-Christ-Church business, God's alleged intervention in history. You acted on it, left all and went away to sojourn among strangers. I can understand this even though I could never accept the propositions (1) that my salvation comes from the Jews, (2) that my salvation depends upon hearing news rather than figuring it out, (3) that I must spend eternity with Southern Baptists. But I understand that you did and even rejoiced in the scandal of it, for I do not in the least mind scandalizing the transcending scientific assholes of Taos and La Jolla. (295)

Sutter goes on, however, to accuse Val of having sold out by now taking financial contributions from these same people: "The reason I am more religious than you and in fact the most religious person I know: because, like you, I turned my back on the bastards and went into the desert, but unlike you I didn't come sucking around them later" (296). Sutter's attitude, of course, is excessively pure, unwilling to engage with the real world, while his desire to figure out the nature of salvation was explicitly rejected in the "Message" essay.

Will experiences a sense of dislocation on reading further entries that repeat the claim that lewdness represents an effort to go from transcendence to immanence and that Sutter's former wife's problem is that she cannot understand the relationship between sin and sex: for her the latter is a purely natural, wholesome activity. He finally comes upon an entry that does interest him: Sutter's comments on the young man's own condition. "Barrett: His trouble is he wants to know what his trouble is. His 'trouble,' he thinks, is a disorder of such a character that if only he can locate the right expert with the right psychology, the disorder can be set right and he can go about his business." Barrett is suffering from being locked into transcendence, wanting to find companionship there, and being unwilling to enter into immanence (and certainly not in the way that Sutter recommends). Will thinks that this is an exaggerated understanding of his condition. "Where he probably goes wrong, mused the engineer sleepily, is in the extremity of his alternatives: God and not-God, getting under women's dresses and blowing your brains out. Whereas and in fact my problem is how to live from one ordinary minute to the next on a Wednesday afternoon." Will tends to think that such exaggeration has "been the case with all 'religious' people" (340). This last statement indicates not only Will's continuing detachment from his own existential plight, but also on Percy's part, perhaps, a self-criticism of an overly simplistic religious analysis of the human dilemma.

The final entry in Sutter's pad, a kind of perverted Guardini-style analysis, casts significant light on his attitude toward religion: "Christ should leave us. He is too much with us and I don't like his friends. We have no hope of recovering Christ until Christ leaves us. There is after all something worse than being God-forsaken. It is when God overstays his welcome and takes up with the wrong people." Sutter goes on to argue that Val is wrong to regard suicide—or at least its "nurtured possibility"—as sinful: it is in fact "the very condition of recovering oneself" (357). When he himself was depressed by Jamie's slow dying, he attempted to end his life, but was unsuccessful—and discovered lewdness. Sutter concludes, however, that he will not fail the next time. Will's response is to burn the book.

When Will finally catches up with Sutter again, the doctor has nothing to tell him and denies his belief in what was written in the pad, using an inaccurate reference to Wittgenstein's life as justification.[13] Sutter tells him that he really

---

13. Sutter remarks, "After his [Wittgenstein's] last work he announced the dictum which summarized his philosophy. He said: Whereof one cannot speak, thereof one should keep silent. And he did. He stopped teaching and went to live in a hut and said no more" (362). Wittgenstein, in fact, though hardly talkative, led quite an active professorial life afterwards (see Ray Monk, *Ludwig Wittgenstein: The Duty of Genius* [New York, 1990]). This is not just Sutter's mistake: Percy himself has noted that Wittgenstein "actually stopped teaching and moved to the coast of Ireland for seven years and said nothing" (Lawson and Kramer, eds., *Conversations,* 43). In fact, it was twenty-five years later, in 1947, that Wittgenstein went to Ireland, and then only for several months (see Monk, *Wittgenstein,* 520–50). Nevertheless, it is of interest that Wittgenstein also had a profound respect for Dostoevsky, that he saw a Catholic priest in his last months, and that he had a Catholic funeral under circumstances quite as ambiguous as Jamie's (*ibid.,* 579–80).

agreed with Val until she gave up waiting in the desert and became hopeful. He too was waiting for a sign, but none had come. Confused as usual, Will persists in getting Sutter to acknowledge that there is nothing wrong with an ordinary married life with Kitty—which Sutter does (ironically, however) because he can see that for now Will is missing the whole point. At this stage, Will is even described as being ready to "rejoin the human race" (371). So when Sutter confirms that he will commit suicide shortly after Jamie's death and wants to know if Will will join him, Will declines. "Perhaps this moment more than any other, the moment of his first astonishment, marked the beginning for the engineer of what is called a normal life. From that time forward it was possible to meet him and after a few minutes form a clear notion of what sort of fellow he was and how he would spend the rest of his life." (374). It may be that confrontation with the very real possibility of death has roused Will's existential appreciation of life, thereby advancing him to Kierkegaard's ethical stage; or, more likely, it may be that he has momentarily lost interest in Sutter's philosophizing and has lapsed back into acceptance of the conditions of ordinary life.

Unlike Binx Bolling, however, Will Barrett does not succeed in arriving at Kierkegaard's religious stage. When Jamie comes to die, the engineer is still an onlooker at the action of grace. Under pressure from Val, however, he has at least reversed his earlier refusal and summoned the hospital chaplain. Nevertheless, Will is relieved that Jamie's poor condition dispenses with the need for asking him about his wishes in the matter of baptism, "for it was of course absolutely the last question to be tolerated by the comradely and stoic silence generated between the two of them" (378). Will even goes so far as to tell the priest that "Jamie professed no faith, so it is all the same which of you ministers, ah, ministers to him" (382). But Jamie does ask—as interpreted by Will—how we know that the Catholic faith is true. Again, the reply echoes "The Message in the Bottle": "The priest sighed. 'If it were not true,' he said to Jamie, 'then I would not be here. That is why I am here, to tell you'" (388).

It need hardly be said that Jamie's "conversion" remains somewhat incoherent, though Will seems more favorably disposed toward it at the end than he had been at the beginning. The priest himself, Father Boomer, possibly based on the priest who attended William Alexander Percy's last moments, is not particularly impressive. But then Catholic theology (and Kierkegaard) teaches that God acts through his ordained ministers, however unworthy they may be.[14] Still, even in the final scene when Will leaves with Sutter, the whole matter of religion remains unresolved. Either Sutter and Will have not been granted the gift of faith by which to make a decision, or else they have failed to understand what has been going on. But, at least, both have rejected suicide.

The difficulty throughout *The Last Gentleman* is that Sutter's religious preoccupations never seem to become central to Will Barrett's interests, and so there is no possibility of a satisfactory solution. If Percy's intention was to show the power of the Christian proclamation to the unconverted, then it is doubtful that the final scene of Jamie's death succeeds in this: the uncommitted onlooker is likely to be suspicious of a conversion that has been dubiously effected at the last moment from a person who showed little previous aspiration toward such a belief (though Jamie's earlier vehement rejection of Val's overtures may indicate more preoccupation than is immediately apparent from the text).[15] In other words, the Catholic theology that is required to undergird this scene demands a prior belief in its efficacy, and the fiction thus fails for those who still remain "outside." On the other hand, it is somewhat difficult to see how this problem might have been overcome. Percy could justly assert that the Christian revelation cannot fully adapt itself to a naturalistic explanation without begging the question it proposes to answer. Thus, for the believer (of a certain orthodox type at least), this *is* how faith and salvation work; for the unbeliever, of course, this is merely how the faithful *think* such influences function. Whatever the truth of the matter, Percy's own religious intent is certainly more obvious now than it had been when *The Moviegoer* seduced a not-yet-polarized audience in 1961.

14. This is the doctrine that the sacraments work *ex opere operato* with God or Christ as their agent, irrespective of the worthiness of the priest administering them (provided, of course, that he has been properly ordained, etc.). Again, W. L. Godshalk's comment that the scene "hardly glorifies the sacraments or gives us any hope of eternal life in Jesus Christ our Lord" misses this point, though I agree that the "outsider" (the "non-Catholic," to use the old common, if somewhat odious, expression) is very unlikely to be impressed (see "The Engineer, Then and Now," in *Walker Percy,* ed. Gretlund and Westarp, 35).

15. A similar case is presented by Wallace Stevens' conversion to Catholicism during his final illness in a Catholic hospital: his daughter, Holly Stevens, attaches no significance to it (see Milton J. Bates, *Wallace Stevens: A Mythology of Self* [Berkeley, 1985], 296–97).

7

THE RHETORIC OF FAITH

Love in the Ruins, published in 1971, suggests in its subtitle a major shift in Walker Percy's exploration of the problems of belief: *The Adventures of a Bad Catholic at a Time near the End of the World* (a subtitle over which the publisher expressed concern since the use of the word *Catholic* might limit sales). If the Percy reader thought that while Binx Bolling may have been baptized a Catholic, there was no indication that the faith ever meant much to him before his supposed final conversion (if then), or saw—rightly—that Will Barrett was always an outsider to the Roman tradition even at the end, there is no doubt whatsoever that Dr. Thomas More, the protagonist of Percy's new novel, is a believer, albeit a lapsed one. Indeed, he is described as having once been quite religious. Thus, Percy has become even more explicit about his underlying concerns than heretofore: Catholicism now moves from background to foreground, and Percy tends hereafter to be seen, for better or worse, as a "Catholic novelist." [1] He has at last made his point.

Just as *The Last Gentleman* engaged in part with the early days of the race problem, its later developments are very much at issue in *Love in the Ruins,* though the story itself is extrapolated into the future (the 1980s). This is the world of Bobby Kennedy's and Martin Luther King's assassinations, of the Vietnam protests, of the notorious Chicago Democratic Convention, of the Watts race riots, of Frantz Fanon's *Wretched of the Earth.* Percy himself, at some personal risk, participates in the local Community Relations Council in his hometown of Covington, Louisiana, supports LBJ, and strongly denies that the race and Vietnam issues are connected. More important—but intimately related—the crisis in religion, particularly in the Catholic church following the Second Vatican Council,

---

1. Percy also told Lewis Lawson that the first two novels had received too Kierkegaardian an interpretation and that his interest in signs and so forth derived more from Aquinas (Jay Tolson, *Pilgrim in the Ruins* [New York, 1992], 337).

is very much present in the pages of his new novel. The relatively stable and seemingly unified Church to which Percy was converted in the 1940s has begun to disintegrate. Changes, liturgical and doctrinal, have caused some of the faithful to become more conservative, while others have felt themselves liberated to adopt what they see as a more radical Christianity. Already John Courtney Murray's nuanced interpretations of the relations between church and state no longer seem relevant to a changed climate. Catholics are prominent on the political scene in ways with which Percy disagrees: the Berrigan brothers (both priests), for example, are leaders in the antiwar movement, as is Thomas Merton, writing from the solitude of his hermitage on the grounds of his Trappist monastery in Kentucky.[2] Priests are leaving in droves to get married—Fr. John A. O'Brien has now shifted from gathering the narratives of new converts to collecting those of departing clergy—and they are often finding that marriage is no less fraught with problems than that institution which they left behind as celibate ministers.[3]

Doctrinally, some of the fundamental beliefs of the faith are being called into question. This is the period of the Dutch Catechism with its controversial presentations on original sin, the virginity of Mary, and the creation of the human soul; of open resistance to Pope Paul VI's encyclical *Humanae Vitae,* which had unexpectedly reaffirmed the traditional Catholic ban on contraception; of the new "death-of-God" theology (in full swing even as close as Emory University in Atlanta).[4] In England, Evelyn Waugh is complaining, mainly in relation to the

2. Percy had great respect for Merton and even visited him at Gethsemani Abbey (and later asked that an interview about his encounter with Merton be included in *Conversations* as it expressed ideas that could not be found elsewhere in his published writings). Both were deeply troubled by the possibility of nuclear war. However, Percy disagreed with Merton's views on the Vietnam War, and he even found his ideas on the future of monasticism typically those of the 1960s (Tolson, *Pilgrim in the Ruins,* 341). The latter judgment shows again how deeply committed Percy remained to most (but certainly not all) of the particularities of code, dress, and dogma that characterized the Catholic church in the 1940s. And indeed, even in his reluctant sympathy for the war in Vietnam, Percy was displaying a more traditional Catholic stance developed during the anticommunist era (nor was he unmindful, perhaps, that many of the upper echelons of South Vietnamese society, however corrupt, were Roman Catholic in faith).

3. John A. O'Brien, ed., *Why Priests Leave* (New York, 1969). Fr. O'Brien, it should be noted, initiated this volume after the American Catholic bishops expressed concern about the phenomenon and requested that it be studied.

4. The Dutch Catechism, the popular name for *A New Catechism* which appeared in Holland in

disappearance of the Latin Mass, that "the buggering up of the Church is a deep sorrow to me and to all I know"; while in France, Jacques Maritain's vehement (and to many, wholly unexpected) attack on the new theologians, particularly on the cosmic Christianity of Jesuit anthropologist Teilhard de Chardin, has appeared as *The Peasant of the Garonne*.[5] It is also, not incidentally, the time of the popular success of the film version of Robert Bolt's *Man for All Seasons,* a play highlighting Sir Thomas More's moral and religious steadfastness when all those around him were willing to accept expedient change.

Early in the novel, Percy presents the situation in terms that suggest a creative adaptation of the Guardini quotation used as epigraph for *The Last Gentleman:*

Is it that God has at last removed his blessing from the U.S.A. and what we feel now is just the clank of the old historical machinery, the sudden jerking ahead of the roller-coaster cars as the chain catches hold and carries us back into history with its ordinary catastrophes, carries us out and up toward the brink from that felicitous and privileged siding where even unbelievers admitted that if it was not God who blessed the U.S.A., then at least some great good luck had befallen us, and that now the blessing or the luck is over, the machinery clanks, the chain catches hold, and the cars jerk forward? (3–4)

1966 and was quickly translated into English, offered a fresh way of presenting Church teaching that was more ecumenical in spirit than the traditional Catholic texts. However, because of a number of ambiguities in the presentation, a corrective supplement was added at the request of the Commission of Cardinals in Rome in 1968 (see *A New Catechism* [New York, 1988]). The incident is symptomatic of the strife within the Church beginning in the 1960s. Indeed, even as late as 1993, the Dutch Catechism is still considered dangerous enough to need to be replaced by a new official handbook.

The "death-of-God" theologians—usually given as Thomas J. Altizer (then an associate professor of religion at Emory and alluded to in this capacity by Percy), William Hamilton, and Paul van Buren—questioned the divine attributes of Jesus, argued that (as the logical positivists had claimed earlier) religious language was meaningless, and advocated a "religionless Christianity" (an idea borrowed from Dietrich Bonhoeffer's *Letters and Papers from Prison* [New York, 1953]). See Jackson Lee Ice and John J. Carey, eds., *The Death of God Debate* (Philadelphia, 1967). These matters were a continuation of issues raised very controversially in England in 1963 with Bishop John A. T. Robinson's *Honest to God* (Philadelphia, 1963). The movement lost much of its momentum after this period, though it continues in England in the writings of the "atheist" Anglican priest Don Cupitt.

5. Quoted in Donald Greene, "Graham Greene and Evelyn Waugh: 'Catholic Novelists,' " in *Graham Greene: A Revaluation,* ed. Jeffrey Meyers (New York, 1990), 15.

In other words, according to Percy, culture is trying to survive without revelation—and (predictably) failing.[6]

Overall, then, Percy has new problems to contend with. It might be said that by extrapolating the action of the novel into the near future, he is suggesting the possible outcomes of current trends and thus upping the ante in his criticism of present myopia (which is probably why William F. Buckley, Jr., sent a copy of the book to President Nixon and recommended that every future presidential candidate read it). Yet, though obviously there is a strong apocalyptic note in the novel, Percy has argued that his intent was not like that of Orwell or Huxley: "What I was concerned with in this novel is something else altogether. What interested me is what can happen in a free society in which Orwell and Huxley have carried the day. Everybody agrees with Orwell and Huxley, yet something has gone wrong. For this novel deals, not with the takeover of a society by tyrants or computers or whatever, but rather with the increasing malaise and finally the falling apart of a society which remains, on the surface at least, democratic and pluralistic." The meanings of words—freedom, dignity of the individual, quality of life—have slipped so that "it is the job of the satirist, as I see it, to detect slips and then to exaggerate them so that they become noticeable."[7]

In 1968, three years prior to the appearance of *Love in the Ruins,* Walker Percy published an essay that turned out to be a preface to his upcoming work (though the resultant novel is different in several ways): "Notes for a Novel About the End of the World." In it, not only does he make important points about how he sees himself as a novelist, but he does so because he feels strongly that the "new theologians"—he uses the then-current term over and over again—are failing in their prophetic mission. He mentions Harvey Cox in particular, then famous for *The Secular City,* which proclaimed that the new age would be religionless and

6. In 1954, Caroline Gordon wrote to Jacques Maritain: "Allen [Tate] is representing the United States at Mayor La Pira's Christian Congress in Florence. His speech will be largely his comments on your new book [*Creative Intuition in Art and Poetry*]: 'It will be just the right thing, for Jacques' theory of art boils down to the doctrine that Culture cannot survive without Revelation' " (quoted in John M. Dunaway, ed., *Exiles and Fugitives: The Letters of Jacques and Raïssa Maritain, Allen Tate, and Caroline Gordon* [Baton Rouge, 1992], 51).

7. Walker Percy, "Concerning *Love in the Ruins,*" in *Signposts in a Strange Land,* ed. Patrick Samway (New York, 1991), 247–48.

that the Christian must shift from supernatural belief to acceptance of a total secularity—an extreme form of Dietrich Bonhoeffer's "religionless Christianity" thesis. Cox had attacked, moreover, the existentialist view favored by Percy. Commenting on Paul Tillich, the liberal theologian associated with the existentialists (who, incidentally, had warmly recommended Percy's "Metaphor as Mistake" to his students), Cox wrote:

> Both philosophical existentialism and Paul Tillich's theology are expressions of the mourning period which began with the death of God of metaphysical theism and Western Christian civilization, but the wake is now over. That is why existentialist theologies and philosophies do not partake of the spirit of the emerging age but symbolize rather the passing of the old. There is a certain validity to the Marxist assertion that existentialism is a "symptom of bourgeois decadence," since its categories of *Angst* and vertigo seem increasingly irrelevant to the ethos of the new epoch.

Cox went on to add—anathema to Percy—that "in the age of the secular city, the questions with which we concern ourselves tend to be mostly functional and operational."[8] Again, in a reply to Michael Novak in a subsequent collection of essays (many of them by Catholics) broadly sympathetic with the argument of *The Secular City,* Cox himself presented his thesis in a way that shows why Percy, among others, took strong exception to it: "I would defend the need to extricate the Gospel from 'religion,' but only if Bonhoeffer's definition of the term 'religion' remains constant in the discussion, *i.e.,* religion as dependency, inwardness and a metaphysical perspective which sees *this* world . . . somehow subsumed within another one. Against this kind of 'religion' the Gospel calls man to maturity, away from a fascinated obsession with his own soul and toward *this* world and this *saeculum* as the appropriate sphere of Christian existence."[9]

Thus, from Percy's perspective, "Since true prophets, i.e., men called by God

8. Harvey Cox, *The Secular City: Secularization and Urbanization in Theological Perspective* (New York, 1966), 70.

9. In Daniel Callahan, ed., *The Secular City Debate* (New York, 1966), 118. The exception here is Andrew Greeley, who sees Cox's thesis as coming from "an Americanized version of Bishop Robinson's marriage of Bonhoeffer and Tillich."

to communicate something urgent to other men, are currently in short supply, the novelist may perform a quasi-prophetic function." The novelist's outlook differs "from the usual views of the denizens of the secular city in general and in particular from the new theologians of the secular city." [10] More explicitly, since the new theologians have sold out to the world, the novelist "is one of the few remaining witnesses to the doctrine of original sin" (106). Now, in short, Percy has to contend even with those whom earlier he could have presumed were by definition on his side.

Throughout the essay, Percy makes clear in considerable detail what he judges the novelist's function to be, and distinguishes his own perspective from the aims and objectives of other novelists. "Not being called by God to be a prophet, he [the novelist] nevertheless pretends to a certain prescience. If he did not think he saw something other people didn't see or at least didn't pay much attention to, he would be wasting his time writing and they reading." And again, "the novelist can make vicarious use of catastrophe in order that he and his reader may come to themselves" (101). The novelist is said to function like the coal miner's canary of old—as a warning sign. He sees the problems of the world (racism and war, for example) as symptoms of a deeper malaise in the human spirit. The kind of novelist Percy has in mind is "a writer who has an explicit and ultimate concern with the nature of man," so that one might describe him with "such adjectives as 'philosophical,' 'metaphysical,' 'prophetic,' 'eschatological,' and even 'religious' " (102). Such writers include Dostoevsky, Tolstoy, Camus, Sartre, Faulkner (a surprising choice, perhaps), and Flannery O'Connor. They are distinct from such English novelists as Jane Austen and Samuel Richardson ("The nineteenth-century Russian novelists were haunted by God; many of the French existentialists are haunted by his absence. The English novelist is not much interested one way or another") or from the American social critics and cultural satirists (103).[11]

Percy's novelist is "concerned with the radical question of man's identity and his relation to God or to God's absence" rather than with the kinds of problems found in Hemingway or Sinclair Lewis (108–109). Again, opposing Harvey Cox

10. Walker Percy, *The Message in the Bottle: How Queer Man Is, How Queer Language Is, and What One Has to Do with the Other* (New York, 1975), 104.

11. Percy does, however, see the American novel in general as being more philosophical than the British and hence liable to greater failures.

explicitly together with the new theologians, Percy asserts that "neither novelists nor anybody else is much interested in *any* theologians, and least of all in God-is-dead theologians. The strenuous efforts of theologians to baptize the computer remind one of the liberal clergyman of the last century who used to wait, hat in hand so to speak, outside the scientific laboratories to assure the scientist there was no conflict between science and religion. The latter could not have cared less." Percy adds, significantly, "Yet the contemporary novelist is as pre-occupied with catastrophe as the *orthodox* theologian with sin and death" (my emphasis) (110).

Moreover, claims Percy, "the 'religion' of the novelist becomes relevant if he is writing a novel of ultimate concerns. It would not have mattered a great deal if Margaret Mitchell were a Methodist or an atheist. But it does matter what Sartre's allegiance is, or Camus', or Flannery O'Connor's. For what his allegiance is is what he is writing about" (110–11). While Percy does not think it his calling "to preach the Christian faith in a novel . . . my world view is informed by a certain belief which cannot fail to be central to any novel I write" (111). And, though he considers that the religious novel suffers from certain "disabilities," Percy feels that because Christianity basically respects the individual and sees him as a wayfarer, it is a better doctrine in which to ground a successful narrative than either Buddhism or behaviorism.

Percy goes on to deal with how the novelist views the world and in doing so seems to have the Guardini essay in mind, though he does not refer to it explicitly. If, as Guardini has argued, we are now at the "end of the modern world" (the world of Descartes and Newton and rationalism), we must be in a *postmodern* world. ("Postmodern" here refers to the era after Einstein and World War I when the values of the seventeenth-century scientific revolution and the eighteenth-century Enlightenment have been called into doubt. It does not refer specifically to the fiction of Thomas Pynchon, William Gaddis, and such like, or the term as used by Jean-François Lyotard, though there is some significant overlap.)[12] The emergence of a "postmodern consciousness" opens "unlimited possibilities for

12. See Brian McHale, *Postmodernist Fiction* (New York, 1987); Jean-François Lyotard, *The Postmodern Condition: A Report on Knowledge* (Minneapolis, 1984). Percy's usage is more akin to that in Huston Smith's *Beyond the Post-Modern Mind* (Wheaton, Ill., 1989), which in fact devotes several pages to a sympathetic discussion of Percy's work.

both destruction and liberation, for an absolute loneliness or a rediscovery of community and reconciliation" (112). Postmodern man has "conquered his present ills" and "finds himself in the victorious secular city," but he wants to blow his brains out. Admitting the truth of the death-of-God premises—that religion is dead—and of the conservatives' views also, Percy sees a third way as necessary in the light of a postmodern consciousness. "The wrong questions are being asked," he says. "The proper question is not whether God has died or been superseded by the urban-political complex. The question is not whether the Good News is no longer relevant, but rather whether it is possible that man is presently undergoing a tempestuous restructuring of his consciousness which does not presently allow him to take account of the Good News." What is happening is

> the absorption by the layman not of the scientific method but rather of the magical aura of science, whose credentials he accepts for all sectors of reality. Thus in the lay culture of a scientific society nothing is easier than to fall prey to a kind of seduction which sunders one's very self from itself into an all-transcending "objective" consciousness and a consumer-self with a list of "needs" to be satisfied. It is this monstrous bifurcation of man into angelic and bestial components against which old theologies must be weighed before new theologies are erected. Such a man could not take account of God, the devil, and the angels if they were standing before him, because he has already peopled the universe with his own hierarchies. (113)

The novel is there to point this out and, perhaps, to correct the situation.

In the end, Percy thinks, the new theology has very little to offer: to "the 'religious' novelist, whether it be Sartre or O'Connor, the positive proposals of the new theology must sound like a set of resolutions passed at the P.T.A." (114). The truth is that the modern age, the "Secular Era," is itself almost over. Percy offers a parable: A group of scientists in the 1940s pass a church and hear the gospel, but it has no relevance for them because they are confident in their new knowledge. Fifty years later, a technician passes, and it does have relevance for him because he is aware of his own lostness ("He is the despairing man Kierkegaard spoke of, for whom there is hope because he is aware of his despair"). Percy even talks of the technician being approached by "someone like the whisky priest in Graham Greene's *The Power and the Glory* who has an answer to the technician's problem." He concludes with a statement that bears direct relationship to "The Message in the Bottle" essay: "It is possible that a different kind of communication-event occurs in the door of the church than occurred fifty years earlier" (116).

Percy acknowledges, of course, that the old language is worn out and that the message has to be presented in new ways—indeed, that is precisely what the novelist is about. Too many people think they already have the message (the fundamentalists), while the Church itself has failed in many ways, especially in the matter of race relations. The question then is how does the novelist set about writing, "having cast his lot with a discredited Christendom and having inherited a defunct vocabulary?" (118). Adapting James Joyce to purposes quite at odds with those of the Irish writer, Percy replies that the novelist "does the only thing he can do. Like Joyce's Stephen Dedalus, he calls on every ounce of cunning, craft, and guile he can muster from the darker regions of his soul. The fictional use of violence, shock, comedy, insult, the bizarre, are the everyday tools of his trade." Thus, in writing a novel about the end of the world, the author makes "vicarious use of catastrophe in order that he and his reader may come to themselves" (118). Indeed, Percy's purposes in writing *Love in the Ruins* seem to have been remarkably like Milton's (as argued for by Stanley Fish) in composing *Paradise Lost*.[13]

Percy intended that *Love in the Ruins* itself should be "less solemn" and "more contemporary" than the essay. In fact, its style frequently seems almost too casual. It is hardly too much to say, however, that this again marks a "religious" purpose. Thus, in "Rediscovering *A Canticle for Leibowitz*," also published in 1971, Percy acknowledges the influence of Walter Miller's science fiction classic (like *A Canticle, Love in the Ruins* too has its opening on a "broken interstate"). Although it is not as good as Katherine Mansfield's stories, or even *1984* or *Brave New World*, Miller's book is of more moment because its "peculiar virtue . . . lies in the successful marriage of a subliterary pop form with a subject matter of trans-

---

13. The reference here is to *Surprised by Sin: The Reader in "Paradise Lost"* (New York, 1967), in which Stanley Fish argues that "Milton's procedure was to render in the reader's mind the action of the Fall of Man, thereby causing the reader himself to fall just as Adam did" (Vincent B. Leitch, *American Literary Criticism from the Thirties to the Eighties* [New York, 1988], 215).

literary import." Percy's reference here is to the Catholic theology that is so much a part of Miller's novel and that is so dramatically presented in its final pages. If, then, *Love in the Ruins* is not quite as "artistic" or "aesthetically pleasing" as *The Moviegoer* or even *The Last Gentleman,* this is in part because Percy is wary of the seductions of art and its required ambiguities: sometimes the truth needs to be highlighted, the reader shocked into a belated awareness of those verities that he has culturally forgotten.[14]

The protagonist of *Love in the Ruins,* Dr. Tom More, is quite clearly a Catholic. He is well informed about his religion, even pondering at one point (with, perhaps, unconvincing accuracy) what St. Thomas Aquinas has written on "killing in self-defense: Q.21, Obj.4, Part I, *Sum. Theol.*" (279).[15] In making him a descendant of St. Thomas More, the English martyr and author of *Utopia,* Percy claimed that he was deliberately trying "to establish an Anglo-Saxon, English-American, Roman Catholic point of view. It was a rather overt attempt to de-Irish the American Catholic Church. . . . Therefore, Thomas More. He is both the most English of Englishmen and *the most Catholic of Catholics*" (my emphasis).[16] Percy has pointed out, furthermore, that Dr. More is "entirely different" from his previous two protagonists, who were experiencing "various losses of identity and lack of belief and alienation, and . . . were seeking one thing or another. . . . From the beginning he knows exactly who he is and what he needs. He has no doubt at all. There's no identity crisis here. He knows exactly. The only problem facing the reader is who is crazy, whether it's Dr. More or the rest of the world" (48). And in the novel itself, More's about-to-be-ex-wife accuses him: "You're not a seeker after the truth. You think you have the truth, and what good does it do you?" [17]

What good, indeed! Dr. More, now a forty-five-year-old psychiatrist who has

14. Tolson, *Pilgrim in the Ruins,* 352; Walker Percy, *Signposts,* 232.

15. He also remarks of a medical colleague: "Max the atheist sees things like Saint Thomas Aquinas, ranged, orderly, connected up" (106). As has already been noted, this is an interesting sidelight on how Percy himself understood Aquinas.

16. "I think a lot of novels, so-called Catholic novels, American-Catholic novels, are usually Irish Catholic. Some of them are very well done indeed. Like Edwin O'Connor. And then there's Flannery—although she's a Georgia fundamentalist" (Lewis A. Lawson and Victor A. Kramer, eds., *Conversations with Walker Percy* [Jackson, Miss., 1985], 46–47).

17. Walker Percy, *Love in the Ruins: The Adventures of a Bad Catholic at a Time near the End of the World* (New York, 1971), 68.

suffered mental illness himself and has even attempted suicide, was once a good Catholic who believed that science and religion could be reconciled. Successful early on as a researcher, he even thought of himself as a "genius" likely to make a distinctly Catholic contribution to science, the equivalent of Einstein's. Perhaps he had been too self-satisfied, however: initially his Catholicism was self-centered, "caring nought for my fellow Catholics but only for myself and Samantha and Christ swallowed" (13). Then times changed and a period of decline set in: "My daughter, Samantha, died; my wife ran off with a heathen Englishman . . . and I left off research, left off eating Christ in Communion, and took to sipping Early Times instead and seeking the company of the fair sex, as they used to say." Alcoholism and lechery, however, are rather traditional vices of religious people. More is still a believer.

> I, for example, am a Roman Catholic, albeit a bad one. I believe in the Holy Catholic Apostolic and Roman Church, in God the Father, in the election of the Jews, in Jesus Christ His Son, Our Lord, who founded the Church on Peter his first vicar, which will last until the end of the world. Some years ago, however, I stopped eating Christ in Communion, stopped going to mass, and have since fallen into a disorderly life. I believe in God, and the whole business but I love women best, music and science next, whiskey next, God fourth, and my fellowmen hardly at all. Generally I do as I please. A man, wrote John, who says he believes in God and does not keep his commandments is a liar. If John is right, then I am a liar. Nevertheless, I still believe. (6)

This declaration has echoes of Val's statement to Will in *The Last Gentleman,* so that, from one perspective at least, one might see Percy's treatment of More as an extension of his investigation of Val's type of character as it undergoes challenge. At the same time, insofar as it asserts the importance of specifically Catholic beliefs—the efficacy of Communion, for example (implied, more than stated, in *The Moviegoer*)—it poses the kind of "very real artistic problems" that David Lodge referred to earlier in writing about Graham Greene.[18] These were *artistic*

18. Quoted in Donald Greene, "Graham Greene and Evelyn Waugh: 'Catholic Novelists,' " in *Graham Greene: A Revaluation,* ed. Meyers, 41.

problems, however, that Percy seems to have been less and less desirous of overcoming.

A flashback to the period when More was still a practicing Catholic emphasizes the seriousness that such a belief had, and still has, for him. Dr. More is engaged in conversation with his daughter, who is dying from neuroblastoma. She asks him about his faith and why he has ceased going to Mass, then tells him that he is in greater danger than his wife (a lapsed Episcopalian) because she is protected by "Invincible Ignorance." Samantha asks him not to commit "the one sin for which there is no forgiveness." This is the sin against grace: "If God gives you the grace to believe in him and love him and you refuse, the sin will not be forgiven you" (373–74). One of the questions in the novel, then, is whether More will open himself to the grace of religious belief in its *fullest* sense and return to the fold.

Since More is confirmed in his *basic* beliefs (he does not accept "the validity of all religions" [272]), he is not so much looking for another philosophy to give meaning to his life—in the sense that Binx and Will were—as striving to return to what might be termed, in southern parlance, his "church home." One might even argue that now, with the Church in relative disarray, Percy's main character, however flawed, has to be "fixed," since it is no longer obvious that there is anything steady in the religious sphere toward which he can undeviatingly move. In any case, what this circumstance enables Percy to do is to satirize various trends in religion and the sciences current at the time. These are not temptations for More but rather positions which he sees clearly from the beginning to be false. (More, we are told at one point, is no longer even a moviegoer.) Thus, for example, there is the author's ironic presentation of More's wife, Doris: "Books ruined her [a list given earlier comprised *Atlas Shrugged, Siddhartha,* and *ESP and the New Spirituality*]. Beware of Episcopal women who take up with Ayn Rand and the Buddha and Dr. Rhine formerly of Duke University. A certain type of Episcopal girl has a weakness that comes on them just past youth, just as sure as Italian girls get fat. They fall prey to Gnostic pride, commence buying antiques, and develop a yearning for esoteric doctrine" (64).

The story itself is set "in these dread latter days of the old violent beloved U.S.A. and of the Christ-forgetting Christ-haunted death-dealing Western world" (3). We are told, "Principalities and powers are everywhere victorious. Wickedness flourishes in high places." "Noxious particles" are again in the air. "They do not burn the skin and rot the marrow; rather do they inflame and worsen the secret ills of the spirit and rive the very self from itself" (5). More specifically, blacks (Bantus) have become militant, hippies occupy the nearby swamps, the former Fr. Kev Kevin is now a sexologist (he reads *Christianity Without God,* but also *Commonweal*), white religious fundamentalists (Knotheads) rage against integration with blacks, and euthanasia is commonly practiced. The ready acceptance of euthanasia is, of course, of most concern even to the lapsed Dr. More. He is opposed to his colleagues who are now "Qualitarians," promoting the rational use of abortion and euthanasia. There is an amusing account of how a taciturn candidate for euthanasia turns the tables on his persecutors, though—characteristically of Percy—it is hardly a fair example since this man is in fact quite healthy.

The Catholic church, meanwhile (in which the previously expected Catholic literary renaissance has not taken place), is described as being divided between the ultra orthodox, who stress the rights of property (and include More's mother, a "Catholic Gnostic" who celebrates "Property Rights Sunday") (173), "the Dutch schismatics who believe in relevance but not God," and those described as "the Roman Catholic remnant" (5) who attempt to pursue the gospel unobtrusively. More's sympathies are readily apparent in his report on the situation: "In this Catholic church, the center did not hold. It split in three, Monsignor Schleifkopf cutting out to the right, Father Kev Kevin to the left, leaving Father Smith. There is little to be said about Father Smith since he is in no way remarkable, having been a good and faithful if undistinguished priest for twenty-five years, having baptized the newborn into a new life, married lovers, shriven sinners, comforted the sick, visited the poor and imprisoned, anointed the dying, buried the dead" (139). Fr. Smith is, of course, deeply opposed to the Qualitarians— and emotionally distressed by their plans. More, once a liberal but now alienated from both extremes (the Left believes in "Liberty, Equality, Fraternity, The Pill, Atheism, Pot, Anti-Pollution, Sex, Abortion Now, Euthanasia"), allies himself with Smtih (18).[19] Symptomatic of the overall situation is the fact that at one point

19. At one point we are told that More is not a "liberated Catholic" (51). Percy has frequently expressed his own alienation from both Right and Left.

More, despite his own moral lapses, finds himself discussing "fornication" and "confession" with colleagues who think only in terms of sexual experience and consequent—but unnecessary—psychological guilt (116–18).

When More's daughter died and his wife ran off with the heathen Englishman several years earlier, he lost his religion (or at least the actual practice of it) and turned to the development of what he calls his "lapsometer." This is a device which is supposed to heal the centuries-old rift between man's brain and his body. Or rather, initially, it is merely designed to measure this rift. Dr. More describes what has happened to him: "The period of my decline was also a period of lying fallow and of the germination of some strange quirky ideas. Toynbee, I believe, speaks of the Return, of the man who fails and goes away, is exiled, takes counsel with himself, hits on something, sees daylight—and returns to triumph" (25). The very mention of Toynbee's name here suggests (from various comments in Percy's essays) that there will be something missing in this "triumph."

Dr. More has discovered that heavy sodium ions can have different effects on different brain centers: "For example, Heavy Sodium radiation stimulates Brodmann Area 32, the center of abstractive activity or tendencies toward angelism, while Heavy Chloride stimulates the thalamus, which promotes adjustment to the environment, or, as I call it without prejudice, bestialism" (27). This distinction was suggested to Percy in part by his reading of Maritain's *Dream of Descartes,* in which the Catholic Thomist holds Cartesian dualism responsible for the division between "anthropocentric angelism" and the "materialism of civilization." [20]

20. Elsewhere More refers to "my lapsometer, the first caliper of the soul and the first hope of bridging the dread chasm that has rent the soul of Western man ever since the famous philosopher Descartes ripped body loose from mind and turned the very soul into a ghost that haunts its own house" (191). Jacques Maritain suggests what is wrong with the Cartesian split: "With regard to what is inferior to man, to the world of corporeal nature, Cartesian intellect claims to understand everything exposed to the core, through the substance, through the essence itself. Matter lies naked before it as before the angels" (*The Dream of Descartes,* 142)—hence matter is devalued and eventually takes its revenge. See also Dunaway, ed., *Exiles and Fugitives,* in which Gordon, in a 1969 letter to Maritain, reports a conversation that her daughter had with then-presidential candidate Eugene McCarthy: "Their conversation, which lasted three hours, was mostly about angels—and angelism, she said. (At this point I was reminded of what you said in print years ago, that our chief danger was not from the atom bomb but from 'angelism,' man's effort to use his own intellect as if it were an angel's intellect.) McCarthy, whether or not the idea is original with him, seems to be in complete accord with you on that" (95). The distinction also comes from Arthur Koestler's *Ghost in the Machine* (New York, 1968) and from Allen Tate's essays "The Angelic Imagination" and "The Symbolic Imagination" (in *Essays of Four Decades* [Chicago, 1968]).

What More's Qualitative Quantitative Ontological Lapsometer does is to give a quantifiable reading for each condition. He himself is naturally enthusiastic about his discovery:

> If you measure the pineal activity of a monkey—or any other subhuman animal—with my lapsometer, you will invariably record identical readings at Layers I and II. Its self, that is to say, coincides with itself. Only in man do we find a discrepancy: Layer I, the outer social self, ticking over, say, at a sprightly 5.4 mmv, while Layer II just lies there, barely alive at 0.7 mmv, or even zero!—a nought, a gap, an aching wound. Only in man does the self miss itself, *fall* from itself (hence *lap*someter!). Suppose—! Suppose I could hit on the right dosage and weld the broken self whole! What if man could reenter paradise, so to speak, and live there both as man and spirit, whole and intact man-spirit, as solid flesh as a speckled trout, a dappled thing, yet aware of itself as a self! (36)

More's intention, then, is to heal this Cartesian split between mind and body (a traditional aspiration of neo-Thomists). To this end he examines a number of people with his lapsometer to find out their particular readings. Ted, a hippie, is discovered to be predominantly in an abstracted mode, while a churchgoing fellow doctor is found to indulge his sexual lusts at regular intervals. The "reports" here are remarkably similar to those in Sutter's notebook in *The Last Gentleman,* suggesting that the diagnoses could have been made without the help of any such device, though the device does "confirm" what has already been suspected. On the positive side, the lapsometer is supposed to help physicians "make early diagnoses of potential suicides, paranoiacs, impotence, stroke, anxiety, and angelism-bestialism" (83). What More does not have at this stage is a way of *curing* such conditions. His problem, then, is "to hit on a therapeutic equivalent of my diagnostic breakthrough" (115).

At the time the story begins, such an equivalent has just been found, but it has been offered to Dr. More by the Mephistophelean figure of Art Immelmann. Not only has the real condition of the people in the area been revealed as their social pretenses are seen through, but their actions have been radically altered by the indiscriminate use of More's improved machine. Here, as previously noted, Percy has a wonderful opportunity not only for satirizing the sexologists, liberals, ex-priests, behaviorists, and other denizens of the age in showing what they *really* think when their social inhibitions are removed, but also for introducing many of the themes and insights of his philosophical essays in imaginative ways. Thus, for example, in the essays Percy constantly argues that modern man lives in a mode of abstraction—"theory" has replaced "thing"—which allows him to perpetrate all kinds of horrors in his daily life, from impersonal fornication, to abortion, to threatening nuclear warfare. In the novel, Dr. More asks Immelmann what a plus ten dosage at the level of the prefrontal abstractive centers would do to a man ("especially a student"). Immelmann says that it "would render him totally abstracted from himself, totally alienated from the concrete world, and in such a state of angelism that he will fall prey to the first abstract notion proposed to him and will kill anybody who gets in his way, torture, execute, wipe out entire populations, all with the best possible intentions, in fact in the name of peace and freedom, etc." (328). This is, in practice, more or less what threatens to happen when Immelmann freely distributes the lapsometers against More's wishes.

For much of the narrative, More is on the run from the anarchy that has ensued from Immelmann's activities. His immediate mission is to try to protect three women for whom he is responsible. Each woman also represents a possible future for him as either hedonistic, cultural, or Christian companion, respectively, though there is little doubt even in his mind about what is the right decision in the matter.[21] It is his capture by black militants and his symbolic escape through the return duct of a compressor in an abandoned Catholic chapel that leads More to a rebirth as a functioning Christian. He comes to realize that he must change the habits he has contracted since his daughter's death and his wife's departure. This he does first of all in choosing Ellen, the most worthy of the three women. She is a Presbyterian who does not worry whether God exists or not, but who has a down-to-earth concern with what is good in human life. More has to realize also that the perfectibility that he is attempting to achieve with his lapsometer is impossible. Indeed, Art Immelmann has shown how dangerous it can be. This last discovery brings him to an awareness of his dependence on faith and to a reaffirmation of his practical religious belief:

---

21. There is also the less developed option of pagan Hester (48).

"Let's go, kids," says Art. One hand touches Ellen.

"Don't touch her!" I cry, but I can't seem to move. I close my eyes. *Sir Thomas More, saint, best dearest merriest of Englishmen, pray for us and drive this son of a bitch hence.*

I open my eyes. Art is turning slowly away, wheeling in slow motion, a dazed hurt look through the eyes as if he had been struck across the face. (376)

The novel ends somewhat unsatisfactorily in that the period of crisis and doom is skipped over without further comment. Instead, we are shown Dr. More some five years later. He is now married to Ellen, and his medical practice in a black neighborhood is small and relatively impoverished. He is still working on his project, however:

Despite the setbacks of the past, particularly the fiasco five years ago, I still believe my lapsometer can save the world—if I can get it right. For the world is broken, sundered, busted down the middle, self ripped from self and man pasted back together as mythical monster, half angel, half beast, but no man. Even now I can diagnose and shall one day cure: cure the new plague, the modern Black Death, the current hermaphroditism of the spirit, namely: More's syndrome, or: chronic angelism-bestialism that rives soul from body and sets it orbiting the great world as the spirit of abstraction whence it takes the form of beasts, swans and bulls, werewolves, blood-suckers, Mr. Hydes, or just poor lonesome ghost locked in its own machinery. (382–83)

Perhaps one can say that what he now hopes to achieve with his machine is at least worthy, though one must still doubt the appropriateness of his approach.

On Christmas Eve, Dr. More goes to confession to the moderate, sensible Fr. Smith, who merely groans at the prospect of listening to the long recitation. The encounter progresses in the usual tired way of such happenings with the priest running through his pat answers and questions and anecdotes. "Damn, where does he come off patronizing me with his stock priestly tricks because he reels 'em off without even listening" (398). But More is jolted into sorrow for his sins when the priest reminds him that there are other more important things in the world than the doctor's narcissistic self-examination. Then, in what is referred to as a post–Vatican II revival of public penance, Fr. Smith gives him a sackcloth to wear. Ellen, meanwhile, is said to be suspicious of such Catholic reliance on "*things*" for salvation, and the world, with its customary political and religious divisions, is shown to be back to normal after "the past peculiar years of Christendom" (403).

What we have here, then, is a movement *within* the Christian believer to a rediscovery of his faith. It is noteworthy that two of the people instrumental in this rediscovery are Ellen and Fr. Smith, both of whom derive their "authority" from their extreme sobriety, a virtue especially commended in "The Message in the Bottle." Significantly also, the world at the conclusion of the novel, for all its imperfection and in spite of its racial realignments, is remarkably like that of the period of Percy's conversion.

It is with *Love in the Ruins* that Walker Percy begins to be seen as a distinctly Catholic writer. Thus, in an interview with John Carr in 1971, Percy stated his position as follows:

> I'm a Roman Catholic, although many Roman Catholics don't understand how I could write the novels I do and be a Roman Catholic. Of course, it's an interesting subject in itself. What is a Catholic novelist? Is he a novelist who happens to be a Catholic, or is he a novelist who is first a Catholic before he's novelist? All I can say is, as a writer you have a certain view of man, a certain view of the way it is, and even if you don't recognize it or even if you disavow such a view, you can't escape that view or lack of view. I think your writing is going to reflect this. I think my writings reflect a certain basic orientation toward, although they're not controlled by, Catholic dogma. As I say, it's a view of man, that man is neither an organism controlled by his environment, not a creature controlled by the forces of history as the Marxists would say, nor is he a detached, wholly objective angelic being who views the world in a God-like way and makes pronouncements only to himself or to an elite group of people. No, he's somewhere between the angels and the beasts. He's a strange creature who[m]

both Thomas Aquinas and Marcel called *homo viator,* man the wayfarer, man the wanderer. So, to me, the Catholic view of man as pilgrim, in transit, in journey, is very compatible with the vocation of a novelist because a novelist is writing about man in transit, man as pilgrim.[22]

The opening sentences of the above quotation call to mind Graham Greene's remarks on the relationship between his writing and his religion, though Percy's Catholicism has always been far more strongly asserted than has that of the English novelist.[23] In any case, now that he was firmly established as a Catholic novelist, Percy was eager to make a temporary return to philosophical speculation—or, if not to pure speculation as such, at least to a more discursive form of intellectual persuasion.

22. Lawson and Kramer, eds., *Conversations,* 63.

23. Greene has expressed greater reservation concerning the influence of Catholicism on his writing: "If I may be personal, I belong to a group, the Catholic Church, which would present me with a grave problem as a writer were I not saved by my disloyalty.... As a novelist ... doubt and even denial must be given their chance of self-expression, or how is one freer than the Leningrad group?" (quoted in A. A. DeVitis, *Graham Greene* [Boston, 1964], 44).

8

Philosopher Redux

With the publication of *Love in the Ruins*, Walker Percy had pretty much covered the entire range of his interests, both philosophical and fictional. However, there was still a need in regard to the fiction of achieving more satisfactory and explicit terminations for his characters' wayfarings, while in regard to philosophy there was an opportunity to reassert, and even develop, his earlier claims in the face of newer opponents. Besides, a message—as opposed to an observation—stands in constant need of reiteration. In any case, although between *The Moviegoer* in 1961 and *Love in the Ruins* in 1971 Percy did not publish any new philosophical essays, he had continued to be preoccupied with the subject to the extent even of writing fiction in the morning and philosophy in the afternoon throughout the 1960s. When *Love in the Ruins* appeared, it was seen by several critics as a very imperfect exercise of the fictional mode, as though Percy had found himself confined by its artistic restraints and was seeking a way of escape.[1] The philosophy— or at least the sense of the author having an all-too-clear set of ideas on certain issues—was showing through. Then, between 1972 and 1975 Percy published three new philosophical essays and collected his various articles in the field to make *The Message in the Bottle*, to which he gave the subtitle *How Queer Man Is, How Queer Language Is, and What One Has to Do with the Other*. By using the title of his most religious essay for the book itself, he was leaving no doubt about what the main purpose of his argument would be.

The new philosophical essays add up to almost one hundred pages—a considerable effort by any standard, amounting to a short book on the subject—and, more important, they represent modest but definite developments of his earlier work. Percy, of course, repeats many of his former insights and examples on the

---

1. Thomas McGuane's comment that *Love in the Ruins* offers a "friendly sociology" of types captures the sense that it is more a novel of ideas than of people. See "This Is the Way the World Will End," *New York Times Book Review,* May 23, 1971, pp. 7, 37.

topic of language, but he also introduces new names, or has more to say on old ones, such as Charles Sanders Peirce, and confronts new theories, Noam Chomsky's in particular. He has obviously kept up with his serious reading in the discipline over the years. Now and then he even draws attention to some important revisions in his own thinking on the subject.[2]

The first of the new essays, "Toward a Triadic Theory of Meaning," was published in *Psychiatry* in 1972. It is a rather technical (and at times tedious) piece, aimed at a professional audience of working psychiatrists. It also uses narrative examples that are strikingly similar to those to be found in the early pages of *The Last Gentleman* (where Will Barrett confronts his psychiatrist, for example), suggesting a possible mid-1960s provenance. Percy's basic point is that since psychiatrists, more than other medical practitioners, use language in their treatment of patients, a theory of language might be useful to them. Because the theories offered by behaviorists such as B. F. Skinner and semioticians such as Charles Morris are unsatisfactory, one needs to look to the nineteenth-century founder of semiotics, Charles Sanders Peirce, for guidance, particularly to his "triadic theory" of language.

According to Peirce, the use of language requires a triadic relationship between "a sign, its object, and its interpretant" as opposed to dyadic relationships of the stimulus-response kind (Peirce does not use such terminology, however). In the case of stimulus-response, the two things—stimulus and object stimulated—are materially connected; in the case of triadic relationships, a *symbol* (here equivalent to a *sign*) intervenes as the third element, "connected with its object," Peirce wrote, "by virtue of . . . the symbol-using mind." Building on this analysis, Walker Percy acknowledges that dyadic energy exchanges are involved in triadic relationships—"sound waves in air, colloidal synaptic event, efferent nerve impulse, muscle contraction, or glandular secretion"—but claims also that there is something more to the transaction. Dyadic theory, he asserts, "can account for perhaps 98 per cent of natural phenomena. Unfortunately the phenomenon of talking-and-listening [*i.e.*, using symbols] falls in the remaining 2 per cent" (162). Percy is not claiming here, it should be noted, that this "2 per cent" is anything

---

2. See, for example, *The Message in the Bottle: How Queer Man Is, How Queer Language Is, and What One Has to Do with the Other* (New York, 1975), 166n.

other than natural. Shortly afterwards, he offers one of his standard examples of the problem: spelling the word "cake" on Helen Keller's palm and her then going to fetch the item can certainly be explained in terms of sign-response, dyadic behavior, but such is not the case when, having learnt the name of one thing, she wants to *know* the names of other things without having any desire to go and fetch them. Thus the "2 per cent," the wanting to *know*, needs an explanation, albeit again a *natural* one.

By dividing up the phenomenon of language usage so that its separate components are dealt with by specialists in such disciplines as logic, math, syntax, and learning theory, the real issue of explaining triadic behavior is evaded, Percy thinks. As a scientist himself who has the task of accounting *fully* for linguistic behavior, Percy is not willing to "yield the field to formalists, logicians, and transformational linguists" (163). So, after attacking such philosophical linguists as Ogden, Richards, Korzybski, and Stuart Chase, Percy offers a loose set of more than twenty postulates as alternative ways of thinking about the problem. Thus, for example, echoing Saussure, Wittgenstein, Bakhtin, and others (and in apparent contradiction of some of his own claims both earlier and later), he contends, "The basic unit of language is the sentence" (166); "There is no necessary relationship between a name and that which is named beyond the coupling of name and thing by namer" (168); "A sentence may mean anything it is used to mean" (169); "It is impossible to think of an exchange of sentences occurring otherwise than between two or more persons" (172); "A sentence is received and uttered in a *world*" (173). He argues with Chomsky, Russell, and Wittgenstein along the way, objecting in particular to Chomsky's postulation of "innate ideas" in the form of a "Language Acquisition Device" (LAD) to account for how a child can achieve complex speech patterns though exposed only to a limited, and often incorrect, variety of sentence structures: "I wonder whether Chomsky's LAD . . . is nothing more nor less than the unique human ability to couple sentence elements, to couple symbols with things, symbols with symbols" (170). This, as I hope to show later in the present chapter, is a misunderstanding of Chomsky's LAD and its function: it is Percy's attempt to replace it with Peirce's schema of symbol and object being connected by mind, but without much actual explanation of that "unique human ability" to make such a connection.

When Percy comes to deal with psychiatric analysis as such, he sees it as a special case of the use of language that may throw light on its more normal occurrences. The new "linguistic" problem in psychiatry is that, because modern man is so eager to identify himself in terms of Freudian symbols, to surrender his sovereignty and confess his complexes, the whole function of the original process has been distorted and perhaps rendered counterproductive. Thus, according to Percy, it is only through fictional technique or phenomenological description that the limitations of both behaviorism and Freudianism can be overcome, for it is only here that language is understood in all its complexity and deviousness. In comments that closely resemble those of another recent critic of Freudian analysis, Jeffrey Masson, Percy suggests that insofar as the analyst succeeds in his task, it is because he has already begun to observe his patient in such a contextual way: "But is it not the case that when all is said and done and all theories aside, what happens is that the therapist gets to know his patient pretty well, understands him, intuits him, can talk with him and about him—and that behavioral theory can never say much about it?" (186).

Thus, once again, the tools of scientific analysis (assuming for the moment that the Freudian enterprise falls within this category) are shown not to account for the complexity of *individual* behavior. Where Peirce's triadic theory could be useful—Percy rather disconcertingly avoids specifics at this critical point—is that it "might bestow order and system upon the phenomenologizing which to the behavioral scientist must seem closer to novel writing than to a science of behavior" (187). In all, the details of the approach taken here are relatively new, but the main thrust of the argument is that of Percy's earlier philosophical essays: man is an absolutely unique creature, qualitatively distinct from the rest of creation, and hence endowed with a correspondingly unique destiny; a true *natural* explanation of his existence would lead implicitly to a recognition of his *supernatural* origins.

The second new essay, "The Delta Factor," though it only appeared originally in the *Southern Review* as late as 1975, is appropriately placed at the beginning of *The Message in the Bottle* for in it Percy sums up the themes of the rest of the essays and of a good deal of his fiction as well. The subtitle for the piece indicates its nontechnical content: "How I Discovered the Delta Factor Sitting at My Desk One Summer Day in Louisiana in the 1950's Thinking about an Event in the Life of Helen Keller on Another Summer Day in Alabama in 1887" (3).

The essay begins with a typical series of Percy queries, some of them referring to themes that have been touched on in the novels: Why do men feel good in bad environments and bad in good environments?; more specifically, "Why is it that the only time I ever saw my uncle happy during his entire life was the afternoon of December 7, 1941, when the Japanese bombed Pearl Harbor?" (4); "Why is it difficult to see a painting in a museum[,] but not if someone should take you by the hand and say, 'I have something to show you in my house,' and lead you through a passageway and upstairs into the attic and there show the painting to you?" (5) (a scene that had appeared in different form in *The Last Gentleman*). The situations resemble one another in that each is counter to what one would expect and hence requires explanation.

Percy finally asks, with Arnoldian overtones, what a man should do when he is caught powerless between the old and the not-yet-formulated new theories of man? Man as organism is no longer acceptable (such a theory could not account for the situations alluded to above), but neither is talk of man's "soul, mind, freedom, will, Godlikeness." Thus, Percy replies, "What a man does is start afresh as if he were newly come into a new world, which in fact it is; start with what he knows for sure, look at the birds and beasts, and like a visitor from Mars newly landed on earth notice what is different about men" (7).

Adopting the stance of such a "terrestrial Martian" in order to undertake this search, Percy discovers in his new guise that, of course, man *is* different from the other animals because of his use of language and in spite of the fact that the scientists, including Darwin, have been trying to deny this uniqueness for the last one hundred years. It is this difference—Percy sees it as a unique "gap" in nature—that explains both man's hopes *and* his problems: "If you know why this creature talks, thinks the Martian, you might also know why he behaves so oddly" (18). Moreover, this difference needs to be spelled out for those who can no longer accept the traditional Judeo-Christian view.

The old consensus view of man and his purposes that no longer exists (though it seems to exist for people like Percy himself) was "the belief that man was created in the image of God with an immortal soul, that he occupied a place in nature somewhere between the beasts and the angels, that he suffered an aboriginal catastrophe, the Fall, in consequence of which he lost his way and, unlike the beasts, became capable of sin and thereafter became a pilgrim or seeker of his own salvation, and that the clue and sign of his salvation was to be found not in science or philosophy but in news of an actual historical event involving a people, a person, and an institution" (18). What is happening now, according to Percy, is that we are living in the new world on old beliefs (a point that both Guardini and Nietzsche had made): "The denizens of such a time are like the cartoon cat that runs off a cliff and for a while is suspended, still running, in mid-air but sooner or later looks down and sees there is nothing under him" (19). Clearly, Percy wants to reintroduce in some new way the previous Christian understanding of man.

Percy elaborates on what he sees as the uniquely modern contradiction thus: most people in the West would agree with both the proposition that man is an evolutionary organism possessed of certain needs and drives, *and* the proposition that he is in some way unique with certain rights, freedom, and dignity. But, asserts Percy, "the conventional wisdom expressed by these two propositions, taken together, is radically incoherent and cannot be seriously professed without even more serious consequences" (20). Thus, Percy maintains, "When the scientific component of the popular wisdom is dressed up in the attic finery of a Judeo-Christianity in which fewer and fewer people believe, and men try to understand themselves as organisms somehow endowed with mind and self and freedom and worth, one consequence is that these words are taken less and less seriously as the century wears on, and no one is even surprised at mid-century when more than fifty million people have been killed in Europe alone. In fact there is more talk than ever of the dignity of the individual" (21–22). Here, obviously, one would want to question Percy's leap from describing an empty "faith" to accepting the Holocaust; that the transition follows is not clear by any means. One might also notice that Percy does not yet explain how the two propositions to which most people supposedly subscribe *are* to be reconciled—one seems to need to reject one or the other, a conclusion that Percy himself would hardly accept.

Whatever the inconsistencies or omissions in Percy's argument, however, his contention that modern man is alienated seems to be confirmed by the experience of many human beings. Man is *not* at home in his environment, and this circumstance must be accounted for by any acceptable theory. Nevertheless, having admitted that the Christian view is no longer a consensus one, Percy argues that an ethical Unitarianism (loosely the prevailing moral code among liberals), the remnant of a defunct Judeo-Christianity, is no substitute for a vigorous belief, and that only Judeo-Christianity deals with ongoing alienation. In Judeo-Christianity "the experience of alienation was . . . not a symptom of maladaptation (psychology) nor evidence of the absurdity of life (existentialism) nor an inevitable consequence of capitalism (Marx) nor the necessary dehumanization of technology (Ellul). Though the exacerbating influence of these forces was not denied, it was not to be forgotten that human alienation was first and last the homelessness of a man who is not in fact at home" (24).

Percy's assertion above is problematical, however, since it seems more a reaffirmation of traditional Christian doctrine than a new presentation that would appeal to the unconverted and the disaffected. Thus, his eventual argument for religious belief is in part based on the consequences of its absence: because people don't accept the idea of a Fall, they have no way of dealing with the disasters of the twentieth century. Even poets and artists who, unlike scientists, have long recognized man's loneliness and alienation have had no alternative to offer. Thus, when with the shock of World War I the "old modern age" came to an end and it was found that men often preferred war to peace, "the theorists of the age had only one recourse: to search for explanations either within the 'organism' or within the 'environment.' Accordingly, it did not strike anyone as peculiar when scientists sought an explanation for man's perversity and upsidedownness in this or that atavism from man's evolutionary past. Man blamed the beasts for his madness" (27). In a sense, Desmond Morris' 1967 *The Naked Ape* became the explanatory text to read, an answer that Percy cannot accept (though one that is not thereby rendered unacceptable).[3]

A Martian, in contrast, might think that since it was language that made man different, it was there that the problem lay. Pursuing this "clue," Percy again turns to the phenomenon of Helen Keller, making the extraordinary claim that "if one had an inkling of what happened in the well-house in Alabama in the space of a few minutes, one would know more about the *phenomenon* of language than is contained in all the works of behaviorists, linguists, and German philosophers"

---

3. Desmond Morris, *The Naked Ape: A Zoologist's Study of the Human Animal* (New York, 1967).

(35–36). At eight years of age, "Helen made her breakthrough from the good responding animal which behaviorists study so successfully to the strange name-giving and sentence-uttering creature who begins by naming shoes and ships and sealing wax, and later tells jokes, curses, reads the paper, writes *La sua voluntade e nostra pace*, or becomes a Hegel and composes an entire system of philosophy" (35). Helen's case distills the essence of the experience that all have and "the breakthrough of the species itself" (38). A stimulus-response explanation will not account for the event. Charles Sanders Peirce, according to Percy, had said essentially the same thing, but his statement was lost in his heavy metaphysic. In any case, the original breakthrough to language "was a natural phenomenon *but a nonlinear and nonenergic one . . . that is to say, a natural phenomenon in which energy exchanges account for some but not all of what happens*" (39) (my emphasis).

It is human language, the "Delta phenomenon," that is responsible for our triumphs and disasters: all our sorrows and delights, our boredom and our ecstasy. Percy links Delta with our evolutionary progress: "Life has existed on the earth for perhaps three billion years, yet Delta . . . could not be more than a million years old, no older certainly than *Homo erectus* and perhaps a good deal more recent, as late as the time of *Homo neanderthalensis*, when man underwent an astonishing evolutionary explosion which in the scale of earth time was as sudden as biblical creation. Was not in fact the sudden 54 per cent increase in brain size not the cause but the consequence of the true urphenomenon, the jumped circuit by which Delta . . . first appeared?" (42). Again, it is important to note that, for Percy, this breakthrough into language is a *natural* event—a "2 per cent" difference that is the result of dramatically increased brain size.

In language, man unites thought, symbol, and thing. Thus, in talking about a *balloon*, for example, a boy is using a generalized term—which cannot be equated with an animal responding to a buzzer. The boy, according to Percy, "couples *balloon* with balloon. But who, what couples? Who, what is the coupler? Do you mean some part of his brain does the coupling? I could not say whether it is his brain which couples, his 'mind,' his 'self,' his 'I.' All one can say for certain is that if two things which are otherwise unconnected are coupled, there must be a coupler" (44). Percy ends on a disingenuous agnostic note stating that it is language that makes man to be man, however the breakthrough was originally caused, "whether by pure chance, the spark jumping the gap because the gap was narrow enough, or by the touch of God, it is not for me to say here" (45). The peculiarity of this view—of which Percy is very much aware—is that since language makes humans human, and beasts cannot sin, it is in language that we must locate all our troubles.

Again, Percy's third new essay is placed appropriately enough at the end of the collection, for it is certainly the most difficult of them all. Its simple title, "A Theory of Language," is compensated for by its complex subtitle: "A Martian View of Linguistic Theory, Plus the Discovery That an Explanatory Theory Does Not Presently Exist, Plus the Offering of a Crude Explanatory Model on the Theory That Something Is Better Than Nothing." Percy is still a Martian, and still making the contention—odd, disingenuous, wrong-headed?—that his paper "can commend itself to readers more by reason of its ignorance than its knowledge" (298). This time Percy's concern is to refute not so much the behaviorism of Skinner as the antibehaviorism of the Cartesian Noam Chomsky in his explanation of the origin and functioning of language. Percy finds Chomsky and other transformationists such as Katz and Fodor to be equally in error, though from an opposite point of view to that of Skinner and Morris.

Percy first asserts that language studies have bifurcated. There are those like Bloomfield and Chomsky who are interested in "descriptive," "structural," "transformational" linguistics and who abstract from the actual speakers of the language.[4] The other side, consisting of behaviorists and learning theorists, asserts that "human language must not be different in kind from communication in other species." But Percy claims as usual that neither theory accounts for what actually goes on in human speech. He does not agree with Chomsky that "human language is [so] utterly *unlike* animal communication" that one needs "the old Rationalist notion of innate ideas to account for it" (300). Quite simply, "decrepit mind-body dualism" will no longer do. The transformationist's schema is "no more than a statement of the problem under investigation. The 'LAD' appears to be a black box whose contents are altogether unknown" (302). He explains his problem with Chomsky: "This awarding of the prime role to syntax rules out non-

4. If the coupling of the names of Bloomfield (phonemes and morphemes) and Chomsky (transformational grammar) seems odd, it needs to be kept in mind that Percy is simply claiming that both have taken an abstract view of language, as opposed to that of the behaviorists and learning theorists.

syntactical elements, for example, semological and phonological components, as primitive generative components of deep structures and in effect posits syntax as an underivable and therefore unexplainable given" (304–305).

Percy, on the other hand, argues for a system that begins with "a semological-phonological linkage" as against Chomsky's postulation of "syntax as a central underived component." This seems to conform better with how children acquire speech and to afford the possibility of finding a "neurophysiological correlate," something he actually does at the end of the essay (307). "In the initial naming stage of language acquisition, the first sentences children utter are the linking of semological elements (forms of experience) with phonological elements (forms of sound)," contends Percy (308).

Although Percy stresses the importance of the studies of language acquisition in children, he wonders why their authors also skip over the naming stage, something that is unique to man. Is there nothing to be said, he asks, or is the process simply mysterious? Again, transformationists are limited because they are looking for "grammatical patterns and distributional relations" so that they don't have much to say about the single word (309). Moreover, their rules don't correspond with what goes on inside people's heads psychologically.[5] Nevertheless, picking up from his 1972 essay "Towards a Triadic Theory of Meaning," Percy suggests that Chomsky's LAD is like a coupler. This, he claims (though without the necessary elaboration), would explain the "extraordinary generative capacity" of children (319).

So Percy is led back to Peirce's theory to show how the LAD black box works. Percy asks: "In view of the uniqueness of the human capacity for speech, how different are these workings from the workings of other brains? Are they qualitatively different or quantitatively different? Does the black box hold Cartesian mind-stuff or S-s-r-R neuron circuitry? or both?" (321)[6] He himself wants to offer "a relatively simple and parsimonious model along Peircean lines," who,

5. Percy now spells out his theory, becoming rather technical in the process. Thus, a child's "one-word utterance" is the "earliest appearance of the naming sentence." "The addition of functors to child speech can be understood as the behaviorally necessary substitutes for a diminishing context" (*The Message in the Bottle,* 312, 316).

6. Peirce claims that man is naturally adapted "to imagining correct theories" and that he is inclined toward philosophical realism, both rather Scholastic propositions with which Percy would have agreed (*The Message in the Bottle,* 322).

Percy claims, got it from the medieval Scholastic philosopher Duns Scotus (324). So, in the coupling of semological and phonological elements in the acquisition of language, there must be a coupler, an interpretant.

However, far from regarding this "coupler" as supernatural or immaterial, Percy goes on to seek its neurological basis. It "must be, considering the unique and highly developed language trait in man, something which is present and recently evolved in the human brain and either absent or rudimentary in the brains of even the highest nonhuman primates" (326). Percy thinks he has found an answer in Norman Geschwind's claim that the phenomenon of language depends on "a recently evolved structure, the human inferior parietal lobule, which includes the angular and supramarginal gyri, to a rough approximation areas 39 and 40 of Brodmann . . . areas [that] have not been recognized in the macaque" and which "even in the higher apes . . . are present in only rudimentary form" (326). Although he confesses himself "incompetent" to evaluate these findings, Percy goes on to claim that "if Geschwind is right, what he has uncovered is the cortical 'base' of the triadic structure of the typical semological-phonological naming sentence." But he concludes, as he had in "The Delta Factor," that "the coupler is a complete mystery. What it is, an 'I,' a 'self,' or some neurophysiological correlate thereof, I could not begin to say" (327).

One may reasonably ask, of course, if this assertion doesn't call into question the absolute distinction between man and animal that Percy has been insisting on from the very beginning. While the macaque may not have this cortical area in its brain, the very fact that the existence of such an area might explain the phenomenon of language renders the latter wholly empirical and the product of biological evolution? Put another way, if Percy's argument is that God has given man an extra biological capacity and that its existence has recently been proved by the neurologists, in what sense can such a capacity be said to make him *qualitatively* different from the other animals? It would seem that it cannot. Or, if one concedes that a "spiritual substance" (a soul, an "I") must have a neurological base in order to function at all, and if Percy thinks that having found such in Geschwind's work he thus has an empirical fact that at least allows for the possibility of the existence of a soul (*i.e.*, it has a "place" in which to locate itself), he does not make his point clear against a wholly physicalist explanation of the entire setup. And yet one suspects that this is what Percy wants to do. In accepting the theory of evolution against both the denials of present-day biblical creationists and the simple ignorance of pre-Darwinian philosophers and theologians (*e.g.*, Aquinas and such), and also in accepting the Christian revelation of man as unique, with certain rights, freedom, and dignity, he must find a point of reconciliation between the two. Such a point lies in the "modest" form of evolutionism accepted in the Catholic church since the time of Pope Pius XII, which allows for physical evolution so long as it is affirmed also that each human being is endowed with a soul infused immediately into man by God at conception. This, of course, contrary to the statements of *Humani Generis*, is not a proposition that can easily be proved.

When *The Message in the Bottle* appeared in 1975, gathering together almost all of Percy's philosophical writings since 1954 and with the three new essays placed strategically at the beginning, middle, and end of the collection, it was immediately obvious that there were many repetitions in the pieces and that they badly needed editing. Nevertheless, the very fact that these essays were collected and published in this form is a statement of how serious Percy himself had always taken his philosophical thinking to be. Most important, the volume did indeed elicit a response from professional philosophers and linguists that was more critically sophisticated than that offered earlier by Percy's sympathetic expositors, though one suspects that had Percy not been by this time a successful novelist, the essays would not have received the same degree of attention. I have dealt briefly in Chapter 4 with these criticisms in so far as they concerned Percy's earlier philosophical writings, so I will confine myself here to what the critics had to say about the essays discussed in the present chapter.

Whatever the confusions and simple lack of knowledge on the subject of linguistics of which Percy—rightly, it seems to me—has been accused (his "crackpot" view according to one critic), it is important to keep in mind that his basic intent is to defend the notion that man is distinct from the other animals and that he in some way has an immortal soul. The easier it is to justify this assertion in empirical terms, the better as far as Percy is concerned—which is a mark of the period of his religious conversion in the 1940s. It is this sense of the matter that Hugh Kenner (himself from the same conservative Catholic tradition, but hardly an unsophisticated judge) captures in his remark that Percy, like Copernicus, may have "a lot of the facts wrong, and most of the details . . . [but] what we honor him for is having drawn a picture with just the main essential correct," though Kenner's speculative prediction that *The Message in the Bottle* "may one day rank with *De Revolutionibus Orbium Coelestium* and 2475 be marked by semi-millennial celebrations" is surely wildly exaggerated.[7] It is equally obvious that for this very reason—the largeness of Percy's claim—a critic such as Thomas Nagel would be thoroughly opposed to Percy's point of view quite apart from the validity or otherwise of any of its individual arguments.

Yet, it should be borne in mind that, contrary to what some Percy defenders (and the author himself) have implied, Nagel shares many of Percy's desires: that of making philosophical argument more accessible to a wider public, an opposition to a naïve positivism and to a scientism (defined with a somewhat different, though related nuance, as putting "one type of human understanding in charge of the universe and what can be said about it"), and a distrust of a total objectivity that refuses to take account of man's irreducible subjectivity.[8] Indeed, Nagel sees the current interest in language as a response to this need of reconciling objectivity with subjectivity, though the way in which the reconciliation is achieved does not satisfy him. Nagel agrees that there "may be something to Percy's claim that a modern form of disorientation is caused by the swallowing up of the familiar human world by a centerless, objective world disclosed by physical science" and that "since we are parts of this objective world it swallows us too, with the apparent consequence that the less specifically human our view of ourselves is, the more scientifically accurate it will be (as is true of our knowledge of water or light)." He cautions, however, that "this contrasts uncomfortably with the type of religious conception that puts the stamp of objectivity on a human view of the world by asserting that man is created in the image of God, who sees things as they really are." [9] Still, Nagel is accusing Percy of being *overly* objectivist, some-

---

7. Hugh Kenner, "On Man the Sad Talker," *National Review,* September 12, 1975, p. 1,000.

8. Thomas Nagel, *The View from Nowhere* (New York, 1986), 9. I disagree with Tolson's judgment that "Nagel seemed almost to resent Percy's presumption and ambition for attempting so much, for trying to consider all aspects of language" (*Pilgrim in the Ruins,* 401). It seems to me rather that Nagel is simply saying that Percy is wrong in many instances and that he just doesn't know enough about that whereof he speaks.

9. Thomas Nagel, "Sin and Significance," *New York Review of Books,* September 18, 1975, p. 56.

thing that Percy does also with his Martian example: Percy's Martian stance is incoherent since only a human being could understand the workings of a human language, and, besides, the belief that "the best way to achieve understanding is to become like a Martian is, in extreme form, to elevate scientific objectivity and detachment into a universal method" (56).

A more specific criticism that Nagel makes is that, in relation to the Helen Keller example, "there is no hope of understanding how the word 'water' means water by concentrating on an individual act of speech." But when he speculates more broadly—"It may be thought, for example, that if man is really a machine, it does not make sense to assign him moral worth. But why isn't it plausible to conclude that if men are machines, some machines (those that are men) have moral worth?"—he is open to Percy's legitimate rebuttal that such thinking would prove extremely weak in the defense of our moral system against the threat of a Hitler, and is indeed an instance of the unacknowledged presupposition (see Guardini) of an earlier Christian moral foundation (54).

In a more technical critique of Percy that objects in passing to his Thomistic pairing of word and thing, Frank Parker finds him inaccurate on Chomsky and other linguists and that, in general, he "just does not seem to understand the basics of what he is attacking."[10] Thus, Percy is wrong in his claim that the contents of Chomsky's LAD are unknown. "On the contrary," Parker asserts, "numerous universals have been formulated over the past twenty-five years"— and he proceeds to list several of them (150). On Percy's attempt to liken his coupler to Chomsky's LAD, Parker comments that Percy's theory is deficient in two ways: "First, it is so ill-defined that at best it can be subsumed under Chomsky's theory and at worst it is without empirical content. Second, although it may be capable of generating an infinite number of grammatical strings, it cannot restrict its generative power to all and *only* the grammatical sequences" (156). Then there is the problem that the kind of referential theory of language that Percy is proposing was long ago refuted by Frege with his famous "morning star/evening star" analysis in which both terms are seen to refer to the same object though

10. Frank Parker, "Walker Percy's Theory of Language: A Linguist's Assessment," in *Delta*, XIII (November, 1981), 146. In an essay that may suffer a little from overkill, Parker rightly criticizes a number of Percy's other significant commentators for their too easy acceptance of Percy's pronouncement on linguistics.

they obviously have different meanings (158). Finally, Percy's use of Geschwind's work is considered dubious and beyond what the scientist himself claimed, since the latter "has admitted that 'It would be difficult to conceive of grammar as depending on intermodal transfers [of the type mediated by the inferior parietal lobule]' " (164). Parker's conclusion is that if Percy's book "raises interesting philosophical questions about language, it does so despite its insubstantiality as a linguistic study" (163). Here again, it seems to me, Percy's lapses have resulted from his rushing to make current linguistic findings, or at least his view of them, fit prior theological convictions.

In a more sympathetic commentary, Jonathan Culler observes that Percy's problem "is insoluble in the form proposed" since "it is the contrast between signs that allows signs to emerge, so that the individual sign or name is not the unit in whose terms the problem should be posed." He reaches the heart of the matter when he notes insightfully that "direct perception is something Mr. Percy longs for"—although Culler cautions that there is "no perception outside of symbolic systems." [11]

What effect such criticisms had on Percy is difficult to tell, though a year later, in a self-interview, he referred irreverently to practitioners of "transformational generative grammar, formal semantics, semiotics" as those who "by and large have their heads up their asses and can't even be understood by fellow specialists." Moreover, the fact that he kept reiterating his main points suggests not only stubbornness but also the conviction that his total view was greater than its specific arguments. In any case, in a 1976 interview with Marcus Smith, Percy defended his idea of a "coupler" that connects word and perception. Indeed, Percy argued that his approach was more objective than Descartes' since one can't see the latter's "I," while the existence of the coupler is obvious. [12] But, while still being

11. Jonathan Culler, "Man the Symbol-Monger," *Yale Review*, LXV (Winter, 1976), 263, 264. Culler does not elaborate on Saussure's theory here, but it should be noted that his own interpretation has been tellingly criticized by Robert Scholes in *Textual Power: Literary Theory and the Teaching of English* (New Haven, 1985), 86–92. Walter Benn Michaels makes similar criticisms, remarking that Percy's problem is that he is more aware of Bloomfield than of Saussure, of Tarski rather than Barthes (*Georgia Review*, XXIX [Winter 1975], 974). See also Jonathan Culler, *Framing the Sign: Criticism and Its Institutions* (Norman, Okla., 1988), 161–65.

12. Lewis A. Lawson and Victor A. Kramer, eds., *Conversations with Walker Percy* (Jackson, Miss., 1985), 178, 130–31. When it was pointed out to Percy that the Helen Keller example wasn't quite right since she had had two years of normal child development before her impairment began,

vague on the matter and appealing to Chomsky, he denied that the coupler can be explained mechanistically. Then he went on to make the assertion that seems to me to lie at the core of his arguments on language: "to say man is different is not to split him into mind and body"—he *is* part of a continuous order—"but neither Aquinas nor Scotus are acceptable to twentieth century scientists because their realism depends on positing a psyche, an immaterial psyche or soul, so that in order for you or me to know something, we know it by some operation of this immaterial substance. This may or may not be true. . . . Once you open your mouth about Aquinas and how you know things by their essences and by the unions of the immaterial elements in the psyche, communication ceases for most scientists" (135). It is here that Percy's fundamental intent is exposed and one sees also the reason why he would continue to have problems with his professional critics.

---

the novelist admitted as much but asserted, "What was important to me was that the well-house episode distilled the essential elements of the normal naming experience."

9

SECOND COMINGS

The fact that *Love in the Ruins* marked a kind of creative end point for Walker Percy, in that with it he had presented all of his major themes, led him to tell Shelby Foote on one occasion that he was contemplating engaging with philosophy exclusively from now on. But, shortly afterwards—long before he was persuaded by the harsh professional critiques that *The Message in the Bottle* received and which, however unfair or misdirected he may have thought them to be, did not bode well for his future endeavors in the discipline—he found himself reverting to the fictional mode. Besides, Percy had been stung by the criticism that *Love in the Ruins* dealt with the theme of evil in a rather "sentimentalist" way (V. S. Pritchett's comment) and felt a need to vindicate himself.[1] Again, given his philosophical and theological premises, it is more than likely that he was eager to achieve some kind of closure on the issues that he had dealt with more ambiguously than he might have wished in his novels to date. Thus, the three novels that Walker Percy would write in subsequent years are to a large extent repetitions and intensifications of the earlier ones. *Lancelot* is about another "moviegoer," a kind of perverted Binx Bolling who takes the Stoic ethic to its logical and self-destructive limit, a dramatic extrapolation of Aunt Emily's stance with little possibility left for misinterpretation of that philosophy's intent. In *The Second Coming*, a continuation of the story of Will Barrett, the latter comes fully to terms with his father's suicide and converts to Christianity, thus going well beyond the confusion of *The Last Gentleman* (Percy remarked in an interview that whereas *The Last Gentleman* had been "inconclusive," *The Second Coming* "solves the problems").[2] And in *The Thanatos Syndrome*—though the novel

1. See Jay Tolson, *Pilgrim in the Ruins: A Life of Walker Percy* (New York, 1992), 358; V. S. Pritchett, "Clowns," in *Critical Essays on Walker Percy,* ed. J. Donald Crowley and Sue Mitchell Crowley (Boston, 1989), 48.
2. Lewis A. Lawson and Victor A. Kramer, eds., *More Conversations with Walker Percy* (Jackson, Miss., 1993), 19.

strikes one in part as an unplanned afterthought—the social evils of the age are presented with more immediate examples and more historical justification than was the case in *Love in the Ruins*. Overall, then, issues are resolved in ways satisfactory to Percy—by now a successful writer with ready access to the publishing markets—ways that may not have been available to him earlier because of a variety of artistic, emotional, and commercial constraints.

In 1977, the year in which *Lancelot* appeared, Percy also published an essay entitled "The State of the Novel: Dying Art or New Science?" Here he insists again that "art is cognitive; that is, it discovers and knows and tells, tells the reader how things are, how we are, in a way that the reader can confirm with as much certitude as a scientist taking a pointer reading."[3] It does so even in the present age when "the very enterprise of human life itself" is being questioned in novels and when there is "a diminished sense of significance" in the work of art (141, 142). This was not so earlier with Sartre's Roquentin or Faulkner's Quentin Compson, for their "illnesses" *had* significance "because they are held to possess certain insights not yet shared or perhaps only dimly shared by most of their fellow denizens of the Western world" (146). But a new age needs appropriate new signs and symbols, so that Percy's next novel, while still presented in a relatively conventional format, will sacrifice an appeal to existentialist *Angst* for a more immediately threatening mode: that of a secular and religious apocalypse.

Thus, however repetitious the theme of *Lancelot* may be, the novel presents character and issue with a ferocity quite unlike anything in *The Moviegoer*. This intensity arose from a number of circumstances surrounding the novel's composition. To begin with, *Lancelot* was written at a time when Walker Percy was experiencing problems in his own emotional life: he was writing at an office in downtown Covington rather than at home, and was dangerously (though probably innocently) close to a young female artist in the same building; she would subsequently paint his best-known portrait, one that Percy himself would describe as "a kind of composite of the protagonists of my novels, but most especially Lancelot."[4] Such upheaval may account for the extraordinary rage over sexual matters

---

3. Walker Percy, *Signposts in a Strange Land,* ed. Patrick Samway (New York, 1991), 140.
4. See Tolson, *Pilgrim in the Ruins,* 402; Percy, *Signposts,* 422.

that is so characteristic of Lancelot and quite absent in Percy's other male characters, who are driven by more restrained lusts. In fact, Percy wrote to Foote at the time with what Jay Tolson describes as "a rare burst of coarseness": "Don't you ever want to (1) shoot your wife (2) burn your house (3) run off with 2 26-year-old lovely Foote-admiring graduate N.C. students . . . (3) [sic] shoot your mother-in-law (4) move to Greece . . . ? Christ, you sound like Ralph Waldo Emerson. Please forward the secret of your maturity to a demoralized Catholic" (405–406). And Lois Parkinson Zamora has argued in *Writing the Apocalypse* that Percy's style here reflects on the author himself:

We know that apocalyptic visions incorporate sexual imagery: Revelation images the most opprobrious of spiritual and social offenses in lurid sexual terms. The result of such imagery is not a sense of sexual licence so much as a palpable undercurrent of repressed sexuality, the psychological analogue of the political impotence of the apocalyptist. Lancelot's phallic bombast must be understood in terms of impotence, in his case actual rather than figurative. . . . Indeed, in his novelistic epitomizing of the spiritual ills of contemporary culture in sexual terms, Walker Percy himself, not just his narrators, would seem to participate in and extend this characteristic apocalyptic narrative device.[5]

Again, in the early seventies Percy had been invited to write an introduction to a new edition of his cousin's *Lanterns on the Levee*. This obviously brought to mind once more the full force of William Alexander Percy's thoughts on the condition of the modern world and perhaps the continuing appeal of such a position even for Walker Percy himself. In any event, Percy now undertook to push his cousin's Stoicism to the limit to explore its supposed inadequacies. Many readers had responded positively to Aunt Emily (William Alexander Percy's surrogate) in *The Moviegoer* and condemned confused, but searching, Binx. The new novel, in which the main character's preoccupation with the decline of the modern world—and especially with its sexual decay—is an aggressive version of a con-

5. Lois Parkinson Zamora, *Writing the Apocalypse: Historical Vision in Contemporary U.S. and Latin American Fiction* (New York, 1989), 138.

dition that William Alexander Percy tended to accept rather regretfully, would correct this erroneous judgment on the Stoic tradition.

Most important of all, Percy was having difficulties—though hardly doubts—with his faith, manifested in an uncharacteristic grumpiness over reciting grace at meals (not particularly significant in itself, but symptomatic of a deeper malaise), failure to attend Mass, and excessive drinking. Since Percy has affirmed on several occasions that his belief has been unusually constant, one surmises that part of Percy's religious troubles at this time derived from the ongoing upheaval in a Church which he had expected to remain unwavering—not only were clergy and nuns continuing to depart in large numbers, but even traditional dogmas were being called into question (Percy's beloved Eucharist being demoted—unofficially, of course—from a case of transubstantiation to one of mere "transignification"). Thus, for example, a close Benedictine friend, who later left the priesthood, has observed that his own rather cynical view of the Church tended to distress Percy in their conversations together: though troubled by the Church's ignoring of social problems, "He was reluctant to take the valuable and throw out the rest." In the novel, Lancelot combines a controlled, Stoic fury (not an oxymoron in this case) with anger that the Church has softened its message to suit the times: "I might have tolerated you and your Catholic Church, and even joined it, if you had remained true to yourself. Now you're part of the age. You've the same fleas as the dogs you've lain down with." Percy seems to have shared a sentiment that Caroline Gordon expressed in a letter to Jacques Maritain in 1969: "I am certainly glad I entered the Church when I did! The 'new theology' has me baffled"—except that he would have added: "and outraged."[6]

Whether or not Percy was using his new novel to work through his confusions and relieve his irritations, the theme of *Lancelot* is absolutely clear: at the end of the narrative, the protagonist—the advocate of a radical return to the ancient Stoic ethic—remarks to his friend Percival, a Catholic priest: "One of us is wrong. It will be your way or it will be my way." He adds, as if to bring even greater clarification to the proposition: "There is no other way than yours or mine, true?"

6. Tolson, *Pilgrim in the Ruins*, 368; Walker Percy, *Lancelot* (New York, 1977), 168; John M. Dunaway, ed., *Exiles and Fugitives: The Letters of Jacques and Raïssa Maritain, Allen Tate, and Caroline Gordon* (Baton Rouge, 1992), 96.

The priest's response on both occasions is yes (257). Thus, the novel can be seen as an intense dialogue between the Catholic and Stoic positions (the original intention of *The Moviegoer*), though what is peculiar about *Lancelot* is that only one side of the exchange is represented (Lancelot quite obviously repeats or paraphrases Percival's points, however). What is significant about this technique is that it allows a monomaniacal rage to dominate the narration even as it subverts its force. Thus, while Percy is certainly "writing a kind of Jungian drama between a self and a counter-self," there is no doubt that in the end it is the Catholic ethic that is being recommended: the exaggerations in Lancelot's position, his frequent attacks on the Christian view of life, and his terrifying behavior all point to the attractiveness of their Catholic alternative (403–404). Although the eventual fate of Lancelot himself may be uncertain, the "salvation" of the reader—as the epigraph from Dante indicates—has been clearly undertaken by "showing him the lost people . . . [in] the region of the dead."

Lancelot Lamar Andrews is a member of the River Road gentry in Louisiana, an Episcopalian (in the tradition of his namesake, the great Anglican divine beloved of T. S. Eliot) brought up to look down on Roman Catholics. He is a former Rhodes Scholar, an ex-football player, and a lawyer who was once active in civil rights. But as was the case with Binx Bolling, Will Barrett, and Tom More, he has lost direction in his life (he lives in an alcoholic haze) and so is in need of a defining event that will call for decisive action on his part. And as with Binx's father, Lancelot's sire combined romantic, Stoic, and scientific interests: his library, which consisted of volumes of Romantic English poetry, southern history, Saint-Exupéry, Sir Walter Scott's novels, and H. G. Wells's *Science of Life,* is described contemptuously as "a strange collection in which I could detect no common denominator except a taste for the extraordinary and marvelous . . . the extraordinary adventure undertaken by a brave few . . . the extraordinary stunt of H. G. Wells in taking on all of life, the extraordinary glory of a lost cause," though it has obviously left its mark on Lancelot himself (116). One option is closed from the beginning, however. Unlike Dr. More and to some extent Binx, Lancelot has never been able to escape "into the simple complexities of science," which can solve the mysteries of the universe without showing one how to lead an ordinary life (94).

In fact, a large part of Lancelot's quest has already been undertaken and concluded even as the story begins: a year earlier he had been jolted out of his *malaise* and into a renewed awareness of his life by the accidental discovery of his wife's infidelity. The discovery was made literally at the movies in that it came about while a steamy romance involving a hippie Christ-figure was being filmed at their home with Lancelot's Margot as heroine. It seemed to him thus (rather perversely, one is inclined to think) that a good of some kind—his new awareness—could come from evil and that therefore perhaps God was not to be discovered as the Great Watchmaker who had created a beautiful universe. He was to be discovered through the existence of pure evil in the world: "A new proof of God's existence! If there is such a thing as sin, evil, a living malignant force, there must be a God!" (52). The positive witness of an Albert Schweitzer no longer had any significance, nor was Hitler a good example of pure evil since his behavior might have psychological explanations. Thus Lancelot had concluded: "My quest was for a true sin—was there such a thing? Sexual sin was the unholy grail I sought" (140).

Obviously, the world that exonerates Hitler would even more readily excuse mere marital infidelity, so one can only conclude that it is Lancelot himself who judges that such behavior is radically evil and that, for him, Hitler's conduct is less clearly so. The latter perspective is ominous, surely. And indeed, as the story progresses, Lancelot's rational discourse turns more and more to insane rant, especially on the matter of sex. And once again, Percy is both setting up a certain view and behavior—Lancelot Lamar's in this instance—for our appalled rejection *and* venting (for complex psychological reasons) his own fury against the decadence of the times.

In his quest for further damning evidence against his wife, Lancelot decided to make his own home movie in which she, unwittingly, would also have a starring role. The chapter in which Lancelot looks at the result is entitled "Friday Afternoon at the Movies: A Double Feature." There, but in reverse because of a technical blunder that has rendered black images white and vice versa, Lancelot found out not only that his wife had been unfaithful but also that his daughter was involved in a triangular sexual relationship. Thematically, the reason for the movie being shown negatively is that in this situation "dark is light and light is dark" (190)—it is the dark, the evil, that reveals the godhead. Or rather, such should have been the case. But Lancelot failed to discover the evil he had sought. When, later, he killed Margot and her lover, he discovered simply nothing: "There was no 'secret' after all, no discovery, no flickering of interest, nothing at all, not even any evil. There was no sense of coming close to the 'answer.' . . . As I held that wretched Jacoby by the throat, I felt nothing except the itch of fibreglass particles under my collar. . . . There is no unholy grail as there was no Holy Grail" (253). Lancelot even failed to find that evil in himself—when his house exploded and he was thrown into the air, he is described as Lucifer—which had led to his killing four people.

Thus, when the novel opens, Lancelot has rediscovered himself and taken his decisive action a year earlier, and as a consequence he is now confined to a mental institution where he is recovering from "shock, psychosis, disorientation." Something obviously has gone wrong with his search. Although he is looking forward to his imminent release and a new life, he still cannot understand the recent past (with no self-knowledge, he himself is a symptom of the shortsightedness of the times). His friend Percival—who comes from the same social background (and a family prone to suicide) and had converted to Catholicism in a leap of faith, become a priest, preached the Gospel in Uganda, but who seems to have fallen from grace at some point along the way—is to act as his "leverage point" and "companion" in this examination (and so recover his own faith in the process).

Lancelot's initial quest was for evil, the evil that his wife had committed by being unfaithful to him. He set out as the Knight of the Unholy Grail to find an answer "to the most fundamental question of all." The question, he explains, is whether people are "as nice as they make out and in fact appear to be, or is it all buggery once the door is closed?" (131). Nevertheless, Lancelot initially saw the possibility of discovering evil as a path to religious knowledge, though in a peculiar, if not perverted, form. He contrasts his own obsession with Percival's: "You always got it backward: you don't set out looking for clues to God's existence, nobody's ever found anything that way, least of all God" (216). But it is only in Lancelot's view that Percival, the priest, has always got it "backward." The whole point of the novel is to show that Lancelot's approach is the wrong one. The fact, of course, that Lancelot was not satisfied when he finally encountered "evil" indicates that perhaps Percival had been right after all.[7]

---

7. In his presumption that the world is evil and must be restored by man, Lancelot is a gnostic heretic. See Cleanth Brooks, "Walker Percy and Modern Gnosticism," in *The Art of Walker Percy: Stratagems for Being,* ed. Panthea Reid Broughton (Baton Rouge, 1979), 260–72.

His quest for evil having reached its unsatisfactory conclusion, however, the confined Lancelot now seems to take up a new position that is equally objectionable. As Lois Parkinson Zamora remarks, "Lancelot's apocalyptic plan for a 'new order' provides him with comfortingly absolute answers to ultimate theological and philosophical questions, as well as with the justification for murder."[8] Claiming (incorrectly) that it was only Lancelot and Percival who, in the Arthurian legend, saw the Holy Grail, he proposes a sterner form of religious belief that is really a combination of ancient Stoicism and militant Counter Reformation Catholicism. According to Lancelot, "There is going to be a new order of things and I shall be part of it. Don't confuse it with anything you've heard of before. Certainly not with your Holy Name Society or Concerned Christians Against Smut. This has nothing to do with Christ or boycotts. Don't confuse it with the Nazis. They were stupid." Then Lancelot offers—in words that echo "The Message in the Bottle" essay and so suggest Percy's at least speculative identification with Lancelot's project—his own solution: "What if one, sober, reasonable, and honorable man should act, and act with perfect sobriety, reason, and honor? Then you have the beginning of a new age" (156).

When Lancelot outlines the new order and invites Percival to join with him in the enterprise, there are echoes of Aunt Emily's phrasing: it will be characterized by "a stern code, a gentleness toward women." But more troubling statements follow.

You have your Sacred Heart. We have Lee. We are the Third Revolution. . . .
I cannot tolerate this age. And I will not. I might have tolerated you and
your Catholic Church, and even joined it, if you had remained true to yourself. Now you're part of the age. You've the same fleas as the dogs you've
lain down with. I would have felt at home at Mont Saint-Michel, the Mount
of the Archangel with the flaming sword, or with Richard Coeur de Lion
at Acre. They believed in a God who said he came not to bring peace but
the sword. (157)

After Lancelot's release from the institution, he will be able to get this new order

8. Zamora, *Writing the Apocalypse,* 132.

under way, an order based not on Catholicism or any other fashionable ideology, "but simply on that stern rectitude valued by the new breed and marked by the violence that will attend its breach" (158). He has come to the conclusion that both the decadent way of modern America and the Baptist way of loving Jesus must be rejected. "There is only one way and we could have had it if you Catholics hadn't blown it: the old Catholic way. . . . Then we knew what a woman should be like, your Lady, and what a man should be like, your Lord. I'd have fought for your Lady, because Christ had the broadsword. Now you've gotten rid of your Lady and taken the sword from Christ" (176–77).

Lancelot wants a "new Reformation" that will combine the best of himself and the best of Percival with that of Lee, Richard, Saladin, Leonidas, Hector, Agamemnon, Richthofen, Charlemagne, Clovis, Martel, and a nonemasculated Jesus. This attitude, as Lewis A. Lawson has pointed out, is derived from Joachim de Flora's millenarianism and was the subject of William Alexander Percy's long poem, "Enzio's Kingdom," in which he identified the plight of Frederick II of Sicily with that of his own senatorial father in Mississippi. In presenting this ideal in all its harshness and brutality, then, Walker Percy is asserting "a total rejection of 'Enzio's Kingdom.' "[9]

When at the last moment Lancelot's next-door companion—a woman who is suffering the psychological effects of gang rape—rejects his offer to start a new community in the Shenandoah Valley, he comes up with a "solution" that "is as clear and simple as an arithmetic problem." He uses a Scholastic syllogism to show that God, if he exists, will not continue to accept the Sodom of the present world. If he does not intervene, Lancelot "will start a new world single-handedly." Meanwhile, he will give God some time. The priest, on the other hand, like Fr. Smith in *Love in the Ruins*, having rediscovered his faith through the negative witness of Lancelot's dementia, is going off to take a little church in Alabama to preach the gospel there, "forgive the sins of Buick dealers, administer communion to suburban housewives" (256).

At the end of the novel then, as was pointed out earlier, it is asserted that there are really only two ways, the priest's or Lancelot's (the latter is given a slight

9. Percy has said that Lancelot is a fascist, even at the end. He is both better and worse than Aunt Emily (see Lewis A. Lawson and Victor A. Kramer, eds., *Conversations with Walker Percy* [Jackson, Miss., 1985], 207).

modification in that it is suggested that Lancelot will go off with the woman and be joined later by his child). He questions Percival about whether there is anything he wishes to tell him. Percival replies yes but without sequel. This may seem puzzling, but in fact the whole novel can be seen as a brilliant and consistent example of reversal: it is the unspoken ideals that are the important ones, and it is the very radicalness of the reverse alternatives that both alerts us to their unacceptability but also to the seriousness of our predicament. For his own part, Percy has succeeded both in showing that he did not hold the views on religion and sexuality with which we might all too easily be inclined to associate him— or at least that he did not hold them as naïvely as we might have thought—while at the same time he has been able to exercise an unrestrained polemic against the myopia of the age.

In December, 1977, Percy published a self-interview in *Esquire*. The fact that he called the piece "Questions They Never Asked Me *So He Asked Them Himself*" suggests that the items discussed were especially important to him. The piece indicates, among other things, how Percy felt about matters of belief after he had completed *Lancelot*. Here, then, he confesses his faith in the dogma of the Catholic church—a sign of the Church's divine origins is that it survives periodic disasters—and claims that scientific humanism is not a rational and honorable alternative. Although belief is a gift from God, "I asked for it, in fact demanded it. I took it as an intolerable state of affairs to have found myself in this life and in this age, which is a disaster by any calculation, without demanding a gift commensurate with the offense. So I demanded it."[10] What attracted him to the Church was "Christianity's rather insolent claim to be true, with the implication that other religions are more or less false" (177).

The above is an aggressive Catholic proclamation indeed, one very much in keeping with the ideas of Jacques Maritain on the matter, and one in its vehemence and certainty not wholly unrelated to Lancelot's agenda. Indeed, Percy himself has often claimed affinity with Lancelot rather than with his near namesake Percival. He has also stated that it was his own faith that ultimately kept him from being like Lancelot. At one point in the novel, Lancelot says to Percival: "You know the main difference between you and me? With you everything seems to

10. *Ibid.*, 176.

get dissolved in a kind of sorrowful solution. Poor weak mankind! The trouble is that in your old tolerant Catholic world-weariness, you lose all distinctions. Love everything. Yes, but at midnight all cats are black, so what difference does anything make? It does make a difference?" (131). Perhaps the answer is that while Percy understands Lancelot's rage and is himself inclined to make radical distinctions in matters of faith and morals, he is also aware, like Percival, that even a tolerant Catholicism does not accept everything. In the end he cannot be against—as is the case with Lancelot—Christian love.

The partial crisis of faith that Walker Percy had experienced in the seventies caused him to become even more religiously committed during the remaining years of his life. Perhaps his religious renewal was inspired by the arrival of Polish Cardinal Karol Wojtyla in Rome in 1978 as Pope John Paul II, a pontiff clearly intent on halting the slide into relativism that, from some perspectives, had plagued the Catholic church since the end of the Second Vatican Council. Percy now began to attend Mass on a daily basis and, as Tolson remarks, his "whole-hearted return to the fold seemed to include an almost penitential commitment to serving and defending the faith. For Percy, this service would consist largely of vigorous affirmations of the authority, dogma, and magisterium of the church, and particularly of the Holy Father himself, all of which he thought were under attack both from without and within the church" (434). So, whereas *Lancelot* had offered a destructive account of a distorted religious faith, Percy's next novel would provide a constructive rendering of a true belief and would have an un-ambiguous ending. Percy intended, in fact, to write his first unalienated novel. One could also argue that, just as in *Lancelot* Percy wanted to bring the Stoic ethic to its logical conclusion to show its ultimate dangers, in *The Second Coming* he wanted to explore fully (and even ridiculously) his own desire for certainty, his being troubled that God remains so closemouthed, so that he himself could eventually reject such desire for religious verification.

The Second Coming, published in 1980, has Will Barrett of *The Last Gentleman* for its chief protagonist.[11] There he was left as a witness to the advent of grace

---

11. Percy has claimed, however, that it was only in the writing of the new novel that he discov-

without being quite aware of its presence; there he was left also as looking to Sutter Vaught for guidance. The new novel takes up the question decades later when Sutter has gone to seed and can no longer function as a guide. Will, however, still finds himself engaged in the same quest as before, though this time it is much more explicitly religious.

Older, widowed, rich (through his marriage, though not to Kitty Vaught of *The Last Gentleman*), and successful (through his former New York law practice), Will Barrett is now seriously contemplating suicide. "How," asks the narrator, "could Will Barrett have come to such a pass?" and withholds an answer. While the fact that Will is now close to the age at which his father had killed himself explains his greater preoccupation with the matter than was the case in *The Last Gentleman*, the authorial intrusion, which occurs on a number of occasions in the novel, alerts the reader to the fact that what he has before him is essentially a philosophical exploration, partly in the manner of Thomas Mann's *The Magic Mountain*. Thus, later, in re-presenting the same scene, the author again intrudes to remind his reader that a philosophical quest is in progress: "What to make, reader, of a rich middle-aged American sitting in a German car, holding a German pistol with which he will in all probability blow out his brains, smiling to himself and looking around old Carolina for the Jews whom he had imagined had all disappeared?" (134). The alert reader, noting the more than two hundred remaining pages, must seriously doubt this threat. He or she may also feel that Barrett's role as a mere cipher for Percy's philosophical speculations is becoming all too obvious. Indeed, it sometimes seems as if it is the author himself rather than Will who is determined to keep the religious question in the foreground and move it toward what Tolson judges a forced resolution.[12]

In the scene alluded to above, Barrett is prevented from taking his life by the fact that just then someone else apparently tries to kill him. The shock releases him into the freedom to make one more attempt at living. He still needs to understand his father's suicide, however, and it is this need that establishes the basic theme of the novel: memories of what happened on that occasion seep into his

---

ered that he was talking about an older Will Barrett, and there are some technical inconsistencies in the narrative. The story itself is actually based on the life of a former schoolmate (Tolson, *Pilgrim in the Ruins*, 416).

12. Walker Percy, *The Second Coming* (New York, 1980), 15; Tolson, *Pilgrim in the Ruins*, 432.

consciousness at regular intervals throughout the novel. As the authorial voice declares at one point: "Only one event had happened to him in his life. Everything else that had happened afterwards was a non-event" (52). Earlier, Will had sought to escape from his father's suicide by searching for, and finding, "another way" (72, 132). He had gone up North to make money and had "even tried to believe in the Christian God because you didn't, and if you didn't maybe that was what was wrong with you so why not do the exact opposite?" (73). He had managed to do everything—except believe in the Christian God. The point is, however, that the effort to come to terms with his father's suicide *and* his search for faith are intimately connected (though I prefer to think of this connection in terms of a conflict between philosophical viewpoints—Stoic and Christian—rather than psychologically as an inadequate earthly father being replaced by a perfect heavenly one).

In his new crisis, Will finds himself again confronted with the choice between the convenient Episcopal faith of his ancestors and the Stoic humanism of his father. But what Will realizes now is that his father, like Binx's in *The Moviegoer*, had also been excessively, even romantically in love with the idea of death, and it is this new perception of him that leads Will again to seek "another way." Besides, mere humanism, he realizes, leads to Buchenwald, since we now know that many of the worst atrocities of Nazi Germany were perpetrated by men who had a refined taste for Goethe and Mozart. This Stoic humanism was as much a part of the SS colonel's character as it had been of the ancient Romans and is, for that very reason, suspect. Indeed, *Lancelot* was designed to portray its potential follies. Jack Curl, an Episcopal priest, presents, on the other hand, a Christian alternative that, in its comfortable no-nonsense attitude, in its belief that God is to be found in other people rather than transcendentally in prayer, holds equally little attraction for Will.

There are a number of other characters in the early part of the book who are secondary representatives of the Christian and Stoic choices. Thus, Will's friend Lewis Peckham sees himself and Will as having the same problem: "We're the once-born in a world of the twice-born. We have to make our way without Amazing Grace. It's a lonely road but there are some advantages along the way. The company, when you find it, is better. And the view, though bleak, is bracing. You see things the way they are." Will, however, finds Lewis' lack of belief "unpleasant": "It was no better than the Baptists' belief"; "At least, believers were consistent" (151). Later, Percy's ultimate condemnation is passed on Peckham: we learn that he takes Erich Fromm more seriously than God, Dante, or even Virginia!

Barrett's late wife had been an old-style Episcopalian who believed in *The Book of Common Prayer* and sought to win her way to heaven through the performance of good works. For a while Will even imagined that he believed what she believed, "taking for his own [and for its outlandishness] a New York Episcopal view of an Anglican view of a Roman view of a Jewish happening"—which is a distinctly Roman Catholic way of understanding the Christian tradition that would not necessarily be accepted by the other denominations mentioned (156). Again, his daughter Leslie is a "new-style Christian who believed in giving her life to the Lord through a personal encounter with Him and who accordingly had no use for church, priests, or ritual." Then the narrator adds slyly: "She believed this and Jason [her boyfriend] believed a California version of this" (158). Neither of these solutions will work for Will, though he cannot yet say why: "What was wrong, he asked himself, with opening up and loving everybody? What was wrong with their loving Jesus? I don't know. Something" (160).

Later on, almost as though he were presenting a set of theses to be rejected, Percy lists the various beliefs of the characters in his story: those of Marion, Leslie and Jason, Jason's parents (they were "Californians"), Jack Curl, Kitty (who believes in astrology and reincarnation), Will's servant Yamaiuchi (a Jehovah's Witness who believes in the 144,000 elect), Yamaiuchi's wife (a theosophist), and even Sutter, whom Will had once visited in Santa Fe only to find him sitting in an imitation adobe house watching *M*A*S*H* (159). When, soon afterwards, Will wonders why he himself cannot be a believer in this age of perfunctory faith and Californianism, the very phrasing of the issue makes it clear that he will have to find some other solution to his problems. From Percy's previous work we can guess that it will be a Catholic one, though this time it would be more accurate to call it Anglo rather than Roman Catholic.

On this occasion, however, unlike the case with Percy's other novels, there is a kind of alternative, even antiphonal, search going on with the character of Allie, the daughter of Kitty from *The Last Gentleman*, who is not at all God-preoccupied.[13] She had once been confined to a mental institution from which she later

13.   Percy had somewhat changed his opinion of Jung by this stage and even claimed that "Jung-

escaped. Percy presents her as a more developed version of Lonnie and of Lancelot's neighbor in the rehabilitation center, a young Helen Keller who is rediscovering the nature of language as she tentatively explores her way back to the real world. Whereas her mother has degenerated into a lewd and acquisitive matron, Allie functions as a salvific figure worthy of Barrett's interest and devotion. Early in the novel, when Will literally stumbles upon her, he is helpful to her but does not at all suspect that she will play a major role in resolving his problem.

Will's initial solution, then, is presented in a long letter to Sutter (Percy has admitted — rightly — that this ploy was a risk but that he had to send the ms. off in a hurry), in which Will informs him that he intends "to settle the question of God once and for all" and that he now knows "how to put the question so that it must be answered." "My death, if it occurs, shall occur not by my own hand but by the hand of God. Or rather the handlessness or inaction of God" (186). He continues:

> I will say only that the action I propose to take comes as a consequence of my belated recognition of my lifelong dependence on this or that person, like my father or yourself (who I supposed knew more than I did) or on this or that book or theory like Dr. Freud's (which I thought might hold the Great Secret of Life, as if there was such a thing). My equally belated discovery is the total failure, fecklessness, and assholedness of people in general and in particular just those people I had looked to. This includes you. Maybe you most of all. (187)

Now, at last, Barrett will find out whether his father was right or not. There are only two classes of people, he tells Sutter, the believers and the unbelievers, and he has not yet decided which is the more "feckless." The trouble with the Christians is that they have "killed off more people in recent centuries than all other people put together" (188). Nevertheless, they may still have the truth, though their presence en masse either as Southern Baptists or Irish Catholics offends his Episcopal reticence. Why, he wonders, "if the good news is true . . . are its public

---

ian individuation" was an essential theme of *The Second Coming* (Tolson, *Pilgrim in the Ruins,* 423). Presumably Will and Allie are animus and anima, respectively.

proclaimers such assholes and the proclamation itself such a weary used up thing?" (189).

Still, at least the Christians are not crazy. The unbelievers, on the other hand, are perceived by Will as suffering from madness: "The present-day unbeliever is a greater asshole because of the fatuity, blandness, incoherence, fakery, and fatheadedness of his unbelief." Born into a world of endless wonders, he fails to ask about what his purpose here is. The more intelligent he is, the crazier he is, reading Dante "for its mythic structure," and defending a freedom the origins of which are left uninvestigated. "He is as insane as a French intellectual." Will claims that it has taken him "all these years to make the simple discovery: that I am surrounded by two classes of maniacs. The first are the believers, who think they know the reason why we find ourselves in this ludicrous predicament yet act for all the world as if they don't. The second are the unbelievers, who don't know the reason and don't care if they don't" (190).

However, though Will includes himself in the ranks of the unbelievers, he claims that he is not insane. But since he now knows that the Jews are not leaving North Carolina, the apocalyptic sign that such a removal would represent is gone. In the end, Will discovers a better way: "the first scientific experiment in history to settle once and for all the question of God's existence" (192). Since the wonders of the world no longer serve to prove anything, "what if one should devise a situation in which one's death would occur if and only if God did not manifest himself, did not give a sign clearly and unambiguously, once and for all?" This is to be Will's version of the famous Michelson-Morley experiment that confirmed Einstein's theory of relativity. Barrett sees no flaw in his logic. God will be required to break his silence and to speak at last. Like Jacob, Barrett will wrestle with him for an answer: "My experiment is simply this: I shall go to a desert place and wait for God to give a sign. If no sign is forthcoming I shall die. But people will know why I died: because there is no sign. The cause of my death will be either his nonexistence or his refusal to manifest himself, which comes to the same thing as far as we are concerned. Only you [Sutter] know the nature of the experiment. I give you permission to publish the results in a scientific journal of your choice" (193). Will is pleased that there will at least be an end to this kind of question and that it will no longer be necessary to listen to the preachers "haranguing about God's existence" or to the professors "haranguing people about God's nonexistence and mythic structures" (193). However, if he dies, he wishes Sutter to continue the experiment by monitoring the movement of the Jews and the advent of the last days, a request that seems to render the experiment itself somewhat futile (though perhaps not necessarily so since in that case Sutter would at least be confirming a negative finding).

Afterwards the document is described by the narrator as "outlandish" (195) and we are told that any sensible person might consider Will's preoccupations to be crazy: "So it was that Will Barrett went mad. . . . This unfortunate man, long subject to 'spells,' 'petty-mal' trances, and such minor disorders, had now gone properly crazy" (197).[14] But when the narrator goes on to explain the nature of this craziness—the belief that man is the only species bent on his own self-destruction in the names of peace and freedom—the reader must wonder how ironically the description is intended:

> This is how crazy he was. He had become convinced that the Last Days were at hand, that the world had fallen into the hands of the only species which knew how to destroy itself along with all other living creatures on earth, that whenever in history this species had invented a weapon, it had forthwith used it; that it was characteristic of this species that, through a perversity or an upsidedownness peculiar to it, while professing a love of peace and freedom and life, secretly it loved war and thralldom and death . . . that the end would come by fire, a fire such as had not been seen in all of history until this century of demons, a fire which would consume the earth. The very persons who spoke most about "people's democracy" or "the freedom and sacredness of the individual" were the most likely, he was convinced, to be possessed by demons.

The ironic narrative voice concludes: "Madness! Madness! Madness! Yet such was the nature of Will Barrett's peculiar delusion when he left his comfortable home atop a pleasant Carolina mountain and set forth on the strangest adventure of his life, descended into Lost Cove cave looking for proof of the existence of

---

14. Although Will rejects the Christian Pentecostal type of love to which Leslie seems committed, he acknowledges, "If the result of the experiment is positive, then she and I will have found common ground. I will acknowledge her Lord" (227).

God and a sign of the apocalypse like some crackpot preacher in California"
(197–98).

Will's crawling into the cave is described in terms of a rebirth. Then, when he
has arrived in the belly of the cave and is sitting waiting, the narrator again
intrudes to ask: "Who else but a madman could sit in a pod of rock under a
thousand feet of mountain and feel better than he had felt in years?" Again one
senses a certain irony in the voice. Convinced that there is no way in which his
plan can fail, Will waits for an answer while sustaining himself with narcotics.
The nature of his plan is repeated in the following terms: "His plan was simple:
wait. The elegance of it pleased him. As cheerfully as a puttering scientist who
hits on a simple, elegant experiment which will, must, yield a clear yes or no, he
set about his calculations. The trick was to devise a single wait which would force
one of two answers, not more, not less" (212). Will is even certain that his answer
will be more satisfactory than those experienced by the mystics in the desert or
by suicides. But he still concludes that if God does not speak and the Jews are
not a sign, "then that too is an answer of sorts. It means that what is at hand are
not the Last Days but only my last days, a minor incident to be sure, but an event
of importance to me" (213). Once again, one wonders whether Will is not making
a prior excuse for the possible failure of his search?

Things go wrong, of course. As the narrator of the story explains, this can
happen even with an "experiment most carefully designed by a sane scientist."
The upshot of Will's investigation is that it is intruded upon after seven or eight
days (Percy's indefiniteness about time here seems to suggest excessive concern
with theme) by a toothache: "A clear yes or no answer may not be forthcoming,
after all. The answer may be a muddy maybe" (213). Whether the toothache is
intended to be taken as a response from God, a kick in the pants to tell Will not
to be such an asshole, remains unclear from the narrator's point of view. In the
meantime, however, having taken several capsules to relieve his pain, Will lapses
into a state of semi-consciousness in which many of the scenes from his earlier
life, and some imaginary ones that represent his anxieties, are replayed and a
resolution is achieved. In a dialogue with his father, for example, in which the
latter argues that there is no place left to go—not Santa Fe, home, Israel, Aix—
Will contends, "There must be a place" (215–16). Still, we are told eventually
that there was no sign, the toothache returns, and Will groans aloud to be let out

"with no thought of God . . . or the Last Days" (223). Like Lancelot, he has come upon no pure experience of the Godhead, but only the overwhelming reality of his own material circumstances.

In making his exit, Will falls—described in comic apocalyptic terms—into Allie's greenhouse. She asks him later:

"Did you find the answer?"
"Yes"
"What was it?"
"I don't know." (246)

Even several pages later it is not clear what he actually learned in the cave, but he does at least know what he has to do. The experience has brought him to a new humility and to engagement in a truly intersubjective relationship—"this gift of yours and mine"—with the innocent Allie (300).[15]

In a further conversation with Allie (in which her Aunt Val, a member of the Little Eucharistic Sisters of St. Dominic, is mentioned affectionately), Will tells her that nothing can defeat him now since he has defeated his father. The solution is to recognize the enemy as the love of death. Will cries out against death in all its forms—his father, the Church (it has the smell of death), Christendom, old and new Christianity, various isms, and even Norman Rockwell.

But Will's resolution of his problems is not immediate. He sets out for the swamp in Georgia where his father tried to kill him, only to realize on his way there that he needs to go back home to catch something or someone. Disoriented, he ends up in a hospital where his medical friends diagnose him—they tell Will that there are pills for what ails him—as suffering from Hausmann's Syndrome (a kind of epilepsy), the symptoms of which are depression, fugues, certain delusions, sexual dysfunction, and "inappropriate longing," an explanation that prompts him to think that the illness ought to be called not Hausmann but Housman, "the disorder suffered by the poet [a favorite of William Alexander Percy]

15. This resolution seems to put Will a little in the Jack Curl camp since he now recognizes that it is through loving a fellow human being—and only in that way—that one loves God. See my essay "Is Love of Man the *Only* Way to God?" (*Catholic Mind* [February, 1978], 29–37) for an overview of this theological development.

who mourned dead Shropshire lads and rose-lipt maids and his own lost youth" (302). Barrett is at last relieved of his Stoic inheritance, though the relief is ambiguous in that it makes him feel, not unpleasantly, that his life has been taken out of his own hands. Afterwards he is curious if everything might be attributed to chemistry. "Had this longing for Allie been a hydrogen-ion deficiency, a *wahnsinnige Sehnsucht?*" His answer is no (307). The climax to his decision-making process comes when, staying at a motel with Allie, he has a dream in which his father urges him to kill himself, like a Roman, for Christ's sake! Instead, Barrett rises, leaves the motel, and throws the guns down an overlook without waiting to hear them reach bottom.

Having rejected suicide and established a truly intersubjective relationship with Allie, Will is at last ready to go even further. He approaches the retired Fr. Weatherbee, a great believer in the Apostolic Succession, and tells him that he himself does not believe and does not want to enter the Church. Still, Barrett adds that "it does not follow that your belief, the belief of the church, is untrue" (358). He is willing to listen to Fr. Weatherbee because he seems to know something—and Jack Curl does not. With a rather too overt bow to "The Message in the Bottle," Will adds: "We are also willing to take instructions, as long as you recognize I cannot and will not accept all of your dogmas. Unless of course you have the authority to tell me something I don't know. Do you?" (358). Reluctantly, the priest speaks about his old parish in Mindanao: "They believed the Gospel whole and entire, and the teaching of the church. They said that if I told them, then it must be true or I would not have gone to so much trouble. During my absence betrothed couples remained continent and cheerful of their own volition" (359). The passage not only echoes "The Message in the Bottle" but also the scene with Jamie and the priest in *The Last Gentleman;* it is, indeed, its fulfillment.[16] When an overexcited Will then wants to know if the priest believes in Christ's Second Coming, the latter becomes uncomfortable. There is no gentlemanly reserve this time, however, in Will's attitude: "What is it I want from her [Allie] and him, he wondered, not only want but must have? Is she a gift and therefore a sign of a giver? Could it be that the Lord is here, masquerading behind this simple silly

---

16. See, however, Norman Lewis' book *The Missionaries: God Among the Indians* (New York, 1990) for a less sympathetic view of such evangelistic activities.

holy face? Am I crazy to want both, her and Him? No, not want, must have. And will have" (360). With this ending, Will Barrett has at last arrived home.

Yet it is a *willed* conclusion, more a manifestation of its author's own faith and intentions than an artistically achieved development. Percy does not appear to have been fully engaged with his subject, and it is hard to balance the seriousness of Will's questions against the ridiculous means (especially from an informed theological viewpoint) he uses to answer them. Furthermore, as Tolson remarks: "We need to hear from the Christian ironist before this novel ends; but we don't. Instead, we have Adam going off to join his Eve. What one distrusts most about this in some ways brilliant and beguiling novel is that it serves too therapeutic an end rather than the harder truth as Percy saw it" (432). Not surprisingly, *The Second Coming* is a Percy novel that seems to have had an especial appeal for those sympathetic with a New Age style of Christian gnosticism, an outcome that would hardly have pleased its by now ultraorthodox author.

Mention of "orthodoxy" also raises a serious problem: why has such an explicitly Roman Catholic author settled for Will's conversion to the Episcopal church rather than his own? This seems especially odd in a novel in which that church is very clearly criticized not only in the person of Jack Curl but also in the type of Christianity it professes. In a comment full of rich ironies, Will remarks, "The main virtue of Episcopalians is their gift for reticence. Seldom can an Episcopalian (or an Anglican) be taken for a Christian. Perhaps that is what I like about them" (219). Attempting to answer this question, Jay Tolson offers this reflection:

> Percy cuts against his own grain, against the bias of his own belief, in order to play with possibilities beyond his knowing. . . . What does it mean, for instance, that the Episcopalian Barrett gets what he wants in this world while, in other novels, assorted Catholic protagonists seem to settle for something less? . . . Percy was . . . very close to [Newman's] outlook . . . summed up in the . . . dictum, 'we succeed by failing.' To think that defeat in this world is the best preparation for happiness in the next is Stoicism with a Christian reward attached to it. It is easy to see why Newman's Catholicism appealed to the adoptive son of Will Percy.[17]

17. Tolson, *Pilgrim in the Ruins*, 425. John Edward Hardy has also tied himself into unnecessary knots trying to answer this question (*The Fiction of Walker Percy* [Urbana, 1987], 222).

Here, however, it seems to me, Tolson is stretching things mightily, though there *is* a real difficulty that has no easy answer. Perhaps it was just too cumbersome for Percy to have Will jump through all the hoops in one novel. What it is important to note about Fr. Weatherbee (employing Newman in a slightly different way from Tolson) is that he has a deep interest in the Apostolic succession and thus belongs to the more Catholic-leaning and less Protestant element in the Anglican communion, a group that disputed Pope Leo XIII's Bull in 1896, *Apostolicae Curae*, which denied the validity of Anglican orders. In other words, Fr. Weatherbee is a very Catholic kind of Episcopalian priest, and his life's work in Mindanao suggests the genuineness and unpretentiousness of his Christian commitment.

Having said all of the above, a problem still remains—especially in the light of several of Percy's late comments on the doctrinal and disciplinary inadequacies of Episcopalianism. Perhaps—and I mention this with deep skepticism and professional hesitation—Percy deemed that the most theologically obtuse of his protagonists was unworthy to become a member of the church of the great St. Thomas Aquinas! Were one to venture even farther, one might risk the proposal that in both *Lancelot* and *The Second Coming* the Catholic faith is most present by its relative absence: the radical inadequacies of *all* alternatives reinforce its supreme necessity. Whatever the solution, it is clear that both *Lancelot* and *The Second Coming* rest conclusive in their respective Christian affirmations.

10

Lost in the Cosmos?

The Second Coming marked a watershed in Walker Percy's career: he had come to terms with his father's suicide by writing it out, so to speak, and his embrace of the Christian faith had been strongly reaffirmed. It is not surprising, therefore, that he should now begin to write more explicitly about religion. In the section of *Signposts* entitled "Morality and Religion," only one of the ten essays included was composed before the 1980s, quite unlike the balance of decades to be found in the other two sections. In short, Percy was now a Catholic advocate. And he was such, as Tolson noted earlier, not just because of the Church's external foes, but also because the institution was under attack internally. His own stance within the various controversies could be described as moderate conservative, though he maintained an unwavering identification with the positions of the current Roman pontiff, John Paul II.

Two essays, published in 1981 and 1983, respectively, show how explicitly Catholic Percy had become (while his comment on the suicide of John Kennedy Toole in his foreword to the latter's *Confederacy of Dunces*—"It is a great pity that John Kennedy Toole is not alive and well and writing. But he is not, and there is nothing we can do about it"—suggests his own freedom from further preoccupation with that matter). In "A View of Abortion, with Something to Offend Everybody," which appeared in the New York *Times* on June 8, 1981, Percy makes his position on the issue clear from the very beginning: "A twentieth-century novelist should be a nag, an advertiser, a collector, a proclaimer of banal atrocities."[1] Legalized abortion, he asserts, is such a banal atrocity. An indication that his position is specifically Catholic in nuance and sentiment rather than merely on the religious Right (even though his appeal is on natural humanistic rather than religious grounds) is that he also attacks pro-lifers—the antiwelfare

---

1. Walker Percy, *Signposts in a Strange Land,* ed. Patrick Samway (New York, 1991), 226, 340.

Reagan administration, Jesse Helms, and the Moral Majority—because they "don't seem to care much about born life" (341).[2]

Arguing that there is nothing private about the decision to abort a fetus, Percy appeals to modern biology for a determination of when life begins. "Such vexed subjects as the soul, God, and the nature of man are not at issue. What we are talking about and what nobody I know would deny is the clear continuum that exists in the life of every individual from the moment of fertilization of a single cell" (341). Arguments about the onset of life were legitimate in the past because no one knew exactly when it began, but now it is science, ironically, and not the Church per se that is providing us with this information. "Compared to a modern textbook of embryology, Thomas Aquinas sounds like an American Civil Liberties Union member," Percy notes, referring to the medieval theologian's belief that the male fetus did not acquire a soul until forty days after conception (the female had to wait ninety days) and that while it was sinful to abort at any time, it was not homicidal to do so at an early stage. Nowadays, in any case, it is the Church that is most accepting of the new scientific information on conception, while the "secular juridical-journalistic establishment" opposes it. Percy makes no acknowledgment that not all scientists are agreed that the progress from the original DNA to the mature person is direct, nor is he at all in sympathy with those Catholic theologians (such as Father Charles Curran) who would favor a less dogmatic approach to the issue.[3] Indeed, Percy concludes with the rather provocative statement that the pro-abortionists are probably going to win but that "you're going to be told what you're doing" (342).[4]

2. See also Lewis A. Lawson and Victor A. Kramer, eds., *More Conversations with Walker Percy* (Jackson, Miss., 1993) where Percy criticizes Justice Blackmun for his decision in the *Roe* v. *Wade* case and declares that his own position on the issue is not a "theological, Catholic" one but has rather been dictated by general humanistic principles (184). My point is that the *tone* of Percy's objection *is* Catholic.

3. Dr. Charles A. Gardner, for example, has argued that since much depends on the subsequent interaction of cells and molecules, "the fertilized egg is clearly not a prepackaged human being. There is no body plan, no blueprint, no tiny being pre-formed and waiting to unfold. . . . [T]he particular person that it might become is not yet there." Quoted in Laurence H. Tribe, *Abortion: The Clash of Absolutes* (New York, 1990), 118.

4. Otherwise "liberal" philosophers such as Elizabeth Anscombe and Anthony Kenny are in agreement with Percy on this issue. See Anscombe, "You Can Have Sex Without Children: Christianity and the New Offer," in *Ethics, Religion, and Politics* (Minneapolis, 1982), 82–96, and Kenny, "Abortion and the Taking of Human Life," in *Reason and Religion: Essays in Philosophical Theology* (Oxford, 1987), 153–66.

The other piece, from 1983, has a more distinctly religious provenance: "A 'Cranky Novelist' Reflects on the Church," a speech delivered to a group of seminarians at the Benedictine abbey near Percy's home and on the grounds of which he would one day be buried. Percy begins by noting how few in number the seminarians are. He then refers to a suggestion in *Newsweek* that "the standards of the priesthood, standards of education, the rule of celibacy, ordaining women, and so on" be relaxed in the light of this crisis.[5] Percy, however, is opposed to such a move—he likens the priesthood to the Marines—and proposes, in the Guardini tradition, that the decline in numbers may even be a good thing: "It, the Church, will be seen increasingly as what it was in the beginning, a saving remnant, a sign of contradiction, a stumbling block, a transcultural phenomenon, a pilgrim church" (319–20).

Registering along the way his disapproval of the post–Vatican II changes in nuns' habits and in their names, and expressing his hope that "Catholic" novelists will begin to create a literature of "affection and celebration" (such as exists among Jewish writers) rather than dwell, immaturely, on their supposed mistreatment as children at the hands of priests and nuns, Percy explains that he is concerned with the excessive interest that people now have in the occult and with the rise of the new fundamentalists (321). His criticism of popular occultism as a rejection of true science in favor of "pseudo-science" is couched in the language of 1940s Catholicism: Percy declares that he prefers the traditional religion-science problem since the truth can never be contradictory. Again, his objection to the new television evangelists has the same tenor: they have devalued the language of the Good News by "pandering to a crude emotionalism divorced from reason" (323). Even when Percy confesses his own upset at some of the recent liturgical changes and his preference for "the very understatement of emotion in the quiet corporate worship, and, above all, the ancient, enduring liturgical form of the Mass," in typical 1940s loyalist fashion he criticizes Auberon Waugh (Evelyn Waugh's son who had temporarily left the Church in protest against the changes in ritual) for his excessive attachment to such forms (324). The Church, Percy is convinced, carries on regardless. Then he adds: "And let the Holy Father, this marvelous man, appear anywhere and there occurs all over the world a tumult

5. Percy, *Signposts*, 317.

not of despair and division but of rejoicing and hope, and not merely among Catholics" (325).

In all, this is a piece that rings through and through of the Church of the 1940s. There is no hint whatsoever that the nature of the Catholic priesthood might be open to revaluation on general biblical and historical grounds; indeed, the explicit assumption is that the Church is a "transcultural phenomenon." Moreover, Percy seems to have hardly been aware of some of the widely acknowledged problems in Catholic seminaries during the 1980s, *e.g.*, the fact that many of those admitted were active homosexuals. It would not, of course, have been appropriate for Percy to have mentioned this issue on such an occasion, but everything indicates that his tradition-bound outlook prevented him—like so many others—from even recognizing the problem.[6]

Although fundamental to Walker Percy's outlook, the essays discussed above were merely occasional pieces. However, since *The Second Coming*, he had had in mind a more comprehensive work that would examine the root cause of the modern malaise and that would also be continuous with *The Message in the Bottle*. Indeed, there is a very strong sense of yet another repetition in this third phase of Percy's life: philosophical essay, fictional creation, and especially interviews all give the impression of a man who has fixed his views on most issues and is simply seeking more functional ways of disseminating his already-arrived-at message (though his opponents *are* frequently changing). In any case, Percy referred to this project as his most important work, his *Novum Organum*, a kind of coming to terms with the displacement of man that the ideas of Copernicus, Darwin, and Freud had brought about.[7] Its focus would be some kind of study of consciousness and an attack on those who deny the existence of a self (Levi-Strauss and Michel Foucault), or present a naïve cosmology (Carl Sagan), or assert that apes have the same sign-using capacities as humans, or offer confused accounts of contempo-

6. See Paul Wilkes, "The Hands That Would Shape Our Souls," *Atlantic,* CCLXVI (December, 1990), 80. Wilkes is referring to a 1987 essay in *Commonweal* by Fr. Richard McBrien, chair of Notre Dame's theology department, in which McBrien poses this question: "What impact does the presence of a large number of gay seminarians have on the spiritual tone and moral atmosphere of our seminaries?"

7. Lewis A. Lawson and Victor A. Kramer, eds., *Conversations with Walker Percy* (Jackson, Miss., 1985), 223.

rary moral issues on television (Phil Donahue). All of these represented consciousness gone astray, though, as I stress later in this chapter, Percy nowhere refutes the specific arguments of his acknowledged opponents. Perhaps the most important motivation for the book was the fact that Percy's own involvement with philosophy and fiction had arisen initially from the realization that science took no account of the individual, the person, the self, the soul. So what he now needed was simply to defend these realities anew.

In preparation for his opus, Percy attended a conference on primatology in New York in 1980 and spent some time with semiotician Thomas Sebeok in Toronto in the following year. The resulting study, *Lost in the Cosmos: The Last Self-Help Book* (the original subtitle was *Why Carl Sagan Is So Lonely*), appears at first sight to be a reworking of all of Percy's previous material in that it contains both philosophical reflection and narrative detail (a mix similar to that found in Kierkegaard's *Either/Or*), a further attempt by Percy to bring home to the reader those themes that had been central to his essays and his fiction: the realization that man is in some way unique, that he is not at one with himself and needs to be shocked into a realization of this fact, that the options he is currently pursuing can have consequences that he is not willing to live with, and that some kind of conversion to a belief in a Savior—and very much a Catholic form of this belief— is required.[8] There are, however, some new elements in the present book that help give coherence to ideas that were merely hinted at in his earlier writings.

Percy's intent now was just as serious as in the case of *The Message in the Bottle*. However, because *Lost in the Cosmos* is also a spoof on self-help books (and on the "100 million Christian fundamentalists"), its own presentations all too often seem frivolous, casual, lacking in reflective seriousness. Indeed, the book itself sold significantly more copies on the West Coast than on the East Coast and seems to have appealed to the very audience of which Percy was most critical. The reader resents being urged by Percy to answer questionnaires and engage in incessant judging, while submitting to being criticized in the process. Of course,

---

8. Walker Percy, *Lost in the Cosmos: The Last Self-Help Book* (New York, 1983). When Sagan later heard that he had been criticized by Percy, he wrote to the novelist about the matter: "He said if I could show him any cited evidence that God was ever there or ever in a being, he would have to consider it." Percy's comment was that Sagan doesn't realize how mysterious human beings are (Lawson and Kramer, eds., *Conversations*, 297).

this is simply a more accelerated version of the approach that Percy had taken all along, now visible in its full nakedness.

Opening with an epigraph from Nietzsche that sets the theme—"We are unknown, we knowers, to ourselves"—*Lost in the Cosmos* will tell about the strange case of this unknown self as it exists in a world where it knows so much about everything else besides itself. Among other things, Percy promises to give "a semiotic theory of the Self" to account for this phenomenon. Thus, Percy prefaces the work with a preliminary questionnaire that is supposed to help the reader determine whether or not his self is lost in the Cosmos, whether or not he knows himself. The answer, quite obviously, is that we do not know ourselves, and so the reader is asked to identify with one of several descriptions of the self. These include the Cosmological self of the tribesman living in a primitive society, the Christian or Jewish self as a creature of God destined for happiness, the illusory self ("the conviction that one's sense of oneself is a psychological or cultural illusion and that with the advance of science, e.g., behaviorism, Levi-Strauss's structuralism, the self will disappear"), the Jeffersonian self that expects happiness through effort and right living, and the lost self (13). The latter is the kind of self that Percy feels is the most interesting and perhaps the only real self that it is possible to have nowadays:

With the passing of the cosmological myths and the fading of Christianity as a guarantor of the identity of the self, the self becomes dislocated . . . is both cut loose and imprisoned by its own freedom, yet imprisoned by a curious and paradoxical bondage like a Chinese handcuff, so that the very attempts to free itself, e.g., by ever more refined techniques for the pursuit of happiness, only tighten the bondage and distance the self ever farther from the very world it wishes to inhabit as its homeland. The rational Jeffersonian pursuit of happiness embarked upon in the American Revolution translates into the flaky euphoria of the late twentieth century. Every advance in an objective understanding of the Cosmos and in its technological control further distances the self from the Cosmos precisely in the degree of the advance—so that in the end the self becomes a space-bound ghost which roams the very Cosmos it understands perfectly. (12–13)

Percy's choice of the lost rather than the Christian self indicates that he does not see a simple return to religion as an answer to all of our problems, but rather that the matter is far more complicated than that. Christianity can no longer function as an *automatic* guarantor of the identity of the self and is, in fact, itself caught up in the universal dilemma.

The core of the book consists of twenty questions "to test your knowledge of what to do with your self in these, the last years of the twentieth century" (15). Each of the questions—which are about, for example, the amnesic self or the self that is subject to the whims of fashion—is designed to show how the self is not at one with itself. By asking the reader to conduct little "thought experiments," Percy hopes to make him aware of this fact. Many of the situations, of course, resemble those found in his novels. Thus, Percy speculates on the amnesic self as it is presented in the movies, wonders about fashion (à la Sartre's Roquentin: "The nought which is you has devoured the style and been sustained for a while as a non-you until the style is emptied out by the noughting self"), and wonders about members of the audience on *The Tonight Show* who cheer at the mere mention of their hometowns (25).

As might be expected, the Promiscuous Self of contemporary sexuality provides Percy with his most useful example. He presents an entertaining parody of Phil Donahue's show in which the subject of sex (*i.e.*, extramarital affairs and homosexuality—which are said to be more common now than in the Weimar Republic) is under discussion. Toward the end, three apparent strangers walk into the studio and are asked to give their opinions on what has been said. Each of their attitudes can be identified with a position that Percy has already examined at an earlier point in his career. While the first two strangers—John Calvin and a Confederate officer—roundly condemn the licentious discussion, their respective theories of predestination and northern aggression allow them to refuse personal responsibility (the Confederate is a Stoic who sees Richard Coeur de Lion as Lee). The third visitor, on the other hand, described as the "Cosmic Stranger," asserts that the current religious and sexual crises are but symptoms of a deeper disorder in this "sentimental, murderous, self-hating, and self-destructive" species (54). Although the Stranger predicts disaster and recommends a new beginning, Donahue's show, itself a symptom of the disordered times, continues unperturbed to its conclusion when the host announces the human-interest topic for the following day.

Percy himself proceeds to offer interesting reflections on the envious self and the depressed self, among others. The depressed self—the word *boredom* did not enter the language until the eighteenth century, the so-called age of reason—is the inheritor of the cultural and scientific riches of the Western world and yet "sits in the ashes like Cinderella yielding up ownership of its own dwelling to the true princes of the age, the experts." (Although Percy does not say so here, this phenomenon is an example of Whitehead's "fallacy of misplaced concreteness," which was mentioned in "The Loss of the Creature.") The consequence is that one comes to think that "*they* know about science, *they* know about medicine, *they* know about everything in the Cosmos, even me" (74–75). The thought-experiment recommended at this point is that "the only cure for depression is suicide." Such a serious choice awakens a person to the reality of his or her existence. If the individual chooses not to go through with it—but has *really* considered it—then Percy asks:

> Are you not free for the first time in your life to consider the folly of man, the most absurd of all the species, and to contemplate the comic mystery of your own existence? And even to consider which is the more absurd state of affairs, the manifest absurdity of your predicament: lost in the Cosmos and no news of how you got into such a fix or how to get out—or the even more preposterous eventuality that news did come from the God of the Cosmos, who took pity on your ridiculous plight and entered the space and time of your insignificant planet to tell you something. (78)

This description of the situation (echoing once again "The Message in the Bottle") is a brief anticipation of the Christian and Catholic conclusion toward which, of course, the entire book points.

As a preparation for such an outcome, the author immediately goes on to indicate that it is no longer a question of choosing between scientific and religious explanations of the human phenomenon:

> The traditional scientific model of man is clearly inadequate, for man can go to heroic lengths to identify and satisfy his needs and end by being more miserable than a Calcuttan. As for the present religious view of man, it begs

its own question, the question of God's existence, which means that it is not only useless to the unbeliever but dispiriting. The latter is more depressed than ever at hearing the good news of Christianity. From the scientific view at least, a new model of man is needed, something other than man conceived as a locus of bio-psycho-sociological needs and drives. (81–82)

Citing Mother Teresa's claim that people in advanced societies where all their biological needs are met are very unhappy, Percy therefore interrupts his progress to ask the reader to consider "a more radical model than the conventional psychobiological model, a semiotic model which allows one to explore the self in its nature and origins and to discover criteria for its impoverishment and wealth" (82).

In offering this semiotic model of the self, Percy credits Ernst Cassirer, Charles Sanders Peirce, Ferdinand de Saussure, Hans Werner, Susanne Langer, Sir John Eccles, and George Mead as his mentors in the field; he names his foes as Charles Morris, the French structuralists, Michel Foucault, and the deconstructionists, all of whom appear to deny on ideological grounds the very concept of the human subject. He also includes among his foes those who suggest that other animals can use language in any true sense; animals, he contends, are still involved in the same kind of dyadic interactions that have characterized the cosmos since its beginning.[9]

Percy proceeds to make his usual point about the consequences of the appearance of human language in the universe: the advent of man initiates *triadic*, or Delta, behavior. While it is possible that this development may have occurred elsewhere in the cosmos or among other animals on earth, we do not *know* this "despite heroic attempts with [teaching 'language' to] chimps, gorillas, and dolphins." Percy does not think, however, that triadic behavior is necessarily unique to man. What is essential, and what semiotics proposes, is that "where triadic behavior occurs, certain new properties and relationships also come into existence" (94–95). Thus, as a result of this development, man now lives not simply

9. Percy refers here to the seminal work of Herbert Terrace and Thomas Sebeok. See also Terrace's *Nim* (New York, 1987). For criticism of their approach, see Eugene Linden, *Silent Partners: The Legacy of the Ape Language Experiments* (New York, 1986).

in an environment like the other animals but in a *world*, a sphere that is "segmented and named by language" (99). Again, in opposition to Descartes, Percy concludes that "semiotics provides an escape from the solipsist prison by its stress on the social origins of language" (102).

Unfortunately, however, in the evolutionary process which Percy is here describing, signs undergo a *devolution*. At first they are vehicles of discovery, but then there is "a hardening and closure of the signifier": *only* appears in speech as in the sentence "This is only a tree." The unique is assigned to its class. A recovery from this state of affairs is possible through catastrophe: "The German soldier in *All Quiet on the Western Front* could see an ordinary butterfly [this example had been presented in slightly different form in *The Moviegoer*] as a creature of immense beauty and value in the trenches of the Somme" (105). Poets, painters, and even scientists can perform this recovery. The implication is that all of us should attempt to do so.

There is yet a further problem, the central problem of the book, namely, that the sign-user is unknown to himself: "Semiotically, the self is literally unspeakable to itself. One cannot speak or hear a word which signifies oneself, as one can speak or hear a word signifying anything else. . . . The self of the sign-user can never be grasped, because, once the self locates itself at the dead center of its world, there is no signified to which a signifier can be joined to make a sign. The self has no sign of itself" (106–107). The result of this state of affairs, Percy claims, is that "the signified of the self is semiotically loose and caroms around the Cosmos like an unguided missile." In semiotic terms, the situation is that there has appeared "for the first time in fifteen billion years (as far as we know) a creature which is ashamed of itself and which seeks cover in myriad disguises." Indeed, following on with this line of thought, man's exile from Eden is explained as "the banishment of the self-conscious self from its own world of signs" (108). Percy speculates on whether it might even be the breakthrough itself into language which is the catastrophe that has brought about this banishment, "the price of naming and knowing," or that perhaps it is the result of "a subsequent event, a bad move in the exercise of its freedom by the sign-user . . . a turning from a concelebration of the world to a solitary absorption with self" (109). The self, in any case, is at the center of the problem.

A true explanation of what has happened, and an escape from it, can only be achieved, according to Percy, through myths and religion, from Totemism to Christianity. But, in the West at least, since we live in a postreligious age, such explanations are no longer available to us. In this case the only apparent escape is through art or science. Both, however, have problems, Percy thinks. In the case of science, the "problematical self," if it is that of a genius like Einstein, totally "transcends the world" of the here and now. If it is that of a less inspired practitioner, it reenters the world imperfectly (bestially) after the elation of discovery (angelism).[10] The matter is even worse when one thinks of the scientists at Los Alamos and their detachment from the consequences of their atomic research.

The artist, on the other hand, is the "suffering servant" of the age, the canary in the mine shaft, in that he sees the darker side of things. Initially, his situation appears to be better than that of the scientist in that, by "naming the predicament of the self," he can reverse the process of alienation. But his is only a transient salvation: "After a while, both the artist and the self which receives the sign are back in the same fix or worse—because both have had a taste of transcendence and community." Hence the successful poet is tempted to commit suicide, while his readers enjoy an exhilaration that lasts only "twenty minutes, an hour at most." Unlike the scientist whose projects may require very long periods of pursuit, the artist has "reentry problems that are frequent and catastrophic" (121).

While Percy offers a number of cases for the reader's consideration as to how well the "self" has been handled, he does not provide any conclusion to his inquiry. The important point to recognize, as far as he is concerned, is that the problem of the self is unique to humans (in our experience thus far, at least): "the impoverishments and enrichments of a *self* in a *world* are not necessarily the same as the impoverishments and enrichments of an *organism* in an *environment*" (122).

Following this long and inconclusive excursion, Percy elaborates further on this supposed "reentry" problem, arguing that "the present world is in some sense

10.   Percy's description of such a case suggests that the early, unredeemed Dr. More belonged to this class: "The divorced wife of an astronomer at the Mount Wilson Observatory accused her husband of 'angelism-bestialism.' He was so absorbed in his work, the search for the quasar with the greatest red shift, that when he came home to his pleasant subdivision house, he seemed to take his pleasure like a god descending from Olympus into the world of mortals, ate heartily, had frequent intercourse with his wife, watched TV, read Mickey Spillane, and said not a word to wife or children" (115).

deranged, the center is not holding, that the plight of the self of the artist-writer is at least in part a historical phenomenon and not an essential property of being an artist-writer; that there may have been other times and other places, whether one wishes to call them an age of faith or an age of myth, in which man perceived a saving relationship to God, the Cosmos, the world, and each other" (145). Indeed, qualifying what he said earlier about the religious option no longer being available, Percy contends that the *ordinary* Catholic (and unusual spiritual seekers such as Simone Weil, Martin Buber, Dietrich Bonhoeffer, and Flannery O'Connor) may still have an experience that has been lost to the artist-writer:

> The Catholic is content to practice his faith in a dumpy church in York [England], while the tourists gape at the great nacreous pile of the York minster, an artifact of a former Catholic culture, as beautiful as the shell of a chambered nautilus and as empty. It is not argumentative, I think, to note the niceness of the ambiguity because, if the Catholic is content to have it so, so is the unbeliever. Thus, the esthetic delight of, say, Hemingway in the Catholic decor of Pamplona would perhaps be matched by his contempt for actual Catholic practice in Oak Park, Illinois. It is an ambiguity because it can be given two equally plausible interpretations, Catholic and non-Catholic. The Catholic: what matters to me is faith and practice; the cathedrals and fiestas are incidental. The non-Catholic: what is attractive to me is the Catholic decor, cathedrals and fiestas; what I want no part of is the belief and practice, which is often in bad taste, if not vulgar. Both are right. Catholic practice is often drab or outlandish, drab in Oak Park, Illinois, outlandish in Chichicastanango. And yet the beautiful York minster is empty. (150)

But this solution (based, incidentally, on a fundamental contrast between the dead Anglicanism of York minster and the vibrant worship of that city's local Roman Catholic community), available to some ordinary and extraordinary believers, is not so to those committed to the abstracted, noninvolved consciousness of contemporary man; nor does the all too apparent "ignorance" and "obnoxiousness" of the "God-party" help in the matter (157).

In attempting to explain further the nature of this abstracted consciousness and its difficulties in accepting the religious option, Percy proposes that the rivalry between the scientific and religious mentalities is not as innocent as some historians would have us believe. Thus, in dealing with what he calls the "Exempted Self" of the scientist, Percy wonders why the latter is often troubled when, for example, the facts seem to indicate that man may have appeared on the earth "suddenly and lately" (163). In this case, Percy indicates his own preference for Alfred Russel Wallace over Darwin (while accepting Darwin's greatness) since Wallace, though a pioneer evolutionist, allowed for a certain discontinuity between man and his animal ancestors.[11]

Percy goes on, however, to offer a number of possible answers to explain why scientists in general refuse to accept "facts" that go against their theories. It may be that science cannot tolerate discontinuities or that "scientists find it natural to deal with matter in interaction . . . and don't know what to make of such things as consciousness, self, and symbols and even sometimes deny that there are such things, even though they, the scientists, act for all the world as if they were conscious selves and spend their lives transacting with symbols" (163). But the answer that in tone and character seems nearest to what we know of Percy's own way of thinking runs thus:

> Because scientists in the practice of the scientific method, a non-radical knowledge of matter in interaction, often are not content with the non-radicalness of the scientific method and hence find themselves located in a posture of covert transcendence of their data. . . . Hence, scientists operate in the very sphere of transcendence which is not provided for in their science. Given such a posture, it is not merely an offence if a discontinuity turns up in the sphere of immanence, the data, but especially if the discontinuity seems to allow for the intervention of God. A God is already present. A scientist is a God to his data. And if there is anything more offensive to him than the suggestion of the existence of God, it is the existence of two Gods. (164)

11. "Darwin was a very great scientist . . . Wallace was a little nutty, sometimes obnoxiously occult, but in the end may have been closer to the truth about man" (Percy, *Signposts,* 164).

Percy's accusation against the scientists may have a certain plausibility, of course. Even so, he himself recognizes that there is a genuine problem between the claims of the scientists and those of religious believers. He suggests that a high-school student might pose the question thus (and in so doing arrives at the heart of the matter himself): how did it come about "that matter in interaction, a sequence of energy exchanges, neurones firing other neurones like a binary computer, can result in my being conscious, having a self, being able to utter sentences which are more or less true and which you can understand. . . . Or, if there is a soul, please tell me what evidence there is that it exists, and if it does, how it is connected with this compact mass of billions of neurones which is my brain?" (165).

Percy himself does not answer either question, but further considers instead why the scientific objectivist tends to dislike God even when the facts may point in his direction. He offers as example the hostile reaction at Harvard to Sir John Eccles' contention that evolution cannot account for mind. It might be, Percy allows, that religion has a bad name from past excesses. He thinks it more likely, however, that it is because of the reason he has already given: "while the scientific method may be officially neutral toward God, scientism, an attitude which extrapolates from the objectivity of the scientific method to an all-construing transcending objectivism, cannot be neutral. There is no room in the Cosmos for an absolutely transcending God" (167). The consequence of this rejection of God, Percy adds, is that man is lonely in the cosmos, which may explain why he wants to teach chimps how to use signs or why Carl Sagan wants to make contact with ETIs. He concludes with Chesterton's dictum: "When man stops believing in God, he will believe in anything at all" (172).

A more serious consequence, in Percy's view, is that there is now also a "Demoniac Self" which is possessed "by the Spirit of the Erotic and the Secret Love of Violence" (175). Whether one is a believer or not, it should be possible to see "that in an age in which the self is not informed by cosmological myths, by totemism, by belief in God—whether the God of Christianity, Judaism, or Islam—it must necessarily and by reason of its own semiotic nature be informed by something else" (178). Thus, for example, because of the failure of the churches, many selves have chosen a "reasonable" sexuality as an alternative. But in a technological age in which sin has been banished as a category of experience, this new sexuality tends to see the other person as a mere source of need-satisfaction while sex becomes the new absolute. The demoniac, ever present in human experience in spite of its denial, may erupt again in these circumstances with very serious consequences. Percy offers a brief history of the erotic and its relationship with violence, asking finally: "Will World War III erupt because of the suppressed fury of the autonomous self, disappointed now even in the erotic, that very demoniac spirit which is overtly committed to peace and love but secretly desires war and apocalypse and nourishes hatred of all other selves and perhaps of its own self most of all?" (192). Again, just in case the reader finds his prognosis unacceptable, Percy concludes by asking the reader how *he* would explain the anomalies of our murderous age.

In the final section of *Lost in the Cosmos*, entitled "A Space Odyssey," Percy returns to the fictional mode, offering two more extended "thought experiments" (though they are not so called) that are alternatives to one another. Both have been provoked by Sagan's *Cosmos*, the "scientism" of which Percy considers sophomoric because it shows "too little malice and too much ignorance" (202). Percy is, of course, sympathetic with Sagan's enthusiasm for science and with his rejection of fashionable astrological superstitions. But he objects to the "history" of science that Sagan offers, one that gives little importance to the Christian contribution, and, more generally, he finds it "deplorable" that "these serious issues involving God and the nature of man should be co-opted by the present disputants, a popularizer like Sagan and fundamentalists who believe God created the world six thousand years ago" (202).

The first of these thought experiments asks what the self marooned in the Cosmos would say if it met someone from another planet. The tentative reply provides a summary of the argument of the book, namely, that a flaw has somehow developed in man's consciousness since the "Sy" (the ability to use symbols) breakthrough—something that Sagan denies, since he does not admit the existence of a soul or psyche. Indeed, Sagan's answer (in Percy's book) to queries about man's present condition is this: "We do not recognize the existence of a 'soul' or 'psyche' if these entities be interpreted as anything other than a property of the organization of the DNA and other molecules of the organism." [12]

The second question ("A Space Odyssey II") deals with the alternative situ-

---

12. Percy, *Lost in the Cosmos*, 217.

ation in which man encounters no such aliens in space. A mission has been sent out under a Stoic captain and three women (the supposedly ideal mix and, incidentally, the same situation as that in *Love in the Ruins*). "An open and free sexuality was programmed, based on Prescott's statistical analysis of pre-industrial societies," the author explains, referring to one of Sagan's more provocative sources (232).[13] The mission fails to colonize and returns to a devastated earth in which remain only a few stray monks (three Benedictines, "the remnant of a thriving community which at its peak, a period of religious revival after the second of the great wars of the twentieth century, had as many as three hundred men" [242]), scientists, and deformed children. The captain is described as "a Christian who has lost his Faith in everything but the Fall of Man" (229). The climax comes in two choices: to begin again in an imperfect world as suggested by the Jewish-Catholic abbot (who believes in the Big Bang and that God "created man through evolution, in the latest moment of which, perhaps the last Ice Age, man became ensouled and came to himself as man, body and spirit" [247]—an account similar to Maritain's), or to start out for another planet with only the perfect specimens as the scientist suggests. There is hardly any need to indicate which is the "correct" solution. Percy's description of the remnant community gathered in Lost Cove, Tennessee, with its traditional religious divisions between Jews and Catholics and Protestants suspicious of each other, and the captain now officially married to the Methodist Jane Smith, exactly parallels the final scene of *Love in the Ruins*.

The book ends with a thought experiment in which Percy suggests, very much along the lines of "The Message in the Bottle" essay, that we change our usual perspective and see the preposterousness of the Christian message as a measure of the preposterousness of the age. Religion, he asserts, progresses in its preposterousness as it passes through Judaism to Protestantism to Catholicism:

Catholic Christianity is the most preposterous of the three. It proposes . . . also that the man-god founded a church, appointed as its first head a likable

---

13. The reference is to James W. Prescott's "Body Pleasure and the Origins of Violence," *Bulletin of the Atomic Scientists,* XXXI (November, 1975). Sagan quotes Prescott thus: "The percent likelihood of a society becoming physically violent if it is physically affectionate toward its infants *and* tolerant of premarital sexual behavior is 2 percent. The probability of this relationship occurring by chance is 125,000 to one. I am not aware of any other developmental variable that has such a high degree of predictive validity" (*Cosmos* [New York, 1980], 274).

but pusillanimous person, like himself a Jew, the most fallible of his friends, gave him and his successors the power to loose and to bind, required of his followers that they eat his body and drink his blood in order to have life in them, empowered his priests to change bread and wine into his body and blood, and vowed to protect this institution until the end of time. At which time he promised to return. (253)

Percy proposes, in the tradition of Romano Guardini, that as time goes on and as man increases in his knowledge of the Cosmos, he will find himself more and more alien to it "so that in the end it is precisely the preposterous remedy, it and no other, which is specified by the preposterous predicament of the human self as its sole remedy" (254). This, the conclusion toward which all his arguments have been leading, is as strong a declaration of Christian belief as one can find anywhere. So, in summary, the "theoretically ideal convert to Christianity at the end of the twentieth century" will be, according to Percy, "a person old enough to have exhausted the pleasures of the consumption of science as a world view and the pleasures of the consumption of the art of alienation, but not old enough to have become hopeless or to have committed suicide" (255).

In almost every way, *Lost in the Cosmos* is a very unusual book. It goes beyond Percy's earlier works even while it confirms many of their implications. All of Percy's previous essays and novels had been directed at shocking the reader into an awareness of his own situation and provoking him to make a commitment. It was possible, however, to reject this implication and dismiss the author's views as reactionary and unacceptable, or to enjoy the narrative in itself without worrying about its possible message. What *Lost in the Cosmos* may succeed in doing—if it is taken seriously—is to require the reader to spell out his or her own position, to note its consequences, and to move beyond the realm of a comfortable skepticism. At the same time, and as one would expect from Percy, the general argument of the book is relatively traditional in that it is aimed at defending the orthodox religious understanding of the self or soul as a spiritual entity, warning against its various seductions in the modern world, and in the end suggesting how those "lost in the cosmos" might find their "church home."

As with "The Message in the Bottle" essay, however, Percy's thesis here raises a number of problems. First of all, the self he seems to envisage throughout the book looks, in spite of his many denials, strangely Cartesian. Indeed, his favorable reference to the work of Nobel prizewinner Sir John Eccles seems to confirm this conclusion, for Eccles finds a discontinuity in nature with the appearance of man, a discontinuity best explained by his theory of *Dualist interactionism*, according to which matter and mind "are independent entities and it is proposed that in special sites in the brain, the liaison brain (LB), there is reciprocal interaction." [14] Moreover, Eccles suggests a spiritual origin for the psyche "by infusion into the developing embryo. *This divinely created psyche should be central to all considerations of immortality and of self-recognition*" (366). Although such a position would not quite be in harmony with the official Catholic teaching that the soul is the spirit of the body, it is noticeable that even this latter teaching, especially with the development of modern medicine, lends itself very easily to perversion into Cartesian dualism: physical bodies are presumed to be "ensouled" directly by God a short time after conception (the position taken in Pope Pius XII's *Humani Generis*). In brief, how soul and body could possibly interact remains a topic for serious dispute.

More important, Percy ignores the problem of the self as it has been dealt with since the time of Hume. Thus, Hume's acknowledgment that he was unable to find such an entity within his consciousness has suggested to subsequent thinkers that the question ought to be posed rather differently. Wittgenstein's insistence that the "self" is to be identified with the person as we know him through his "public" actions, Gilbert Ryle's vigorous criticisms of the "ghost in the machine" dualism on similar grounds, even Foucault's contention that the self is simply the product of the cultural forces prevailing at the time—although they come from opposing or unrelated traditions, they need far more detailed refutation than Percy offers anywhere in his book.[15] Percy even fails to mention dual (or double) aspect

14. Sir John Eccles, ed., *Mind and Brain: The Many-Faceted Problems* (Washington, D.C., 1982), 242. A brief and sympathetic explanation of why Eccles favors dualism is presented in Stephen Priest's *Theories of Mind* (Boston, 1991), 6. For objections, see Daniel C. Dennett, *Consciousness Explained* (Boston, 1991), 153–55.

15. Percy may have been provoked by Foucault's claim in *The Order of Things: An Archeology of the Human Sciences* (New York, 1970) that "man is only a recent invention, a figure not yet two centuries old, a new wrinkle in our knowledge, and . . . he will disappear again as soon as that knowledge has discovered a new form" (xxiii). He may also have been provoked by the recommen-

theory—where the mental and the physical are seen as but different properties of the same entity—which has long been a popular philosophical way of overcoming the dualistic problem, avoiding on the one hand a crass, materialistic explanation and, on the other, a semireligious assertion of the existence of a separate soul, mind, or self.[16] Least of all does he consider Daniel C. Dennett's proposal that the self and the brain are identical and that "what you are is the program that runs on your brain's computer" (though Percy mentions the idea in passing and uses it as a theme in his final novel).[17] In all, the possibly flawed but serious examinations of the nature of the self that have recently been proposed escape Percy's critical attention.

Lost in the Cosmos appeared at a time when new theories of the origin of the universe were in competition with that presented in Genesis. Steven Weinberg's book *The First Three Minutes: A Modern View of the Origin of the Universe*, published in 1977, was representative of the trend, while Sagan's *Cosmos* brought it to even wider attention. Percy was right to be concerned with the issue—as opposed to those who thought that science and religion need not interact in this matter—and indeed Pope Pius XII had stated as early as 1951 that the theory of the Big Bang "supported" Catholic teaching on the subject.[18] In subsequent years, eager cosmologists would make all kinds of predictions that extended well beyond their strictly scientific findings, culminating perhaps in Stephen Hawking's well-known conclusion to *A Brief History of Time* in 1988: "If we do discover a

dation in "What Is an Author?" that the (human) subject be analyzed as "a variable and complex function of discourse" (in *The Foucault Reader,* ed. Paul Rabinow [New York, 1984], 118).

16. Recent discussions of the nature of the self that are relevant here include Paul Davies, *God and the New Physics* (New York, 1983), Chap. 7; Colin McGinn, *The Character of Mind* (New York, 1982), Chap. 6; Thomas Nagel, *The View from Nowhere* (New York, 1986), Chaps. 3 and 4; Anthony Kenny, *The Metaphysics of Mind* (Oxford, 1989), Chaps. 2 and 6; Priest, *Theories of Mind*; Dennett, *Consciousness Explained.*

17. Daniel C. Dennett's book *Consciousness Explained* appeared in 1991 (to wide acclaim and criticism), but his ideas have been a subject of discussion since the early 1970s. It is of interest that when Dennett wants to give a concise account of his theory of the Self, he finds it best expressed in a parody of the deconstructionist position offered by David Lodge in his 1988 novel *Nice Work* (410–11). Needless to say, in the course of a David Lodge novel the character's self tends to become more "real" (in the Percy manner) than it had been in its original abstracted conception.

18. See, for example, Paul Davies, *God and the New Physics,* 20. An excellent treatment of the general topic is Ernan McMullin's "How Should Cosmology Relate to Theology," in *The Sciences and Theology in the Twentieth Century,* ed. A. R. Peacocke (Notre Dame, 1981), 17–57.

complete theory . . . we shall all, philosophers, scientists, and just ordinary people, be able to take part in the discussion of the question of why it is that we and the universe exist. If we find the answer to that, it would be the ultimate triumph of human reason—for then we would know the mind of God." [19] But whether or not contemporary scientists see themselves as being in automatic opposition to religion is another matter. Even a convinced atheist such as Weinberg has said recently that his main feeling is one of nostalgia "for a world in which the heavens declared the glory of God." [20] The point is that here again—as also in the cases of animal abilities and the theory of evolution—Percy seriously fails to treat the issues in their current presentation.[21] Nor—in spite of his references to Foucault—does Percy really engage with contemporary literary theory and deconstructionism in the manner promised.

Finally, and on quite a different note, Percy's attempt to explain the Fall of Man in semiotic terms seems strangely naturalistic and inconsistent with the traditional Christian emphasis on the voluntary aspect of man's exile from Eden; it may even be consistent with a position of religious skepticism. Moreover, to suggest that Catholicism be embraced on the grounds of its very preposterousness rings less of Kierkegaardian prophetic radicalism than of a despairing attitude toward the efficacy of the whole of that Church's rich heritage of sophisticated

19. Stephen Hawking, *A Brief History of Time: From the Big Bang to Black Holes* (New York, 1988), 175. In *A Brief History of Time: A Reader's Companion* (New York, 1992), Hawking mentions that when he met Pope John Paul II while attending a conference on cosmology at the Vatican in 1981 (an atheist, he was inducted as a member of the Pontifical Academy of Science in 1986), the pontiff "told us that it was all right to study the evolution of the universe after the big bang, but we should not inquire into the big bang itself because that was the moment of creation and therefore the work of God. I was glad then that he did not know that the subject of the talk I had just given at the conference was the possibility that space-time was finite but had no boundary, which means that it had no beginning, no moment of creation" (120). This proposition has, of course, been criticized in turn as philosophically naïve. See also Mary Midgley's erratic but occasionally insightful comments on the pretensions of contemporary cosmologists in *Science as Salvation: A Modern Myth and Its Meaning* (New York, 1992) and Richard Dawkins' *Blind Watchmaker: Why the Evidence of Evolution Reveals a Universe Without Design* (New York, 1987).

20. Steven Weinberg, *Dreams of a Final Theory* (New York, 1992), 256.

21. In the case of evolution, Percy criticizes the fundamentalists for objecting to it, but does not show how it can be reconciled with the Catholic idea that humans are "ensouled" (see Weinberg on this point in *Dreams of a Final Theory*, 248–49). For a more optimistic view, see Jared Diamond, *The Third Chimpanzee: The Evolution and Future of the Human Animal* (New York, 1992).

apologetics: surely a very unorthodox defense of orthodoxy and certainly not reflective of Percy's own position.

Perhaps, in the end, the problem is that Walker Percy was both drawn to the proverbial leap in the dark and yet committed to intellectual certainty. Although Percy himself has complained about the close-mouthedness of God, and as Jonathan Culler noted earlier in a related context, "direct perception" is something for which he longed, he himself had not really been *lost* in the cosmos since his conversion in the late 1940s.[22]

22. Tolson, *Pilgrim in the Ruins,* 467; Jonathan Culler, "Man the Symbol-Monger," *Yale Review,* CXV (Winter, 1976), 264.

11

FINAL EXIT

By the mid-1980s, Walker Percy was becoming more and more preoccupied with questions of religion and morals, even to the extent of being troubled about the conformist behavior of the English Percys at the time of the Reformation (whether he took consolation from the existence of his putative ancestor, Blessed Thomas Percy, is unclear). He fantasized about monastic life to the degree of wanting to buy a house near St. Joseph's Abbey so that he could hear its bells and live by its routines (not quite as odd or excessively religious a desire as it might at first seem, since there are many comfortable homes along the road that passes by the monastery), and he joined a Benedictine confraternity as a lay member (once a popular practice that had become much rarer after Vatican II). Indeed, he no longer worried if his critics dismissed him as merely a Catholic author, a fact that his writings during the period bear out abundantly.[1]

For example, in the 1984 essay "How to Be an American Novelist in Spite of Being Southern and Catholic," Percy recalls how his publisher had been troubled by the appearance of the word *Catholic* in the subtitle of *Love in the Ruins.* Then, defending his identification with the Church, he claims that Catholicism, since it gives value to the individual human life, is congenial to the novelist in a way that philosophies such as Buddhism, Marxism, behaviorism, or Freudianism are not: "I've never met a believing artist who felt constrained by his belief, but I've met any number who believed in nothing but an abstract freedom and who were not only constrained but paralyzed by some internal inquisition of their own making." [2] But while Christianity may help the writer in general, in the present context of southern writing there is the problem that a debased fundamentalism, exemplified by the likes of Oral Roberts, has replaced the old preachers, so that the

---

1. Jay Tolson, *Pilgrim in the Ruins: A Life of Walker Percy* (New York, 1992), 462, 447, 488, 260.

2. Walker Percy, *Signposts in a Strange Land,* ed. Patrick Samway (New York, 1991), 178.

believing novelist "feels like Lancelot in search of the Holy Grail who finds himself at the end of his quest at a Tupperware party" (180). What the contemporary southern novelist needs, Percy suggests, is the "supervention of a mystery beyond the scope of a sociological or a psychological novel" (182).

In "Diagnosing the Modern Malaise," a talk given at Cornell in 1985, Percy repeats an old theme that while the novelist ought not to be ideological, "the primary business of literature and art is cognitive, a kind of finding out and knowing and telling. . . . The pleasures of literature, the emotional gratification of reader and writer, follow upon and are secondary to the knowing." [3] Diagnosis of our present condition is necessary because, as Guardini has shown, we have come to the end of the modern world: "The Christian notion of man as a wayfarer in search of his salvation no longer informs Western culture" (208). There has been a subtle and radical transformation of the consciousness of Western man so that his goals now are autonomy, creativity, and rewarding interpersonal relations. Again, the advent of science as an all-encompassing worldview has also produced scientism, man's dependency on experts to tell him the most intimate things about his own life, which also, in the form of the loss of self, has led to overdependence on genital sexuality as a way of finding meaning in life. Percy now claims that he had been brought up in the pragmatic tradition of James and Dewey and once wanted to be a psychiatrist, but saw that science—even in the cases of such humanist thinkers as Freud and Sullivan—could not deal with the individual. It is for this reason that the novelist is needed, since it is he who is engaged in "true" sciencing.

At about this time also Percy contemplated composing a refutation of the philosophical and literary deconstructionists, whose enterprise he saw as "little more than rehashed Nietzscheanism, an attempt to get rid of God by first disposing of grammar," but he never got around to writing it. In *Signs of the Times: Deconstruction and the Fall of Paul de Man*, David Lehman remarks that Percy "defined a deconstructionist as an academic who claims that texts have no referents, but who leaves a message on his wife's telephone answering machine requesting a pepperoni pizza for supper. The message is a text, writes Percy, and the pizza is a referent." However, it is fair to say, I think, that by any objective

3. *Ibid.,* 207.

standard, Percy, like many other intellectuals of a traditional public mode, was not particularly well informed about the new movement and tended simply to isolate its apparent contradictions for easy ridicule. On the other hand, a program (and here I am lumping disparate enterprises together in a way that will irritate the scholar but that has a certain truth to it and would, I imagine, have satisfied Percy himself) that was opposed to the "metaphysics of presence" and in which Jacques Derrida quite intentionally called into question the very notion of a deferred Christian *parousia* at the end of time, or that, in so far as it had any religious interest at all, was concerned with developing an "a/theology" that would not require even the existence of God, could hardly have been expected to appeal to a person with Percy's beliefs.[4] The later Foucault may have accused Christians with their aspiration toward another life of failing to care properly for the bodied "self," but the general thrust of his speculation on the subject hardly provided much comfort to those committed to the existence of the self as *substance* with all the rights and privileges that such a designation entails. Again, however unfairly, Percy was surely confirmed in all his suspicions of the new movement by the revelations about Paul de Man's Nazi affiliations before and during World War II. In short, Percy's thinking on these matters seems to have been in line with Tzvetan Todorov's remark that contemporary literary theory is "dominated by what we may as well call by its rightful name, antihumanism. . . . I am simply saying that it is not possible, without inconsistency, to defend human rights with one hand and deconstruct the idea of humanity with the other." [5]

Percy would surely have been amused too—and perhaps consoled—to learn that the great Marxist theoretician Louis Althusser had regularly visited a convent of nuns near the Ecole Normale, while the fact that the "Dirty Harry" of American literary theory, Frank Lentricchia, has recently confessed to no longer reading criticism and taken to attending retreats at Trappist monasteries would likely have provoked his belated scorn.[6] In all, while there are occasional similarities between

4. See, for example, Jacques Derrida, *Writing and Difference,* trans. Alan Bass (Chicago, 1978); Mark C. Taylor, "Denegating God," *Critical Inquiry,* XX (Summer, 1994), 592–610.

5. Tolson, *Pilgrim in the Ruins,* 460; David Lehman, *Signs of the Times: Deconstruction and the Fall of Paul de Man* (New York, 1991), 113; Tzvetan Todorov, *Literature and Its Theorists: A Personal View of Twentieth-Century Criticism* (Ithaca, N.Y., 1987), 190.

6. Douglas Johnson, Introduction to Louis Althusser's *"The Future Lasts a Long Time" and "The Facts,"* ed. Olivier Corpet and Yann Moulier Boutang (London, 1993), xiv-xv; Frank Lentricchia, *The Edge of Night* (New York, 1994).

some of Percy's observations and those of contemporary theorists (perhaps Jean Baudrillard's most of all), the entire enterprise must have struck him as sheer folly and totally unexpected from one of the sources most traditionally associated with the defense of the infinite value of the human person.

One of Percy's last essays, published in 1986, was entitled "Novel-Writing in an Apocalyptic Time." [7] Percy's final piece of fiction, *The Thanatos Syndrome*, which appeared a year later and was dedicated to Robert Coles, is also a novel about an apocalyptic time (there is even a reference in it to the recent Marian apparitions in Yugoslavia), one in which also "there is a lot of death around." [8] It is quite repetitious of his earlier themes and in some ways rather casual in reexpressing them (and there are many careless errors in the narrative), but that very fact allows one to see how, as he moved toward the conclusion of his life, Percy might have wanted simply to reinforce his ideas without worrying too much about "art"; after all, Percy had commended Walter Miller's *Canticle for Leibowitz* for precisely this achievement. In fact, as a straightforward read, this is not at all a bad novel (the Philadelphia *Inquirer* described it as a "new genre, the theological-medical thriller"), while it also throws light on how Percy perceived many of his own views (showing a certain tolerant distance from them) and his family history as he became increasingly free of it. One minor character seems like a mild caricature of Percy himself: Jan Greene, the wife of a gynecologist, is described as "an old-style Catholic who wants to rescue the Church from its messing in politics and revolution, from nutty nuns and ex-nuns, from antipapal priests and malignant heterodox Dutch theologians, and so revive the best of the old Church, that is, orthodox theology, without its pious excesses"—a compendium, surely, of Percy's own views on these subjects.[9]

In several ways *The Thanatos Syndrome* carries on from where Percy left off

---

7. Percy, *Signposts,* 166.
8. The reference here is to the apparitions of the Virgin Mary at Medjugorje, beginning in 1981 and continuing into the 1990s. Although the local Catholic bishop doubted their authenticity, the Vatican has remained cautious on the issue. See "Visitations of the Virgin: Visions in Yugoslavia Roil the Catholic Church," *Newsweek,* July 20, 1987, pp. 54–55. It is of interest that when one of the Croatians who had allegedly seen the Virgin came to Percy's Birmingham, Alabama, for medical treatment, further apparitions were reported in nearby Shelby County.
9. Percy, *The Thanatos Syndrome* (New York, 1987), 108.

in his third novel, *Love in the Ruins*, in 1971. There a certain Dr. Thomas More, descendant of the saintly author of *Utopia*, had apparently been cured of an excessive attachment to the possibility of scientifically improving the lot of mankind in favor of submission to the counsel of a wisely conservative Fr. Smith, who recommended a very traditional repentance in sackcloth. Now, however, it is the early 1990s and Dr. More has lapsed once again from the faith, has spent two years in prison in Alabama for drug dealing, and no longer finds much meaning in Fr. Smith's example (who himself has had trouble with alcoholism). But More still sees his own former scientific preoccupations as Faustian, and he is as concerned as ever with the fact that some of his colleagues in the medical profession are currently applying scientific methods to end "useless" lives. This time, Percy even links the present practice of euthanasia with its forerunners in Weimar and the Third Reich as described in Dr. Frederic Wertham's book *A Sign for Cain*.[10] *Lost in the Cosmos*, of course, has also influenced the new novel in giving it some of its specific detail, while Percy is as usual distractingly playful at times (in referring, for example, to *Doe* v. *Dade*).

Consistent with Percy's recent engagement with the problem of consciousness and the nature of the self, Dr. More, who derives his psychiatric faith from Harry Stack Sullivan and Sigmund Freud and believes in a unique self, is described as living in a world that is bad for psychiatrists in that scientists are still arguing about whether there is a mind at all: "We, who like our mentor Dr. Freud believe there is a psyche, that it is born to trouble as the sparks fly up, that one gets at it, the root of trouble, the soul's own secret, by venturing into the heart of darkness, which is to say, by talking and listening, mostly listening, to another troubled human for months, years—we have been mostly superseded by brain engineers, neuropharmacologists, chemists of the synapses."[11] Thus, under attack from "hard" scientists of the Daniel C. Dennett ilk, Percy here expresses far greater sympathy with Freud than he had ever done before: his Dr. More is pro Freud, "a genius and a champion of the psyche—*Seele*, he called it, yes, soul—even though he spent his life pretending there was no such thing," and against the "horde of Texas brain mechanics, M.I.T. neurone circuitrists" (16). Even later,

10. Frederic Wertham, *A Sign for Cain: An Exploration of Human Violence* (New York, 1966).
11. Percy, *The Thanatos Syndrome,* 13.

when More shows an ambivalence in his preference for Freud over Jung—"I thought Dr. Jung was right in encouraging his patients to believe that their anxiety and depression might be trying to tell them something of value"—he finally ends up in the Freudian camp, emphasizing the latter's *scientific* credentials: "In the end Dr. Jung turned out to be something of a nut, the source of all manner of occult nonsense. Dr. Freud was not. He was a scientist, wrong at times, but a scientist nonetheless" (67).

In addition to his concern with the Qualitarian Centers dedicated to humanely eliminating "useless" lives, More has been noticing lately that his patients answer him in monosyllables, that the most unlikely people can perform prodigious feats of memory and mathematical skill, and that women have, in primate fashion, begun to present themselves rearward to their spouses and to others. More significantly, there has also been a great decrease in the level of self-awareness—a flatness and lack of mystery, people taking their views of the self from others. Percy brings his point home in a fine description of black-white relations: a conversation between More and a black janitor that had previously been "a six-layered exchange beyond the compass of any known science of communication but plain as day to Frank and me" (which is one reason why Percy is so sensitive about the attribution of *language* to other species) has now been dramatically simplified as the janitor expresses merely polite courtesies without any underlying ironic awareness (11).

The problem, then, in Freudian terms, is that the old terrors have been replaced by a "mild fond vacancy" (21). More is reminded of the chimp Lana and wonders if there has been a suppression of cortical function, of Wernicke's area, Brodmann 39 and 40, the major speech center and locus of self-consciousness: "the 'I,' the utterer, the 'self'—whatever one chooses to call that peculiar trait of humans by which they utter sentences and which makes them curious about how they look in a mirror" (22). Former Fr. Kev Kevin (of *Love in the Ruins*) and his ex-nun wife, for example, who previously had a rather bitchy marriage, are now full of "love" toward each other. To More, the couples' community that the pair has organized, with its naïve emphasis on peace and love, also sounds like a chimp colony. In all, people are somehow diminished, like, we are again reminded, Gardner's chimps in Oklahoma. Even More's wife, Ellen, who has become a champion bridge player, shows signs that she has been affected by whatever is going around. This time, however, More has no immediate solution: "Time was when I'd have tested their [those suffering from 'flatness'] neurones with my lapsometer. But there's more to it than neurones. There's such a thing as the psyche, I discovered. I became a psyche-iatrist, as I've said, a doctor of the soul, an old-style Freudian analyst, plus a dose of Adler and Jung" (88).

Newly emergent from prison, then, More can see afresh the various ills of society. Thus, even more than was the case with *Love in the Ruins*, the real issue for Percy is to spell out the dimensions of the problems rather than suggest that More himself has to make a choice among them. The thriller aspect of the story comes in his discovery that the Qualitarian project and the flatness effect in his patients are linked and in the dangers of his attempt to rescue a more traditional (and Christian) medical ethic from the chaos. Thus also, if Fr. Smith on this occasion is a good deal "madder" than in the earlier novel, he is so precisely because the current state of the local community has driven him to such an extreme.

When More visits medical colleagues Bob Comeaux and Max Gottlieb at the Qualitarian center (he needs them to renew his license after his prison term), he finds both quite "normal," unaffected by the new flatness. Comeaux is anxious to argue in favor of "pedeuthanasia," the Supreme Court's allowance of "termination" for infants without a life of quality. He puts the matter to a very silent More: "As you of all people know, as you in fact have written articles about, the human infant does not achieve personhood until some time in the second year for the simple reason, as you yourself have shown, that it is only with the acquisition of language and the activation of the language center of the brain that the child becomes conscious as a self, a person" (35). Whatever More may have written on the issue, of course, Comeaux knows that the ex-inmate does not agree with him or draw the same conclusions; indeed, he accuses More and his other opponents that in using the word *infanticide* to describe his qualitarian program, they "are dealing not with the issue but in semantics, a loaded semantics at that" (36).

Fr. Smith, meanwhile, has been living in a fire tower since his hospice closed three weeks earlier when the government cut Medicare for his inmates; since then he has wanted, rather mysteriously, to talk about the Germans. When More has a discussion with him, the doctor understands the priest's feelings about pedeuthanasia and gereuthanasia. But he also finds out that Smith has ceased preaching because words no longer signify. For Fr. Smith, it is the Jews—not the existence of God—that is now the issue; they are, he argues, a people that cannot be "subsumed," though the Holocaust was an attempt to do so (123). Smith goes on to accuse More of belonging to the first generation of doctors who will kill— the old, the unborn, the malformed—for the good of mankind, and he predicts that they will eventually kill Jews. It is tenderness, he emphasizes, not violence, that leads to the gas chamber.

Fr. Smith's dire warnings are, of course, illustrated in the eventual outcome of the Qualitarian practices. In addition to engaging in both pedeuthanasia and gereuthanasia, the Qualitarians are benignly trying to alter human behavior by injecting heavy sodium into the water supply. This has led to the "flatness" perceived by More. The symptoms of those affected are described on this occasion as "a regression from a stressful human existence to a peaceable animal existence. . . . cases of pure angelism-bestialism; that is, people who either consider themselves above conscience and the law or don't care" (180). When More confronts Comeaux with this information, Comeaux argues—with, significantly, Strauss music in the background—that they are all of the same creed, interested in healing the sick, and so forth, and he lists the reductions in crime, pregnancy, and homosexuality and the increases in I.Q. that have resulted from this experiment. While More wonders about the problem of the civil rights of the individuals affected, Comeaux continues in the vein of the kind of argument offered in *The Naked Ape:*

> The hypothesis, Tom, is that at least a segment of the human neocortex and of consciousness itself is not only an aberration of evolution but is also the scourge and curse of life on this earth, the source of wars, insanities, perversions—in short, those very pathologies which are peculiar to *Homo sapiens*. As Vonnegut put it, the only trouble with *Homo sapiens* is that parts of our brains are too fucking big. . . . We're not zapping the big brain. . . . To put it in your terms, what we're doing is cooling the superego . . . and strengthening the ego by increasing endorphin production. (195)

It is claimed that the old political and religious hassles have been bypassed and that, moreover, one can now kick the hypothalamus into an estrus cycle to achieve population control. When More asks about the Qualitarian centers "disposing" of the old and of infants, Comeaux replies that he prefers to use another vocabulary and stresses human dignity and the reduction of suffering.

Recounting all these facts to Fr. Smith in his fire tower, More grants reluctantly that there is something to be said for Comeaux's scheme and rationale "that a society like an organism has a right to survive" (234). But the priest interrupts in a long section entitled "Father Smith's Confession," one that resembles the unassimilated diaries of Sutter Vaught in *The Last Gentleman* and Will Barrett's letter in *The Second Coming* and that, artistically, is just as problematic. Smith begins to talk about his *Wanderjahr* in Germany in the 1930s, when he stayed at the home of Dr. Hans Jager, a child psychiatrist, in Tübingen. He was not terribly Catholic at the time and was especially impressed by one of the doctor's sons who belonged to the Hitler Youth, while being repelled, as was the family, by the other who was a crude Nazi. After all, the priest adds in an attempt to explain his sympathy, *The Student Prince* and Heidelberg were as much a part of the Southern tradition as the novels of Sir Walter Scott; the movement also resembled the early Jesuits, as he notes later. Although such words as *alien, decadent,* and *foreign body* were used, one was hardly aware of the anti-Jewish aspect of the movement—even some Jews wanted to join. Only the Catholic party objected.

Fr. Smith goes on to talk about the great intellectual excitement in Tübingen when a group of notable German and Austrian psychiatrists, distinguished doctors from the Weimar period rather than Nazis (and some of them admirers of the humanitarian work of Dr. Schweitzer), met there to discuss eugenics; Carl Jung could not be present because he was away collaborating on a project with Hermann Göring's brother. Dr. Jager gave Smith a book to read entitled *The Release of the Destruction of Life Devoid of Value,* which examined the case for eliminating all who were useless against that of only disposing of those suffering from hopeless diseases. The troubling thing about the book (and the meeting) was that it had its origin in the supposedly liberal Weimar Republic of the 1920s, not among the Nazis as such. Painfully aware of the similarity with the present, Fr. Smith now refers to the Qualitarians as the Louisiana Weimar psychiatrists.

In a "Footnote," Smith tells how, subsequently, as an American soldier in the war he was involved in the liberation of a hospital outside Munich where Dr.

Jager had worked. He found that in the room where the doctor had operated on children there was a sunny, large geranium. He had not been horrified at the time: "Soldiers are interested, not horrified. Only later was I horrified. We've got it wrong about horror. It doesn't come naturally but takes some effort" (254). He had become a priest afterwards, since that was the only option. Again, Smith wants to know if the psychiatrists in Louisiana today are really any different from the Germans in the 1920s, 1930s, and 1940s?

A tangential issue—though one that dominates the narrative—related to the Qualitarian project (and one possibly based on statements in Sagan's *Cosmos*) is that Van Dorn, the head of the local private school and Ellen's bridge partner, is engaged in the sexual liberation of a Western civilization that was originally messed up by St. Paul. Van Dorn's desire, predicated on the fact that the greatest achievements of man have been the result of sexual energy, is to combine the force of Don Giovanni with the genius of Einstein. Thus, it appears that More's children may need to be rescued from the school—one based on the European model of a Gymnasium-Hochschule and begun, the author notes slyly, to "revive the traditional Southern academy founded on Greek ideals and to avoid the integration of the public schools" (214). More subsequently discovers pornographic photos and tapes of both children and teachers in a variety of sexual poses, confirming that the sexual liberation of Western civilization has its darker side.

The upshot of More's various discoveries is, of course, that the Qualitarian system in all its ramifications must itself be terminated and the funds used to reactivate Fr. Smith's hospice. Percy has great fun in meting out punishments for the offenders: most are required to work in the hospice; but Van Dorn, who with the other teachers was forced to drink molar strength water to make them regress beyond the primate stage to engage in various forms of pongid behavior, is sent off to the Tulane Primate Center (not far from Percy's Covington). There he lives with Eva, the last of the "so-called talking apes." After two months, Van Dorn recovers, becomes "his old self, his charming, grandiose, slightly phony Confederate self" (344). He goes on to be successful on the Donahue and Dr. Ruth shows and in *Penthouse*, and he is pardoned by the governor. Gordon, the researcher who had studied his behavior, goes to Yale, while Eva is sent to Zaire where she is shunned by the other gorillas!

The ending of the novel is similar to *Love in the Ruins* in that the world is restored to its former, imperfect condition. More's patients are back to their "normal" anxious and terrified selves. Percy summarizes with a list that includes some of his pet peeves: there are no longer "human fly" professors on the walls of women's dormitories or women students presenting themselves; LSU has lost games; "writers-in-residence, as well as local poets who for years have been writing two-word sentences like the chimp Washoe and during readings uttering exclamations, howls, and routinely exposing themselves, have begun writing understandable novels and genuine poetry in the style of Robert Penn Warren, formerly of Feliciana" (349); and Kev Kevin is using his background to write successful novels. Kev and Debbie are separated, have abandoned all beliefs, but help with patients now and then. Meanwhile, More himself goes off to Disney World with his wife and family, where he occupies his time reading Stedmann's *History of World War I*, thinking that "the world really ended in 1916," and asking himself, "Why am I beginning to think like Father Smith?" (339). Ellen, now a Pentecostal, is still lusty, however. She opposes Catholics, the Eucharist, and the mixing of spirit with body, and she suspects that the priest has his hooks in her husband. She even contributes money to a television evangelist. The children attend a Christian academy, a circumstance that troubles More.

At the reopening of the hospice, Fr. Smith denounces Satan as the great depriver present in the benevolent, tender-hearted feeling of the audience. Although More kneels beside him like an altar boy, nevertheless we are told that the doctor will not do so every day: he is confused about belief and does not want to be deceitful. Fr. Smith explains to him later: "You have been deprived of the faith. All of us have. It is part of the times." The priest then makes a somewhat incoherent argument: "Just consider. Even if the truths of religion could be proved to you one, two, three, it wouldn't make much difference, would it? One hundred percent of astronomers have discovered that the universe was created from nothing. The explanation is obvious but it does not avail. . . . Ninety-seven percent of astronomers are still atheists. . . . It follows that there must be some other force at work, right?" (364). Smith goes on to talk about the recent apparitions of the Virgin in Yugoslavia. There she told the children who saw her that terrible things had happened in the twentieth century "because God agreed to let the Great Prince Satan have his way with men for a hundred years" (365). But hope must not be lost. More is on the right track: he has something to add to Freud and Jung.

"An Unpublished Letter to the *Times*," written on January 22, 1988, can be seen as a kind of postscript to *Thanatos*. Here Percy declines to rehearse the usual religious and medical arguments against abortion and admits: "Absent these latter, one can at least understand the familiar arguments for a 'woman's rights over her own body,' including 'the products of conception.'" [12] Percy's tack is that since the issue is frozen now, he wants to argue with the *Times*, the ACLU, NOW, etc., about the consequences of present trends. Percy appeals to the experience of democratic Weimar Germany in the 1920s, where jurist Binding and psychiatrist Hoche's book, *The Justification of the Destruction of Life Devoid of Value,* published during the pre-Nazi period, had enormous influence later, though Hitler himself never read it. In other words, once the line is crossed, innocent life may be destroyed for all kinds of good reasons. Opinion polls now favor abortion; they may in time favor euthanasia; so we need to be warned. Whether because the editors felt that Percy was adding nothing new to the discussion, or because his view seemed rather oddball, neither the letter nor its follow-up was acknowledged.

What can be said about the argument of Percy's novel? I have already touched on the relationship between the new cosmology and religion in the previous chapter, and so Fr. Smith's observations on the atheism of the astronomers (*if* it is not, in fact, exaggerated), for example, may be assigned to ignorance of the complexity of the problem. Again, Percy's making fun of the efforts to teach language to chimps has, of course, little relevance to the truth of the connection between them and humans (though it would probably appeal to Chomskyite linguists). It amounts in many ways to no more than the diatribe offered by Bishop Wilberforce in the last century against Darwin's theory of evolution. The euthanasia issue, however, demands more attention.

Percy's argument that the good intentions of Weimar made it at least easier for the Nazi program has received frequent support, though it is not without its critics. [13] Even Derek Humphry's widely read *Final Exit: The Practicalities of*

---

12. Percy, *Signposts,* 349.
13. General support for Percy's position is to be found in Robert Jay Lifton's *The Nazi Doctors* (New York, 1986) and in Donald Dietrich's "Catholic Resistance to Biological and Racist Eugenics in the Third Reich," in *Germans Against Nazism: Nonconformity, Opposition, and Resistance in the*

Self-Deliverance and Assisted Suicide for the Dying would probably have confirmed Percy's worst suspicions. Humphry comments blandly on Nazi euthanasia thus: "The Nazis murdered millions of Jews, gypsies, homosexuals, political dissidents and mentally and physically handicapped people in Germany between 1940 and 1945 mainly by use of cyanide acid gas, which they called Zyklon B. While the Nazi motives were barbarous, ruthless and unforgivable, the actual deaths were swift, though this is small consolation to the families of the killed. The post-war Nuremberg trial and other hearings meted out justice to the Nazi criminals. . . . It was a lapse by a section of the medical profession that must never be allowed to happen again" (43). Indeed, in confirmation of his careless writing and confused thought, Humphry goes on immediately without the least show of compunction or caution to applaud the founding of a new society for euthanasia in Germany in 1980. Furthermore, Humphry's references to Dr. Kevorkian, the physician recently associated with a number of self-induced deaths, fall right into Percy's perception of what is wrong with today's society: Kevorkian showed his suicide machine on Donahue in 1987, and he was dismissed from the University of Michigan at Ann Arbor because "he wanted to persuade men condemned to death for murder in Ohio to volunteer for medical experiments" (133).[14] As usual, however, Percy himself fails to deal with the kinds of cases that lead to sympathy with the euthanasia solution, and so he fails to face the real issue (nor does he make much advertence to how much the Holocaust was a consequence of traditional Christian antisemitism).

During this period Percy was, as ever, also engaged with philosophical problems. Indeed, he was contemplating a new book that would show the inadequacy of the

---

Third Reich, ed. Francis R. Nicosia and Lawrence D. Stokes (New York, 1990), 137–55. Dietrich writes: "While it would be erroneous to attribute the Final Solution to the eugenicists of pre-Nazi Germany, they did help create a climate of opinion within the professions and society that made such horrors as the euthanasia programme and Auschwitz into realities" (140). He adds, however, that the Nazis themselves considered the Church their enemy and that their files suggest "that some members of the Church acted more in accordance with Christian principles than prominent critics have been willing to concede" (150). In *The End of Life: Euthanasia and Morality* (New York, 1986), James Rachels criticizes the relevance of the Nazi example argument, though he fails to mention the Weimar connection.

14. See Derek Humphry, *Final Exit: The Practicalities of Self-Deliverance and Assisted Suicide for the Dying* (Eugene, Oreg., 1991). For criticism of Humphry in relation to his wife's euthanasia, see Rita Marker, *Deadly Compassion* (New York, 1993).

social sciences by way of a prolegomenon to the religious argument. He would use Peirce and Thomas Kuhn and apply triadic theory as rigorously as scientists had applied Newtonian mechanics. Although he seems never to have gotten round to doing this, an invitation to give the 1989 Jefferson lecture to the National Endowment for the Humanities in Washington, D.C., offered an opportunity to gather his philosophical thoughts together for a final declaration (many in his audience were prepared for a less weighty presentation from a novelist they admired).

Percy initially intended using portions of an unpublished earlier piece "Is a Theory of Man Possible?" to lead into his eventual NEH talk. There he had repeated his previous assertions about language as a way of understanding man but added some new "evidence":

The capacity for language seems to be, in the evolutionary scale, a relatively recent, sudden, and explosive development. A few years ago, it was thought to have begun to happen with Homo erectus perhaps a million years ago. Now, as Julian Jaynes at Princeton, among others, believes, it appears to have occurred in Neanderthal man as recently as the fourth glaciation, which lasted from about 75,000 to 35,000 years ago. During this same period, especially around 40,000 years ago, there occurred an explosive increase in the use and variety of new tools. The human brain increased in weight about fifty-four percent, much of this increase occurring in the cortex, especially in those areas around the Sylvan fissure implicated in the perception and production of speech. There are new structures, not present or else extremely rudimentary in even the highest apes. Moreover, recent experiments have shown that if one destroys this cortical region in other primates, it has no effect on vocalization, which is mediated not by a cortical but rather by the limbic system.[15]

Thus, according to Percy, in what seems like a leap to justify his assent to both the Judeo-Christian and Darwinian propositions, "There occurred in the evolution of man an extraordinary and unprecedented event which in the scale of evolu-

15. Percy, *Signposts,* 118–19.

tionary time was as sudden as biblical creation and whose consequences we are just beginning to explore. A fifty-four percent increase in brain weight in a few thousand years is, evolutionarily speaking, almost an instantaneous event. Anatomically speaking, it is perhaps not too much to say that this spectacular quantum jump is what made man human" (119). The approach to the issue that he finally suggests—seeing man as *Homo symbolificus*—opts, he claims rather implausibly, "neither for mechanism nor materialism nor theism, nor any of the perennial quarrels which have always vexed the larger question of man" (129).

In his subsequent NEH lecture, "The Fateful Rift: The San Andreas Fault in the Modern Mind," Percy begins with the proposition that the view of the world offered by the modern social sciences of psychology, linguistics, and anthropology is radically incoherent, and that the source of this incoherence lies in science itself. His purpose, therefore, is "to challenge science, as it is presently practiced by some scientists, in the name of science." [16] He will use the work of Charles Sanders Peirce to contribute "to a new and more coherent anthropology," thus answering the question of how mind and matter are connected (273).

Percy goes on to list various theories of mind—that it is a property of the organization of neurones, that it relates to the brain as a computer to its software (Dennett's idea)—finally quoting a textbook by Neil R. Carlson: "What can a physiological psychologist say about human self-awareness? We know that it is altered by changes in the structure or chemistry of the brain. We conclude that consciousness is a physiological function, just like behavior." Percy comments, using an arresting but inaccurate analogy: "These statements are something less useful than truisms. To say that mind is a property or function of the organization of the brain is like saying that Raphael's *Orleans Madonna* is a property of paint and color" (275). His authoritative conclusion is that "no amount of effort by 'brain' scientists and 'mind' scientists can even narrow the gap" (275–76). Neither is Darwin's claim that a mental act is essentially of the same nature in man and animal any longer accepted, according to Percy, though some still believe that chimps and dolphins have such capabilities. [17]

Thus, one is forced to turn to Charles Sanders Peirce, a scientific realist in the

16. *Ibid.*, 272.
17. See James Rachels, *Created from Animals: The Moral Implications of Darwinism* (New York, 1990), for an up-to-date defense of Darwin's claims.

tradition of the medieval Scholastics. Unlike the English nominalists, and, later, Descartes and Kant, who separated mind from matter and cast doubt on the reality of the world, "the great contribution of Charles Peirce was that he was a rigorous scientific realist and that he preserved the truth, as he saw it, of philosophical realism from Aristotle to the seventeenth century, salvaged it from the medieval language of the Scholastics, which is now all but incomprehensible to us, and recast it in terms familiar to scientists, to the most simpleminded empiricist, and even to us laymen. It, Peirce's realism, cannot now be escaped or fobbed off as Scholastic mumbo jumbo" (279).

Percy proceeds to rehearse the distinction between dyadic and triadic events, arguing as usual for the uniqueness of language—it is species-specific—and for naming as a "new event" (280). The efforts with chimps and the presumption that they are only hindered by lack of a suitable vocal apparatus has been shown by Herbert Terrace's Nim Chimsky to be untrue: both Washoe and Nim were responding to small cues given by their respective trainers.[18] However, in spite of these findings, Percy contends, the leap from neurology to psyche, from biology to grammar has gone unnoticed by scientists. As a result of our being so unaware of this San Andreas Fault between the dyadic and the triadic, the physical and the psychological, Percy extrapolates rather broadly, we are eventually seduced by the likes of Joseph Campbell and New Age religion (presumably because neither pays attention to the animal-human discontinuity) without searching for their inconsistencies.

On the other hand, Percy is equally troubled by those who, in looking for a place for the spiritual, uncritically accept Heisenberg's uncertainty theory as a justification for human freedom or chaos theory which, he claims, enriches rather than contradicts Newtonian determinism. Nor does Freudian theory offer a way out, Percy argues, falling back to his pre-*Thanatos* criticism of the founder of psychoanalysis, since it too can be reduced to a dyadic model "once one accepts

---

18. Although Herbert Terrace's findings have led to the termination of many primate language studies, they have in turn been subject to criticism. See Carl Sagan and Ann Druyan, *Shadows of Forgotten Ancestors: A Search for Who We Are* (New York, 1992), 354–55. See also Jared Diamond's references to studies of the vervet to bridge the gap between animal and human uses of language ("Bridges to Human Language," in *The Third Chimpanzee: The Evolution and Future of the Human Animal* [New York, 1992]). For a criticism of Sagan and Druyan, see Stephen Pinker, *The Language Instinct: How the Mind Creates Language* (New York, 1994), 336.

the immateriality of the entities." He adds: "Valuable though Freudian psychology might be, it must nevertheless be understood as a transposition of dyadic theory to the realm of mental entities, with no account of how it got there" (284).

The fact is that we need to pay attention to language in its neurological, physiological, and evolutionary aspects rather than merely in formal terms. But, though a physiologist such as Norman Geschwind has done this in describing some recently evolved brain structures as "association areas," Peirce "would call such associations dyadic events"—like those made by a computer (Percy's comment on Geschwind's ideas here, which is much less optimistic than before, nevertheless shows that he was engaged in an ongoing effort to fit together physiological and theological views of man) (284). Again, after also referring to Julian Jaynes somewhat critically on this occasion, Percy quotes Richard Leakey: "Speech is controlled by a certain structure of the brain, located in the outer cerebral cortex. Wernicke's area of the brain pulls out appropriate words from the brain's filing system. The angular gyrus . . . selects the appropriate word." [19] Percy questions this use of "pulls out" and "selects" as transitive verbs with subjects and objects: are we to imagine "a tiny little person, a homunculus, doing the pulling and selecting"? Even in the speech-act theory of Austin and Searle, Percy elaborates, there is no questioning of what the *act* is. Percy explains: "An act entails an actor, an agent which initiates the act. Draw me a picture of a speech-act. Where, what, is the actor?" (285). Yet, in spite of his criticisms, Percy says that he himself avoids speculating too much on the brain structures necessary for language, as this would push him in a Cartesian direction.

What, then, Percy asks, links word and object? "Peirce, a difficult, often obscure writer, called it by various names, interpretant, interpreter, judge" and also spoke of "mind" and "soul" (286). Percy calls the link a "coupler." The important point is that "*it, the third element, is not material.*" After all, neurones cannot assert anything: "A material substance cannot name or assert a proposition." Percy concludes: "Peirce's insistence on both the reality and nonmateriality of the third element . . . is of critical importance to natural science because its

19. See Richard Leakey and Roger Lewin, *Origins* (New York, 1977), 178–79. In *Origins Reconsidered: In Search of What Makes Us Human* (New York, 1992), Richard Leakey agrees with Colin McGinn's controversial thesis that "there may be limits to human understanding about nature; the human brain may not be equipped to understand itself" (282).

claim to reality is grounded not on this or that theology or metaphysic but on empirical observation and the necessities of scientific logic." Juxtaposing the "clarity" of Peirce's solution (to which the future will have to pay attention) with the common neurological assertion that mind is "a property of brain circuitry," Percy adds that "it may well turn out that consciousness itself is not a 'thing,' an entity, but an act, the triadic act by which we recognize reality through its symbolic vehicle" (287).

The consequence of the existence of a "soul" (a "coupler," an "I") is that the arts, which deal with such an entity, will have to be taken seriously, "since these are the cognitive, scientific, if you will, statements that we have about what it is to be human" (288). Even if the words we use for this interpreter—soul, ego, and so forth—are not satisfactory, we can still talk about the phenomenon itself. Thus, the traits of a triadic creature are that he is social, has a world (rather than an environment), and engages in lying (something new in the cosmos). And indeed, other philosophers have been on the same track: Heidegger speaks of *Dasein* (human *sein*) with a *Welt* who, unlike an organism, can live authentically or unauthentically; Marcel and Buber contrast "I-Thou" with "I-It" relationships and see man as a wayfarer, something not possible for other species. But it is the hardheaded Peirce who will force psychologists to take account of all this. Then, lastly, "with this new anthropology in hand," Percy suggests—uniting the vocabularies of Peirce and the existentialists in the service of his religious agenda— "one might even explore [this anthropology's] openness to such traditional Judeo-Christian notions as man falling prey to the worldliness of the world, and man as pilgrim seeking his salvation" (290–91).

This last quotation reinforces the point that with Percy philosophy and fiction are always a prelude to religion, and indeed the entire essay is a reiteration of his earliest work. So it is not surprising that most of his final pieces should have been devoted to religion also.[20] For example, in 1987 he contributed a foreword to *The New Catholics*, a volume of convert stories, a genre fallen into disuse in the Church many years earlier. Confessing that it is difficult to write about religious

---

20. See, for example, Lewis A. Lawson and Victor A. Kramer's comment in their introduction to *More Conversations with Walker Percy* (Jackson, Miss., 1993), xiv.

conversion when one hardly understands one's own, Percy identifies in particular with the convert who says: "What else do you expect anything this enormous and this old to be than, at times, something of a horror show?" [21] He notes that "More than one pilgrim finds himself standing at a strange rectory door, wondering how he got there, never having said two words to a priest—and here I have to smile, remembering how it felt and also hoping that he, she, would not run into some exhausted, unhappy, or otherwise messed-up human" (345). He also comments on their preparatory reading, which ran from Aquinas to Merton—but included C. S. Lewis most often—and on a woman who, like himself, read both St. Augustine's complex *City of God* and the rather unsophisticated Catholic pamphlet *Father Smith Instructs Jackson* (the kind of tract that one used to find near the doors of churches and which the Catholic-born Flannery O'Connor had dismissed so contemptuously).

As a product of the Church of the 1940s, Percy had been pleased and relieved with the election of the doctrinally traditional but socially progressive (on some issues at least) John Paul II as pope in 1978. In a 1986 interview with Charlotte Hays for the *National Catholic Register*, Percy remarked: "Most importantly, he's a whole man, a *mensch*. . . . I just like everything about him. I am dismayed by the violence and antipathy toward him in some elements of the Western Church. What comes to mind is the rotten reception he received in Holland. The Pope stands for orthodoxy without oppression. . . . It grieves me to see the Church split this way." The pontiff's visit to the United States in 1987 was intended both to minister to American Catholics and to rein in those clergy and members of religious orders especially who were straying from Roman orthodoxy. For the occasion, Percy and several other prominent Catholics—William F. Buckley, Jr., Avery Dulles, and Theodore Hesburgh among them—were invited by the editors of *America* to contribute short pieces under the title "If I Had Five Minutes with the Pope." In his response, Percy tells the pope not to worry about the Jesuits, the bishops (behaving now as they did in Reformation England), scientists (who should not be messing with life, *in vitro* fertilization, etc.), liberation theologians, or unorthodox theologians in Catholic universities (mere showboaters who are about as important as John Travolta). He should concentrate on ordinary Catho-

21. Percy, *Signposts*, 345.

lics, especially those in the Third World, since it is no accident that their seminaries are full. In the long run youth will get tired and, like Saints Francis and Clare, come back to the Church.[22]

It shows something of Percy's status in official Roman Catholic church circles by this time that he was one of only fourteen international laymen invited to address the Pontifical Council for Culture in Rome in 1988. The result, a paper entitled "Culture, the Church, and Evangelization," is concerned with the problem of the mass media and the fact that so many people spend so many hours watching TV, a phenomenon that must have an impact on the human psyche. Percy notes the loss of the educated classes to secular humanism: academics are not open to the gospel because, he judges, influenced by the movement toward abstractionism, they tend to see historical, unique Christianity "as an instance of such-and-such recurring human proclivity for attributing divine manifestations to particular historical events." The masses, meanwhile, have been lost to scientism. Nevertheless, the Church need not worry too much about science as such, Percy claims, since both are on the side of truth. As he had stated in his previous piece of advice to the pope, secular culture with its scientism and consumerism will eventually exhaust itself and cease to give satisfaction, and people will return because they are lonely and spiritually impoverished. Indeed, with the demise of Christendom, the world now is more promising for religion than in the Victorian era. Meanwhile, he thinks that the Church needs to make more use of TV—which is being misused by the fundamentalists. Percy appeals in this instance, in typical 1940s and early 1950s fashion, to the pioneer telecasts of Monsignor Fulton Sheen. In all, the steadfastness of the Church is more obvious to those outside than to those born within, Percy claims. In the face of the dangers of overacculturation, there is a need to stay on track, to forget the opinion polls, and to pay attention to the poor, the lonely, and the dispossessed. It is hardly surprising that Percy felt that some members of even his audience at the Vatican were upset by the degree of his conservatism.[23]

And so we arrive back at Percy's 1990 essay "Why Are You a Catholic?" published originally in *Living Philosophies,* where Percy answers his own ques-

---

22. Lawson and Kramer, eds., *More Conversations,* 125; Percy, *Signposts,* 346–48.
23. See Tolson, *Pilgrim in the Ruins,* 472–74; Percy, *Signposts,* 298.

tion thus: "The reason I am a Catholic is that I believe that what the Catholic Church proposes is true." [24] When he is asked the question by various unsympathetic persons—members of the KKK, Presbyterian relatives, and so forth—his reply is curt: "What else is there?" (307). When Percy offers a *civil* answer to reasonable inquirers, it is based on science and history: the need for Catholicism as a safeguard against every kind of human evil. He gives his usual account of the problems of the age: scientism, people being more interested in whales than in the starving Sudanese, the fact that nice Americans "have killed more unborn children than any nation in history," that "euthanasia is beginning" now as it did before in Weimar. The killing of the unborn is not considered horrible, he argues, "because in an age of theory and consumption it is appropriate that actions be carried out as the applications of theory and the needs of consumption require." Percy adds, disturbingly, that the only difference between present-day liberals and the Nazis is that "the Nazis favored it for theoretical reasons (eugenics, racial purity), while present-day liberals favor it for consumer needs (unwanted, inconvenient)" (310). The Nazis were the eventual outcome of conditions and thinking not very different from those existing in the contemporary United States.

Repeating statements from *Lost in the Cosmos* and *The Thanatos Syndrome*, Percy claims that there are two signs that resist theory: the self and the Jews. Judaism is offensive because of its claim that "God entered into a covenant with a single tribe, with it and no other"; Christianity is doubly so because of the claim that "God became one man, He and no other" (312). The reason that Hinduism and Buddhism are now more attractive is that science and theory have rejected the singular.

Finally, Percy declares that his reasons (apart from grace) for converting to the Catholic Church "can be described as Roman, Arthurian, Semitic, and semiotic." Thus, he explains that his reading of *Ivanhoe* indirectly influenced his conversion in that it set up a Southern ideal of chivalry which, later, because of finding out what had happened to the Jews in the Holocaust and remembering what had happened to them in the Crusades when real knights killed Jews, he was enabled to "emerge from the enchanted mists of the mythical past, the Roman and Ar-

24. Clifton Fadiman, ed., *Living Philosophies: The Reflections of Some Eminent Men and Women of Our Time* (New York, 1991). For convenience's sake, the in-text page references that follow are to the version that appears in *Signposts* (here, 304).

thurian and Confederate past, lovely as it is" (314). Similarly, this unbelieving age in which we live has the advantage of presenting us with the starkness of the real alternatives that are available to us.

But perhaps the best short account of Walker Percy's religious belief is that found in a "Symposium on Roman Catholicism and 'American Exceptionalism'" in the *New Oxford Review* for March, 1987, which dealt with the trouble over Archbishop Hunthausen (disciplined by Rome for his liberal stances) and Father Charles Curran (the moral theologian removed from his tenured position at Catholic University for doctrinal errors) on such matters as clerical discipline, sexual behavior, abortion, war, and the general area of the Church's noninfallible teachings. Several prominent believers were asked if such events indicated a schism in the Catholic church? Percy's reply was that he did not understand the behavior of Hunthausen and Curran. He would have expected them to set great store by

> the primacy of the Holy See and its magisterium, both on scriptural and historical grounds. . . . I am a convert of 40 years standing. One of the great attractions of the Church for me was its unity-amid-diversity, a mystery indeed but clearly not unrelated to Christ's commission to Peter in Matt. 16:18, both in the founding of the Church and the power to loose and to bind—this and the no less mysterious historical fidelity of the Catholic Church to this commission, through thick and thin, decay and renewal, for some 2,000 years. I do not doubt it will also survive this trial, perhaps not triumphantly, but survive. (4)

Percy's understanding here of the historical development of the Church would be unlikely to satisfy either a contemporary biblical or ecclesiastical historian, of course.[25] And yet, his conclusion is not without its own emotional force: "In a word, if I should now discover, 40 years after entering the Church, that I now belong to a church consisting of a loose federation of flocks and bishops, my first reaction would be that I could have saved myself a lot of trouble if I had become

25. See, for example, Fr. Raymond Brown's conservative but questioning "Scripture and Dogma Today," *America,* October 31, 1987, pp. 286–89.

a Methodist or an Episcopalian—no offense intended" (4–5).[26] Clearly, the *essentially* unchanging Church that Percy had entered in the 1940s was the one in which he ever afterwards remained.

In 1988, Walker Percy was diagnosed as having cancer of the prostate. Irritated at first because his doctor had failed to detect the problem early enough for a cure, he later allowed himself to be subjected to more medical scrutiny than was useful or necessary in the hope that this would benefit scientific knowledge of the disease. Jay Tolson's account of the last few days of Percy's life at his home in Covington suggests the dignity and acceptance with which he faced his own final exit. "Don't ask the Lord to keep me here. Ask Him to have mercy," he requested a short time before his death.[27] When it came at last on May 10, 1990, he was supremely ready. For his friend Shelby Foote, Percy's standing on this "sad height" may have marked the final triumph after a life of aesthetic achievement that had been partly distracted from its true purpose by an unexplainable religious interest; Percy himself, however, must have felt that he had run the race, had fought the good fight, and was coming into his reward.

Two days later, he was buried in the part of St. Joseph's Abbey grounds reserved for members of the Benedictine Lay. Confraternity, which he had joined expressly for that privilege.

26. See Lawson and Kramer, eds., *More Conversations,* for similar comments on the danger of the Catholic church becoming like the Episcopal church (227). In a 1987 interview, Percy observed: "The Church even has St. Peter buried in the basement of a Cathedral in Rome. Other churches can't produce evidence like that" (185).

27. Tolson, *Pilgrim in the Ruins,* 487.

CONCLUSION

The argument of this book has been that not only was Walker Percy the most self-consciously Roman Catholic novelist in America during the past several decades, but that, more important, his version of Catholicism continued right up to the end to bear much—though certainly not all—of the ambiance of the era in which he was converted, the 1940s. Since I have already presented various judgments concerning Percy's effectiveness as a philosopher and a novelist (concentrating less on those characteristics of mood and observation that ensure his artistic reputation than on the ideological content with which he himself was most concerned), it remains to consider where he stood in regard to the variety of Catholic stances that have come into being in recent years and also to evaluate what the future might hold for such a position in terms of novel writing: in other words, I need to justify my claim that he is the *last* Catholic novelist.

As was seen in the previous chapter, in 1987 Percy published a foreword to a volume of seventeen essays by mostly recent converts entitled *The New Catholics*. One notes that almost all the contributors are associated in one way or another with the *New Oxford Review,* a journal brought out in California (with Percy, until his death, among its advisory editors), and dedicated to intelligent discussion of religious matters in the tradition of the original Oxford Movement of Cardinal Newman. In fact, the journal itself claims in its editorials to be socially liberal and theologically conservative.

It is the conservative stance that is most notable about the conversion stories in *The New Catholics*. The contributors are not particularly well known (unlike many of those in the O'Brien books), but they are generally well educated, thoughtful, and sympathetic to other views of human life, views indeed that they themselves may have held at an earlier period. All display a striking need for an authoritative source of religious and moral guidance in their lives, however, and they have all found this in Pope John Paul II, whom they invariably see as the savior of an institution that seemed perilously close to dissolution before his providential arrival—"the white knight of Christendom," as one writer calls him (130). Those who were previously Episcopalians or Anglicans report that they found that church lacking a sense of authority and all too willing to accommodate itself to the modern world—the ordination of women as priests, the condoning and even celebrating (rather than simple forgiveness) of homosexual practices, a laxity on abortion—in short, to treat theological matters as though they were merely issues of sociology. In "The English Channel: Between Canterbury and Rome," Sheldon Vanauken comments that "apart from these 'professional seekers' who value their Seeker's Status more than truth, most of us would be only too glad to have some certain answers straight from the ultimate authority, God. We should welcome an angel very warmly indeed should one stop by." [1] The Roman Catholic church, in the meantime, seems to be the nearest thing to such a celestial announcement. Most interesting of all, perhaps, is the fact that the modern books that influenced these converts—by Chesterton, Belloc, Pieper, Maritain, Guardini, Lewis, Merton—could all have been read back in the late 1940s and early 1950s: there are no names of any significance from more recent times and especially from more recent theological thinking. As a kind of addendum to this and an indication of the peculiar nature of their religious frame of mind, several had the kind of experience described by Richard Gilman: a book "flying" to the prospective convert, a power moving another not to check out of the library a tome on the occult, being "pinned to the pew" in a church, and so on.

Now it would hardly be too much to call this view—that of Percy and the New Catholics—of the Church neoconservative. It almost entirely ignores the work of Karl Rahner, Edward Schillebeeckx, Hans Küng, and all those who have written on the matter in more recent years. [2] It is totally outside any discussion of the Church in terms of its historical and cultural development. In fact, it is a view that is a little to the right of such an acknowledged conservative as Richard John

---

1. Daniel O'Neill, ed. *The New Catholics* (New York, 1987), 136.

2. In a 1986 interview in the *National Catholic Register,* Percy referred to "nutty, heterodox priests . . . people like Fathers Schillebeeckx and Küng, who I'm not sure are Christians, from what I read by them" (Lewis A. Lawson and Victor A. Kramer, eds., *More Conversations with Walker Percy* [Jackson, Miss., 1993], 117).

Neuhaus, Lutheran author of *The Catholic Moment* (subsequently a convert and ordained as a Catholic priest), who quotes Percy's *Lost in the Cosmos* on the radical nature of the Catholic position and who is himself very much in the pope's corner. While sympathetic with Cardinal Joseph Ratzinger's holding the line against extremists such as Küng and Curran (but intelligently invoking Rahner on his own side, too), Neuhaus is a little troubled by Percy's appeal to the *preposterousness* of Catholic claims, and he quotes Reinhold Niebuhr favorably that "it makes all the difference whether one is a fool for Christ or just a plain fool." [3] Thus, in any case, Percy would hardly be seen as belonging to the Catholic mainstream, though what the ultra-orthodox southerner and the conservative Neuhaus would almost certainly agree on is that "John Paul is far ahead of those Christians, including many Roman Catholics, who are only now learning to accommodate the faith to a debased modernity that history is fast leaving behind" (284).

Overall, Percy's religious stance seems to have been remarkably like that of Ratzinger, who was also once a liberal and changed his position only in 1968.[4] In the *New York Times Magazine* for December 27, 1992, Alan Cowell quotes the cardinal as saying: "If you set apart the question of sexuality, or you turn it into an isolated problem of human life, then these issues [sexual conduct, abortion rights, etc.] are given an inflated status and then they become unanswerable. I think they are overly accentuated because the Christian core is not sufficiently in focus and the current life style has placed these problems where they become unsolvable." [5] And again, commenting on the New Catechism, an official text designed to replace the controversial Dutch version, Ratzinger explains: "The novelty is that we have presented a unified and organized vision of faith. It offers a fundamental vision of man, his life, his destiny. Today, Marxism is dead and liberal ideology is so fragmented that it no longer holds a common solid and coherent vision of the human race and its future. Out of this void rises the terrible danger of nihilism" (34). Precisely so, Walker Percy might have added.

---

3. Richard John Neuhaus, *The Catholic Moment: The Paradox of the Church in the Postmodern World* (San Francisco, 1987), 7.

4. Percy has expressed sympathy for Ratzinger's position (see Lawson and Kramer, eds., *More Conversations,* 125).

5. Alan Cowell, "The Vatican: Challenge to the Faithful," *New York Times Magazine,* December 27, 1992, p. 33.

It should be said in fairness that Percy was not by any means alone in this position. For example, Father James Tunstead Burtchaell, implicitly repeating the Catholic claim that Western thought has been off course since at least the sixteenth century, contends that recent moral theology has neglected an exploratory view of moral life and hence has had nothing progressive to say on abortion:

> The most attractive academic alternative has been an ethic descended from Enlightenment liberalism, with its intense priority upon the liberty of the individual. In the atmosphere of an abruptly emancipated discourse within the Church, not a few moralists found this doctrine of moral autonomy attractive, and found that on these terms they could find no very persuasive argument to inhibit the choice of any mother to eliminate a child unwanted and unborn (the more recent extension of abortion advocacy to infanticide for handicapped newborns has extended the issue). Thus there are many ostensibly Catholic theologians whose recent embrace of individualism as a theological starting point has muted their voice on behalf of the unborn.[6]

Taking a similar but wider perspective, the Canadian Catholic philosopher Charles Taylor has made the Guardini- and Percylike argument that today's secular society is unwittingly dependent on the residue of faith from past ages, that it suffers from scientism, and that we need to approach many moral issues from a communitarian rather than an excessively individualistic perspective. Referring to the example of Mother Teresa and Jean Vanier, Taylor asks: "Is the naturalist affirmation conditional on a view of human nature in the fullness of its health and strength? Does it move us to extend help to the irremediably broken, such as the mentally handicapped, those dying without dignity, fetuses with genetic defects?" His final belief is "a hope that I see implicit in Judaeo-Christian theism (however terrible the record of its adherents in history) and in its central promise of a divine affirmation of the human, more total than humans can ever attain unaided."[7]

6. James Tunstead Burtchaell, "Abortion," in *Modern Catholicism: Vatican II and After*, ed. Adrian Hastings (New York, 1991), 274.

7. Charles Taylor, *Sources of the Self: The Making of the Modern Identity* (Cambridge, Mass., 1989), 517, 520–21. The point has also been made by a non-Catholic contributor to the *New Oxford Review*, Robert Bellah, author of *Habits of the Heart: Individualism and Commitment in American Life* (Berkeley, Calif., 1985).

While Taylor has been more willing to accept the basic premise of modern individualism and to work out a new ethic by extrapolating from its presuppositions, the thrust of his vision lies in the same European and Thomistic tradition from which Percy derived much of his viewpoint.

There are, however, other ways of looking at the issues even among those who remain within the Church, and especially of course among those outside it. For example, Catholic journalist Peter Hebblethwaite, following a review of John Paul II's pontificate, gives an altogether more negative judgment on the Bishop of Rome: "It may be that his providential role is to test the conservative hypothesis to breaking-point," he comments acidly (456). Again, there is the kind of questioning of papal infallibility such as Küng has undertaken, the biblical scholarship (such as that by Raymond E. Brown noted earlier) that suggests a rather tenuous link between the New Testament and the present-day Church, and the new thinking on contraception and abortion by theologians such as Charles Curran and Daniel Maguire, none of which carried much weight with Percy, but which cannot thereby be ignored. One might not expect Percy to have agreed with these thinkers—there are good philosophical, theological, and even historical reasons why he should not—but the manner of his resistance to them suggests a blindness to the complexity of the problems he sought to answer so readily. In this, his stance was similar to that of the pope himself, who is said to be preoccupied with Africa because he likes its sense of the supernatural, its simple and *primitive* faith, which has been lost to sophisticated Europeans. But once an apologist for the faith, no matter what his position in the Church, begins to praise the responsiveness of the "unspoiled" inhabitants of some remote and impoverished island, as opposed to the apathy of the sophisticates of London or New York, even the sympathetic reader is likely to call to mind David Hume's observation that the miracles of religion have a curious habit of always taking place among distant and ignorant peoples. And in spite of a heightened awareness of the values of multiculturalism and of the implied racism of Hume's comment, his point retains its basic validity: a body of supposed "truths" that cannot withstand the scrutiny of an educated society deserves profound skepticism.[8]

---

8. The pope's position here (and Percy's also) smacks of—though this is hardly its intent—the strategy of the tobacco companies that, severely restricted in the United States, have increased their exports to Third World countries.

Then again (and very interestingly) there is the question of Percy's own attitude toward religious experience. Tolson stresses that Percy's sense of things here has always been much more intellectual and moral than emotional. Indeed, apart from a religious enthusiasm that embarrassed some members of his family during a trip to the Marian shrine at Lourdes in 1965, the nearest Percy ever came to anything that might be termed a "religious" experience was late in his life when attending Christmas Mass in 1986. He wrote afterwards to Robert Coles that at first everything was quite ordinary. "Then it hit me: What if it should be the case that the entire Cosmos had a creator and what if he decided for reasons of his own to show up as a little baby, conceived and born under suspicious circumstances? Well, Bob, you can lay it to Alzheimer's or hangover or whatever, but— it hit me—I had to pretend I had an allergy attack so I could take out my handkerchief."[9] While the language in which Percy expresses his reaction is somewhat surprising in that it identifies what might be termed basic Christian beliefs that one would have supposed he already held firmly, it is the personal note that is atypical.

Thus, in his actual writings, Percy never explores the kind of doubt that is common in other "believing" writers, in the twentieth century—Georges Bernanos, Brian Moore, Muriel Spark, David Lodge, and, of course, Graham Greene. The journeys of Percy's characters may have their ups and downs and the question of God's existence may even arise from time to time, but one end is always in view: faith is finally arrived at and its further frustrations are left unexamined.[10] His are not really novels of problems within the Church, within belief itself, nor— interestingly—do his characters ever really pray in a truly private way. Percy's protagonists never seem to work out their problems within a context of Catholic orthodoxy: the latter is always the end result. There is not in Percy the kind of religious meditation on suicide that Graham Greene's Scobie engages in in *The Heart of the Matter*, or the kind of searching for faith that one finds in Moore's

9. Jay Tolson, *Pilgrim in the Ruins* (New York, 1992), 466–67. The Lourdes trip is discussed on p. 325.

10. Robert Coles offers a different slant on this phenomenon: "In each of [Percy's] novels the central character, once freed to make his pilgrimage and continue his search, becomes almost impossible to write about any further. From that moment on the character is 'living a life,' a phrase Percy uses in such a way as to set up severe barriers to 'analysis' " (*Walker Percy: An American Search* [Boston, 1979], 235).

The Lonely Passion of Judith Hearne, for example, or even (structurally at least) in Joyce's *Portrait of the Artist as a Young Man;* there is little even of the quiet reflectiveness on the erosion of Western spirituality such as Czeslaw Milosz offers in *Living Philosophies,* and none, of course, of the kind of painful confrontation between personal faith, Church teaching, and emotional desire such as the conservative homosexual editor of the *New Republic,* Andrew Sullivan, has so movingly described.[11] Percy is much more concerned with the social dimension of belief, even if he also has a gnostic inclination. In this, too—that is, in his non-exploration of peculiarly Catholic dilemmas—he resembles Flannery O'Connor. Once again, with Percy one is so impressed with the sense of closure that his own conversion brings that any note of spiritual intimacy and even occasional uncertainty is almost entirely lost.

Whatever its personal dimensions, however, Percy's conversion needs to be criticized from a purely intellectual perspective as well. In this regard, neither the unsympathetic strictures of the naturalists and logical positivists in the 1940s nor the religious inclinations of the literary set—the Waughs, Gordons, and Lowells of the time—seem especially appropriate in judging Percy. I would appeal rather to the more recent example of Anthony Kenny, who in a tone of quiet thoughtfulness has recounted his deconversion from Catholicism in his autobiographical *A Path from Rome.* Kenny was a priest trained in Scholasticism by some of the best of the Church's philosophers and, later, in British linguistic philosophy by some of the best minds at Oxford. He was for many years a concerned pastor until he left the priesthood in 1963 without any of the showmanship that Percy routinely ascribes to wayward theologians; indeed, he remains in good standing in many Roman Catholic circles. As a philosopher at Oxford, however, Kenny decided that the traditional proofs for God's existence were invalid (though Aquinas had still much to teach us), and that therefore the Church's claim to be the recipient of a divine revelation could not be supported. "I am old-fashioned enough to believe," he reluctantly concludes, "that if the Church has been as wrong in the past on so many topics as forward-looking clergy believe, then her claims to impose belief and obedience on others are, in the form in which they

<hr>

11. Czeslaw Milosz, "On Erosion," in *Living Philosophies: The Reflections of Some Eminent Men and Women of Our Time,* ed. Clifton Fadiman (New York, 1990), 96–109; Andrew Sullivan, "Virtually Normal," *South Atlantic Quarterly,* XCIII (Summer, 1994), 659–74.

have traditionally been made, mere impudence." [12] What is relevant about Kenny for Percy is that he is an important and sympathetic philosopher of religion—one who thinks that the discipline has been ill served in recent decades—who is far more in touch with the nuances of current thought than Walker Percy ever was. Kenny—who, incidentally, is opposed to abortion on philosophical grounds—impresses one with a reasoned conviction that Percy never quite achieves, however one may admire the life the southern writer led after his conversion.

Kenny, of course, raises the question of the validity of the faith itself, as does J. L. Mackie, who not only tackles traditional arguments for the existence of God in *The Miracle of Theism*, but also the more recent (and nebulous) thought of Hans Küng on the subject.[13] The actual arguments for and against God's existence do not seem to have engaged Percy that much, but they are very relevant to his case. If they are as weak as current thinking rates them, then Percy's fundamental claims are called into question. Again, in spite of the occasionally excessive statements of self-important scientists, the mainstream positions in both contemporary anthropology and cosmology that acknowledge no originary purpose in the coming into being of either the universe or man, and correspondingly predict a finite end for both the species and the cosmos, do not easily harmonize with Percy's religious faith.[14]

None of this is to say that what Percy proposed could not possibly be true. A resigned skepticism about ultimate questions rather than a dogmatic denial characterizes the present intellectual community. But in so far as this is the case, such positive assertions as the Catholic church makes seem at best of dubious validity.

12. Anthony Kenny, *A Path from Rome* (New York, 1986), 207. Kenny's original arguments against the proofs for the existence of God are in *The Five Ways* (London, 1969). For a criticism of Kenny's arguments, see Brian Davies, *An Introduction to the Philosophy of Religion* (New York, 1982), 40–43.

13. J. L. Mackie, *The Miracle of Theism* (Oxford, 1982).

14. In the light of contemporary scientific findings, for example, recent theologians have tried to come up with new interpretations of survivability. See John Hick's "Theology and Mind-Brain Identity" (in *The Oxford Companion to the Mind,* ed. Richard L. Gregory [New York, 1987], 770–72): "Within a resurrection world, constituting another space, the simplest model for a resurrection body would be an exact 'replica' of the former earthly body, including its detailed brain state" (771). Note other interesting—though hardly consoling—views by theologians Hartshorne, Pannenberg, and Phillips. Percy has little sympathy with these thinkers and hence is burdened with the problems of the older (discredited) theory.

Peter Berger has observed that the result of the Vatican II *aggiornamento* was "to open an eight-lane superhighway through the center of the Catholic ghetto," and that in spite of Rome's subsequent effort to control the traffic "chances are it is too late, at least in Western countries." [15] But, in a deeper sense, we are all bound to a condition of unknowing, nor, as human beings, should we expect otherwise. The situation, as Kenny sees it, is thus: "The agnosticism which I profess is, in philosophical terms, a contingent and not a necessary agnosticism: the agnosticism of a man who says, 'I do not know whether there is a God, but perhaps it can be known.' Contingent agnosticism of this kind is bound to be a restless agnosticism: on a topic so important one is bound to prefer knowledge to uncertainty. So I have never ceased to be concerned about the philosophy of religion, the status of natural theology, and the relations between reason and belief" (208). In other words, the kind of philosophical closure that Walker Percy desired—and that was still available in the 1940s—is no longer viable, though the hunger for it remains.

In *The Fiction of Walker Percy*, John Edward Hardy describes this novelist as a serious author who has "presented so convincingly, so tellingly . . . for believers and unbelievers alike . . . the essential drama of the search for faith." Jay Tolson, in turn, asserts that Percy has deconstructed the Enlightenment idea of man. But such claims are exaggerated (even forgetting for a moment the undesirable company in which such an achievement would place him): both Percy's philosophy and his theology have serious flaws that affect his fiction. A seeker cannot find satisfaction in him unless he or she is prepared to cut off questioning at an unacceptable point. Furthermore, because the notion of an "absolute" truth has been shown to be itself culturally and historically bound, it is unlikely that there can be any more "Catholic" novelists: there is no such goal toward which an intellectually informed and honest human being can now aspire. Anthropologist Stephen Jay Gould claims that "we are an improbable and fragile entity, fortunately successful after precarious beginnings as a small population in Africa, not the predictable end result of a global tendency. We are a thing, an item in history, not

15. Peter L. Berger, *A Far Glory: The Quest for Faith in an Age of Credulity* (New York, 1992), 44.

an embodiment of general principles." This is more convincing than theologian Karl Rahner's assertion that "hominization designates that occurrence in nature in which the universe finds itself in man and is consciously confronted with its origin and goal." Yet understanding the genesis of our science as well as of our religion, knowing the accidental and provisional nature of their respective developments, we are freed from the imperatives of each while at the same time adapting what is useful for our unsponsored, directionless, and disturbing journey. In the end, the trouble with Walker Percy's faith is that it was in large part a defensive strategy in such an uncertain world, a willed resolution of fundamental conflicts that he himself had so honestly and acutely pointed out between a scientific and a religious view of human existence.[16]

Now, unfortunately, among some of his less discriminating readers, Percy may be in danger of appealing in the way that the New Age religions that he has so forcefully dismissed do: for their "mythical liveliness." Thus would this champion of Roman Catholic orthodoxy join that "amorphous group ranging from California loonies like Shirley MacLaine to the classier Joseph Campbell." [17] Far better to see him as a seeker poignantly defined by the already receding Catholicism of his time, a wayfarer more than even he himself ever imagined.[18]

16. John Edward Hardy, *The Fiction of Walker Percy* (Urbana, 1987), 224; Tolson, *Pilgrim in the Ruins,* 491; Stephen Jay Gould, *Wonderful Life: The Burgess Shale and the Nature of History* (New York, 1989), 319; Karl Rahner, "Evolution," in *Sacramentum Mundi: An Encyclopedia of Theology* (New York, 1968), II, 296.

17. Percy, *Signposts in a Strange Land,* ed. Patrick Samway (New York, 1991), 308.

18. Another way of putting Percy's problem—that is, recognizing its existence but offering a different explanation for it—is presented in Thomas Nagel's *View from Nowhere* (New York, 1986): "When we acknowledge our containment in the world, it becomes clear that we are incapable of living in the full light of that acknowledgment" (231).

SELECTED BIBLIOGRAPHY

Ackroyd, Peter. *T. S. Eliot: A Life*. New York, 1984.

Allen, William Rodney. *Walker Percy: A Southern Wayfarer*. Jackson, Miss., 1986.

Allitt, Patrick. "The Bitter Victory: Catholic Conservative Intellectuals in America, 1988–1993." *South Atlantic Quarterly*, XCIII (Summer, 1994), 631–58.

————. *Catholic Intellectuals and Conservative Politics in America, 1950–1985*. Ithaca, 1993.

Anscombe, G. E. M. *Ethics, Religion, and Politics*. Minneapolis, 1982.

Baker, Lewis. *The Percys of Mississippi: Politics and Literature in the New South*. Baton Rouge, 1983.

Bakhtin, Mikhail M. *Problems of Dostoevsky's Poetics*. Translated by Caryl Emerson. Minneapolis, 1984.

Berger, Peter L. *A Far Glory: The Quest for Faith in an Age of Credulity*. New York, 1992.

Bloom, Harold. *The American Religion: The Emergence of the Post-Christian Nation*. New York, 1992.

————, ed. *Walker Percy*. New York, 1986.

Briggs, Kenneth. *Holy Siege: The Year That Shook the Catholic Church*. San Francisco, 1992.

Brinkmeyer, Robert H., Jr. *Three Catholic Writers of the Modern South*. Jackson, Miss., 1985.

Broughton, Panthea Reid, ed. *The Art of Walker Percy: Stratagems for Being*. Baton Rouge, 1979.

Brown, Raymond E. "Scripture and Dogma Today." *America*, October 31, 1987, pp. 286–89.

Callahan, Daniel, ed. *The Secular City Debate*. New York, 1966.

Cantor, Norman F. *Inventing the Middle Ages: The Lives, Works, and Ideas of the Great Medievalists of the Twentieth Century*. New York, 1991.

Carlen, Claudia, ed. *The Papal Encyclicals, 1939–1958*. Raleigh, 1990.

Catechism of the Catholic Church. New Hope, Ky., 1994.

Ciuba, Gary M. *Walker Percy: Books of Revelations*. Athens, Ga., 1991.

Coles, Robert. *Walker Percy: An American Search*. Boston, 1979.

Collins, James. *The Existentialists: A Critical Study*. Chicago, 1951.

Copleston, Frederick C. *Contemporary Philosophy: Studies of Logical Positivism and Existentialism*. Westminster, Md., 1956.

Cox, Harvey. *The Secular City: Secularization and Urbanization in Theological Perspective*. New York, 1966.

Creighton, T. R. M. "Some Thoughts on Hardy and Religion." In *Thomas Hardy After Fifty Years,* edited by Lance St. John Butler. Totowa, N.J., 1977.

Crowley, J. Donald, and Sue Mitchell Crowley, eds. *Critical Essays on Walker Percy.* Boston, 1989.

Culler, Jonathan. *Framing the Sign: Criticism and Its Institutions.* Norman, Okla., 1988.

Davies, Brian. *An Introduction to the Philosophy of Religion.* New York, 1982.

Davies, Paul. *God and the New Physics.* New York, 1983.

Dennett, Daniel C. *Consciousness Explained.* Boston, 1991.

———. *Darwin's Dangerous Idea: Evolution and the Meanings of Life.* New York, 1995.

Diamond, Jared. *The Third Chimpanzee: The Evolution and Future of the Human Animal.* New York, 1992.

Dietrich, Donald. "Catholic Resistance to Biological and Racist Eugenics in the Third Reich." In *Germans Against Nazism: Nonconformity, Opposition, and Resistance in the Third Reich,* edited by Francis R. Nicosia and Lawrence D. Stokes. New York, 1990.

Dunaway, John M., ed. *Exiles and Fugitives: The Letters of Jacques and Raïssa Maritain, Allen Tate, and Caroline Gordon.* Baton Rouge, 1992.

Eccles, Sir John, ed. *Mind and Brain: The Many-Faceted Problems.* Washington, D.C., 1982.

Ellis, John Tracy. "American Catholics and the Intellectual Life." *Thought,* XXX (1955), 351–88.

Fadiman, Clifton, ed. *Living Philosophies: The Reflections of Some Eminent Men and Women of Our Time.* New York, 1990.

Foucault, Michel. *The Order of Things: An Archaeology of the Human Sciences.* New York, 1970.

Gandolfo, Anita. *Testing the Faith: The New Catholic Fiction in America.* New York, 1992.

Garcia, Laura L. "Philosophy and Faith." In *God and the Philosophers: The Reconciliation of Faith and Reason,* edited by Thomas V. Morris. New York, 1994.

Giles, Paul. *American Catholic Arts and Fictions: Culture, Ideology, Aesthetics.* New York, 1992.

Gilman, Richard. *Faith, Sex, Mystery: A Memoir.* New York, 1986.

Gilson, Etienne. *The Christian Philosophy of St. Thomas Aquinas.* 1956; rpr. New York, 1988.

Gould, Stephen Jay. *Wonderful Life: The Burgess Shale and the Nature of History.* New York, 1989.

Greene, Donald. "Graham Greene and Evelyn Waugh: 'Catholic Novelists.' " In *Graham Greene: A Revaluation,* edited by Jeffrey Meyers. New York, 1990.

Gregory, Richard L., ed. *The Oxford Companion to the Mind.* New York, 1987.

Gretlund, Jan Nordby, and Karl-Heinz Westarp, eds. *Walker Percy: Novelist and Philosopher.* Jackson, Miss., 1991.

Guardini, Romano. *The End of the Modern World: A Search for Orientation.* New York, 1956.

Hardy, John Edward. *The Fiction of Walker Percy.* Urbana, 1987.

Hastings, Adrian, ed. *Modern Catholicism: Vatican II and After.* New York, 1991.

Hawking, Stephen. *A Brief History of Time: From the Big Bang to Black Holes.* New York, 1988.

Hellman, John. "The Humanism of Jacques Maritain." In *Understanding Maritain: Philosopher and Friend,* edited by Deal W. Hudson and Matthew J. Mancini. Macon, Ga., 1987.

Hobson, Fred. *The Southern Writer in the Postmodern World.* Athens, Ga., 1991.

———. *Tell About the South: The Southern Rage to Explain.* Baton Rouge, 1983.

Hobson, Linda Whitney. *Understanding Walker Percy.* Columbia, 1988.

Humphry, Derek. *Final Exit: The Practicalities of Self-Deliverance and Assisted Suicide for the Dying.* Eugene, Oreg., 1991.

Hyde, Douglas. *I Believed.* New York, 1950.

Ice, Jackson Lee, and John J. Carey, eds. *The Death of God Debate.* Philadelphia, 1967.

Kazin, Alfred. *Bright Book of Life: American Novelists and Storytellers from Hemingway to Mailer.* Notre Dame, 1980.

Kenny, Anthony. *The Metaphysics of Mind.* Oxford, 1989.

———. *A Path from Rome: An Autobiography.* New York, 1986.

———. *Reason and Religion: Essays in Philosophical Theology.* Oxford, 1987.

Kierkegaard, Søren. *The Present Age.* New York, 1962.

Kobre, Michael. "The Consolations of Fiction: Walker Percy's Dialogic Art." *New Orleans Review,* XVIII (Winter, 1989), 45–53.

Langer, Susanne K. *Philosophy in a New Key: A Study in the Symbolism of Reason, Rite, and Art.* Cambridge, Mass., 1951.

Lawson, Lewis A. *Another Generation: Southern Fiction Since World War II.* Jackson, Miss., 1984.

———. *Following Percy: Essays on Walker Percy's Work.* Troy, N.Y., 1988.

Lawson, Lewis A., and Victor A. Kramer, eds. *Conversations with Walker Percy.* Jackson, Miss, 1985.

———. *More Conversations with Walker Percy.* Jackson, Miss., 1993.

Leaky, Richard, and Roger Lewin. *Origins.* New York, 1977.

———. *Origins Reconsidered: In Search of What Makes Us Human.* New York, 1992.

Lewis, Norman. *The Missionaries: God Among the Indians.* New York, 1990.

Lodge, David. *The Picturegoers.* 1960; rpr. London, 1993.

Luschei, Martin. *The Sovereign Wayfarer: Walker Percy's Diagnosis of the Malaise.* Baton Rouge, 1972.

Lyotard, Jean-François. *The Postmodern Condition: A Report on Knowledge.* Minneapolis, 1984.

Mackie, J. L. *The Miracle of Theism.* Oxford, 1982.

Mariani, Paul. *Lost Puritan: A Life of Robert Lowell.* New York, 1994.

Maritain, Jacques. *The Dream of Descartes.* London, 1946.

———. *The Peasant of the Garonne: An Old Layman Questions Himself About the Present Time.* Translated by Michael Cuddihy and Elizabeth Hughes. New York, 1968.

————. *Art and Scholasticism with Other Essays.* Translated by J. F. Scanlan. 1929; rpr. New York, 1971.

Marker, Rita. *Deadly Compassion.* New York, 1993.

Martin, Luther H., Huck Gutman, and Patrick H. Hutton, eds. *Technologies of the Self: A Seminar with Michel Foucault.* Amherst, 1988.

Masson, Jeffrey. *Against Therapy.* London, 1990.

McGinn, Colin. *The Character of Mind.* New York, 1982.

McHale, Brian. *Postmodernist Fiction.* New York, 1987,

Merton, Thomas. *The Seven Storey Mountain.* New York, 1948.

Midgley, Mary. *Science as Salvation: A Modern Myth and Its Meaning.* New York, 1992.

Monk, Ray. *Ludwig Wittgenstein: The Duty of Genius.* New York, 1990.

Nagel, Thomas. *The View from Nowhere.* New York, 1986.

Neuhaus, Richard John. *The Catholic Moment: The Paradox of the Church in the Postmodern World.* San Francisco, 1987.

Neurath, Otto, Rudolf Carnap, and Charles Morris, eds. *Foundations of the Unity of Science.* Chicago, 1969.

A New Catechism. New York, 1988.

Novak, Michael. *Confession of a Catholic.* San Francisco, 1983.

O'Brien, John A., ed. *The Road to Damascus.* New York, 1949.

————, ed. *Why Priests Leave.* New York, 1969.

O'Connor, Flannery. *The Habit of Being.* Edited by Sally Fitzgerald. New York, 1979.

O'Neill, Daniel, ed. *The New Catholics.* New York, 1987.

Passmore, John. *A Hundred Years of Philosophy.* New York, 1968.

Percy, Walker. *Lancelot.* New York, 1977.

————. *The Last Gentleman.* New York, 1966.

————. *Lost in the Cosmos: The Last Self-Help Book.* New York, 1983.

————. *Love in the Ruins: The Adventures of a Bad Catholic at a Time near the End of the World.* New York, 1971.

————. *The Message in the Bottle: How Queer Man Is, How Queer Language Is, and What One Has to Do with the Other.* New York, 1985.

————. *The Moviegoer.* New York, 1961.

————. *The Second Coming.* New York, 1980.

————. *Signposts in a Strange Land.* Edited by Patrick Samway. New York, 1991.

————. *The Thanatos Syndrome.* New York, 1987.

Percy, William Alexander. *Collected Poems.* New York, 1943.

————. *Lanterns on the Levee: Recollections of a Planter's Son.* Baton Rouge, 1973.

Pinker, Steven. *The Language Instinct: How the Mind Creates Language.* New York, 1994.

Poteat, Patricia Lewis. *Walker Percy and the Old Modern Age: Reflections on Language, Argument, and the Telling of Stories.* Baton Rouge, 1985.

Priest, Stephen. *Theories of Mind.* Boston, 1991.

Quinlan, Kieran. "Is Love of Man the *Only* Way to God?" *Catholic Mind,* LXXVI (February, 1978), 29–37.

————. *John Crowe Ransom's Secular Faith.* Baton Rouge, 1989.

Quinton, Anthony. *Thoughts and Thinkers*. New York, 1982.

Rachels, James. *Created from Animals: The Moral Implications of Darwinism*. New York, 1990.

———. *The End of Life: Euthanasia and Morality*. New York, 1986.

Sacramentum Mundi: An Encyclopedia of Theology. 6 vols. New York, 1968.

Sagan, Carl. *Cosmos*. New York, 1980.

Samway, Patrick. "A Rahnerian Backdrop to Percy's *The Second Coming*." *Delta* (November, 1981), 127–44.

Sartre, Jean-Paul. *Existentialism and Humanism*. Translated by Philip Mairet. London, 1948.

Scholes, Robert. *Textual Power: Literary Theory and the Teaching of English*. New Haven, 1985.

Sheed, Wilfrid. *Frank and Maisie: A Memoir with Parents*. New York, 1985.

Sheen, Fulton J. *Peace of Soul*. New York, 1949.

Shneidman, N. N. *Dostoevsky and Suicide*. New York, 1977.

Sparr, Arnold. *To Promote, Defend, and Redeem: The Catholic Literary Revival and the Cultural Transformation of American Catholicism, 1920–1960*. New York, 1990.

Styron, William. *Darkness Visible*. New York, 1990.

Sullivan, Andrew. "Virtually Normal." *South Atlantic Quarterly*, XCIII (Summer, 1994), 659–674.

Tate, Allen. *Essays of Four Decades*. Chicago, 1968.

Taylor, Charles. *Sources of the Self: The Making of the Modern Identity*. Cambridge, Mass., 1989.

Tharpe, Jac. *Walker Percy*. Boston, 1983.

———, ed. *Walker Percy: Art and Ethics*. Jackson, Miss., 1980.

Todorov, Tzvetan. *Literature and Its Theorists: A Personal View of Twentieth-Century Criticism*. Ithaca, N.Y., 1987.

Tolson, Jay. *Pilgrim in the Ruins: A Life of Walker Percy*. New York, 1992.

Tribe, Laurence H. *Abortion: The Clash of Absolutes*. New York, 1990.

Weinberg, Steven. *Dreams of a Final Theory*. New York, 1992.

Wertham, Frederic. *The German Euthanasia Program*. Cincinnati, 1969.

———. *A Sign for Cain: An Exploration of Human Violence*. New York, 1966.

Wilkes, Paul. "The Hands that Would Shape Our Souls." *Atlantic Monthly*, CCLXVI (December, 1990), 59–88.

Wills, Garry. *Bare Ruined Choirs: Doubt, Prophesy, and Radical Religion*. Garden City, N.Y., 1972.

Wyatt-Brown, Bertram. *The House of Percy: Honor, Melancholy, and Imagination in a Southern Family*. New York, 1994.

———. *The Literary Percys*. Athens, Ga., 1994.

Zamora, Lois Parkinson. *Writing the Apocalypse: Historical Vision in Contemporary U.S. and Latin American Fiction*. New York, 1989.

INDEX

Jung, Carl, 76, 108, 165–66n, 200, 203, 205

Kafka, Franz, 31
Kant, Immanuel, 50, 59, 67, 68, 210
Katz, Jerrold J., 144
Kauffmann, Stanley, 86n, 88, 90, 98
Kaufmann, Walter, 32
Kazin, Alfred, 2, 48, 49, 50
Keller, Helen, 25, 67, 72, 138, 142–43, 149, 150n, 166
Kennedy, John F., 101
Kennedy, Robert F., 117
Kenner, Hugh, 147–48
Kenny, Anthony, 13, 36n, 59, 175n, 192n, 224–25, 226
Keyes, Frances Parkinson, 36
Kierkegaard, Søren: 5, 30, 33, 36, 48, 49, 53, 55, 61, 67, 78, 80, 85, 87, 92, 96, 103, 115, 117n, 124, 193; as influence on Percy's Catholicism, 31–32
King, Martin Luther, Jr., 117
Knox, Ronald, 38, 80n
Kobre, Michael, 98
Koestler, Arthur, 130
Korzybski, Alfred, 75n, 138
Kramer, Victor A., 212n
Kuhn, Thomas, 208
Ku Klux Klan, 19, 27, 106
Küng, Hans, 1, 219, 220, 222, 225

Langer, Susanne K., 31n, 58, 62, 64–65, 66, 182
Lawrence, D. H., 87
Lawson, Lewis A., 13, 86n, 89, 117n, 160, 212n
Leakey, Richard, 211, 211n
Lee, Robert E., 160, 180
Lehman, David, 196
Leitch, Vincent B., 125n
Lentricchia, Frank, 197
Leo XIII, Pope, 36, 173
Levi-Strauss, Claude, 177, 179

Lewis, C. S., 13, 213, 219
Lewis, Norman, 171n
Lewis, Sinclair, 28n, 122
Liberation Theology, 7
Lifton, Robert Jay, 206n
Linden, Eugene, 182n
Locke, John, 50, 62
Lodge, David, 9, 14, 95, 192n, 223
Logical empiricism, 71. *See also* Analytic philosophy; Empiricism; Logical positivism; Positivism
Logical positivism, 58, 60, 62, 64, 119n, 224. *See also* Analytic philosophy; Empiricism; Positivism
Lonergan, Bernard, 7, 36n, 50, 77, 78
Longford, Lady Elizabeth, 1, 4
Lourdes, 42
Lowell, Robert, 5–6, 36, 37, 41, 45n, 54, 60, 224
Luce, Clare Booth, 36
Luther, Martin, 32
Lyotard, François, 123

Mach, Ernst, 58, 71
MacIntyre, Alasdair, 36n
Mackie, J. L., 225
MacLaine, Shirley, 227
Maguire, Daniel, 222
Mann, Thomas, 30, 53, 56, 107, 163
Mansfield, Katherine, 125
Marcel, Gabriel: 31, 33, 34, 38, 53, 57, 61, 63, 65, 87, 103, 135; on intersubjectivity, 68, 96, 212. *See also* Intersubjectivity; Sartre, Jean-Paul
Maréchal, Joseph, 36n
Maritain, Jacques: 5, 7, 36, 37, 38, 39, 47n, 48, 51, 57, 58, 60, 63, 64, 68, 77, 78, 120n, 130, 155, 189, 219; religious dogmatism of, 6–7, 49–50, 55, 119; as viewed by other philosophers, 41, 46. *See also* Gilson, Etienne; Neo-Thomism; Thomas Aquinas, St.; Thomism
Maritain, Raïssa, 39